Selecting Warehouse Software From WMS & ERP Providers

Find the Best Warehouse Module or Warehouse Management System

SECOND EDITION

Philip Obal

www.IDII.com   © 2007 by Industrial Data & Information Inc.

www.IDII.com   © 2007 by Industrial Data & Information Inc.

Research & Training Report

Selecting Warehouse Software From WMS & ERP Providers

Find the Best Warehouse Module or Warehouse Management System

SECOND EDITION

Philip Obal

Industrial Data & Information, Inc.
7217 East 92nd Street
Tulsa, OK 74133

Voice (918) 292-8785
Fax (918) 512-4132

www.IDII.com

www.IDII.com   © 2007 by Industrial Data & Information Inc.

Selecting Warehouse Software from WMS & ERP Providers
Finding the Best Warehouse Module or Warehouse Management System
by Philip Obal

Copyright © 2007 by Industrial Data & Information Inc. All rights are reserved. Except as permitted under the Copyright Act of 1976, no part of this publication may be reproduced or distributed in any form or by any means, or stored in a database or retrieval system, without the prior written permission of the publisher, Industrial Data & Information Inc. All company and product names are the trademarks or registered trademarks of their respective companies.

Cover image is from Voxware & used by permission. See http://www.voxware.com or call Voxware at (609) 514-4100 in North America or +44 (0) 1189 298-353 in Europe.

ISBN: 978-0-9669345-5-7 (Printed)
ISBN: 978-0-9669345-9-5 (PDF)
Library of Congress Control Number: 2007939124
Printed in United States of America
Printing History:
    August 2004   First Edition
    November 2007   **Second Edition**

Quotations must have written permission from the publisher as indicated above. Please send IDII a copy of the publication that the quote appears in. Quotes from this publication must also include the full name of this publication with our website URL:
    "Selecting Warehouse Software from WMS & ERP Providers – 2nd Edition – November 2007 – Publisher: IDII - Website http://www.IDII.com"

Industrial Data & Information, Inc.
7217 East 92nd Street
Tulsa, OK 74133
U.S.A.

918-292-8785 - Voice
918-512-4132 - Fax
www.IDII.com - Website
orders@IDII.com - Order Inquiries

Industrial Data & Information Inc has obtained information from sources believed to be reliable. However, because of continual improvement of software and the possibility of human or mechanical error by our sources, **Industrial Data & Information Inc.**, the author, or others, **Industrial Data & Information Inc.** and the author does not guarantee the accuracy, adequacy, or completeness of any information and is not responsible for any errors or omissions, or the results obtained from use of such information.

www.IDII.com   © 2007 by Industrial Data & Information Inc.

Acknowledgments

I thank God for my **wonderful** wife, Melinda Obal, of 27 years, who has been an inspiration & encouragement to me. It is a tremendous effort to put forth a technical report into easy to understand words. I appreciate Elizabeth Obal for assistance and Ken Ackerman for permission to use some of his warehousing definitions. I also appreciate Blue Sky Logistics, Fluensee, Voxware, Vocollect, and other companies for permission to use their images and screen snapshots, as well as Tompkins Associates for use of an informative article on testing, and The Progress Group & Catherine Cooper for use of an article on the human side of implementation.

Target Audience

This research report can *jump start a Warehouse Management System software selection process* and greatly minimize days and related expenses of exploring possible solutions. **Our mission is to "jump start" the reader in understanding the current warehousing software issues in a single day**, rather than months of the normal, exploratory search & learn process.

This publication is intended for those who are searching for software known as Warehouse Management System (WMS) and Enterprise Resource Planning (ERP). The reader should have a good, working knowledge of either warehouse operations *or* computer systems. The writing within this publication assumes the reader understands the basics of warehousing and goes right into the core issues, including what key functionality makes a better software package and what are missing in most warehousing software today. By getting an up-to-date view on where the warehousing software market is today, one may have confidence in asking pin-pointed questions and knowing what one is investing in.

The following personnel in an organization can benefit from this publication: Operation Management, Warehouse Management, Purchasing Management, Logistics Management, Customer Service Management, 3rd Party Logistics (3PL) providers, 3rd Party Fulfillment (3PF), 4th Party Logistics Providers (4PL), and owners of the company who are involved in the details of warehouse control.

Consultants, Integrators, Information Technology Management and software developers also can benefit from this publication. These computer people will see much time & effort has gone into this report and could utilize this report on "How to Design a Winning Warehouse Management System".

The author welcomes comments and suggestions on warehousing and supply chain issues. Send these to PhilObal@IDII.com or fax to 918-512-4132.

> *We purposely convey <u>detailed</u> consulting & integrator knowledge –*
> *To rapidly <u>raise</u> your "knowledge level" and*
> *For <u>better</u> understanding, questions, & process improvements.*

Table of Contents

TARGET AUDIENCE 1
TABLE OF CONTENTS 2
INTRODUCTION 6
MISSION & GOALS 7
ADDITIONAL HELP IS AVAILABLE 8

DUE DILIGENCE IN NEW WAREHOUSING SOFTWARE SELECTION 9

WAKE-UP CALL 9
COMMON REASONS FOR FAILURE IN DOING A PROPER SEARCH 9
DUE DILIGENCE – LOOK AT ALL OF YOUR OPTIONS 10
DUE DILIGENCE – LEARN ABOUT TECHNOLOGY & WAREHOUSING SOFTWARE 10
HOW TO BE EXTREMELY SUCCESSFUL IN THE WMS SOFTWARE PROJECT 11
WHO ARE YOU? – START THERE – WHAT IS THE BIG PICTURE? 12
START AN INITIAL SCOPE DOCUMENT 13
SEARCH TECHNIQUES 13
HOW TO SELECT WMS SOFTWARE - DIAGRAM 1 14
WHAT IS A WAREHOUSE MANAGEMENT SYSTEM? 15
HIGH LEVEL VIEW - WHAT IS A WAREHOUSE MANAGEMENT SYSTEM? 18
MINDSET OF A CONDUCTOR & ORCHESTRA 20
IMPORTANCE OF SOFTWARE SELECTION STEPS 21
WHAT IS A DIFFERENTIATOR? 22
WHAT IS A COMMON DEFICIENCY? 22
FILLING IN THE GAP – CUSTOM – NEXT RELEASE ENHANCEMENT? 22
WAREHOUSE MANAGEMENT SYSTEMS WILL WORK BEST IF YOU HAVE: 23

CHAPTER 1 24

EXPECTED BASE LINE FUNCTIONALITY 24

ITEMS THAT EXIST IN WAREHOUSING SOFTWARE 24

COMMON EXPECTATIONS TODAY IN WAREHOUSING SOFTWARE 25
CORE FUNCTIONALITY TO EXPECT 25
BUILT-IN UTILITY SOFTWARE TO EXPECT 27
EXPECT LEVERAGING OF 3RD PARTY SOFTWARE PRODUCTS 28

CHAPTER 2 30

DIFFERENTIATORS 30

ITEMS THAT FLUCTUATE IN WAREHOUSING SOFTWARE 30

SUMMARY OF DIFFERENTIATORS 31
FILL IN THE GAP EXPLANATION 34
EQUIPMENT TABLE 35
UNIQUE PATHS 37
SUB-PART NUMBER 37
AUTOMATIC RELEASE TO PICKING FOR EMERGENCY ORDERS 38
AUTOMATIC GROUPING & RELEASE TO PICKING 39
WAVE SELECTION CRITERIA 40
CARTON SELECTION & PICK TO CARTON 41
PICK TO CARRIER SHIPPING LABEL – OPTIMIZED PICK TO CARTON METHOD 43
WEIGH-IN-MOTION CONVEYOR 44
REPACK FUNCTION 45

DIMENSIONS PER PRODUCT UOM 46
BIN LOCATOR SYSTEM 48
LOT CONTROL - DATE CODE MASKING 49
CATCH WEIGHT AND DUAL QUANTITY CAPTURE 50
PART CONDITION - ITEM CONDITION CODE 51
RFID TAG FUNCTION 52
INTERLEAVING OF MULTIPLE TASKS 53
CROSS DOCKING 54
WORK ORDERS & MANUFACTURING 55
USER CONFIGURABLE SYSTEM 56
CONFIGURATION OF THE CLIENT'S CUSTOMER LEVEL 57
LABOR PRODUCTIVITY INFORMATION 58
LABOR PRODUCTIVITY STANDARDS – ENGINEERED LABOR STANDARDS 59
SUPPLY CHAIN EVENT MANAGEMENT (SCEM) - GO PAST FAX, PAGER, & EMAIL 60
SCEM – KPI & NON-COMPLIANCE PERFORMANCE REPORTING 61
SCEM – WORKFLOW 61
METRICS, KPIS, AND DASHBOARDS 62
SCORE CARDS 66
STANDARD XML TRANSACTIONS 67
STANDARD INTERFACE TO MATERIAL HANDLING EQUIPMENT 68
STANDARD INTERFACE TO SHIPPING MANIFESTING SYSTEM 69
VOICE ENABLEMENT 71

CHAPTER 3 72

COMMON DEFICIENCIES 72

ITEMS NOT FOUND IN MOST WAREHOUSING SOFTWARE 72

SUMMARY OF COMMON DEFICIENCIES 73
DOCUMENT IMAGING = PAPER CLIPPING IMAGES 75
MATERIAL SAFETY DATA SHEET (MSDS) PROCESSING 76
CERTIFICATE OF COMPLIANCE AND CONFORMITY (CERT) PROCESSING 80
HAZARDOUS MATERIAL HANDLING 81
ERROR ANALYSIS TABLE 82
YARD MANAGEMENT ON TRACKING TRAILERS 83
ORDER ENTRY – ENTER AN OUTBOUND ORDER 85
AUTOMATIC RE-WAREHOUSING OPTIMIZATION 86
INVENTORY VALUATION REPORT 87
STANDARD INTERFACE TO LOAD OPTIMIZATION SOFTWARE 88
STANDARD INTERFACE TO ROUTE OPTIMIZATION SOFTWARE 88
STANDARD INTERFACE TO DIMENSION & WEIGHING EQUIPMENT 89
STANDARD INTERFACE TO SAP, ORACLE, BAAN, PEOPLESOFT 91

CHAPTER 4 92

WMS STRENGTHS VS. ERP 92

UNDERSTANDING WMS & ERP DIFFERENCES 93
WAREHOUSE MANAGEMENT SYSTEMS STRENGTHS 93
1. ADVANCED BIN LOCATOR 94
2. SLOTTING OPTIMIZATION 94
3. DYNAMIC RF TASK QUEUE 94
4. CONFIGURABLE WAREHOUSE TASK "WORK FLOW" 95
5. EMPLOYEE CERTIFICATION SETUP 95
6. ENGINEERED LABOR STANDARDS & LABOR PERFORMANCE 96
7. WAREHOUSE ACCOUNTABILITY – TRANSACTION HISTORY 96

- 8. Recall & Traceability 96
- 9. Warehouse Equipment Definition 97
- 10. Driving Material Handling Equipment via Interfaces. 97
- 11. Dock Scheduling 98
- 12. Trailer Yard Management System 98
- 13. Work Centers 98
- 14. 3rd Party Logistics Product Ownership 99
- 15. 3PL Contract Rates & 3PL Billing 99
- 16. Advanced 3PL Inventory Allocation Methods 100
- Private Warehousing Needs 3PL Functionality 100
- 17. Outbound Order Picking Methods 101
- 18. Reverse Truck Loading Sequence 101
- 19. Transportation Management System 101
- 20. Eliminate Computer Down Time 102
- 21. ERP Interfaces 102
- Conclusion - Focus on Needed Functionality 102

CHAPTER 5 103

READY… SET… SEND RFP 103
- Step By Step Process Explained - Diagram 9 104

REALITY CHECK 105

REMEMBER THE BASIC FUNCTIONALITY 106
- Internationalization 106
- Part Number Size 106
- 3rd Party Logistics (3PL) – Public & Contract Warehousing 106
- Lot Controlled Items 106
- Serialized Items 106
- Bonded Warehouses 107
- Common API for Data Push & Pull 107
- Compliance Labeling & Packing Lists 107
- Shipping Labels 107
- Standard Operating Systems 107

PREPARE THE RFP 108
- Develop Cover Letter 108
- Provide Company Background 108
- Provide Warehouse Details & Statistics 109
- Reminder - Tailor the RFP 116
- While Waiting for the Responses 116
- Scoring the RFP 117
- Analyze the RFP Responses 118
- One Page Cost Summary 119
- How To Select WMS Software - Diagram 10 120
- Minimum Number of Installed Customers 121
- Customers in Your Industry 121
- Excellent I/O Data Throughput Performance 121
- Clean Financial History 121
- Good Revenue to Employee Ratio 121
- Excellent References 121

FINAL SELECTION 122
- Selecting the Site to Tour – Site Visit Selection Tips 123

- Site Visit Benefits 124
- Site Visit Questions... 125
- Headquarter Visit Benefits 127

UNDERSTANDING THE SOFTWARE CONTRACTS PROCESS 129
- Contract Provisions from the User's Perspective.. 130
- Customizations and the Contract 133
- Software Selection Conclusion 134

CHAPTER 6 135

IMPLEMENTATION OF NEW SOFTWARE 135
- Can You Increase the 41% Satisfaction Factor?... 136
- Implementation Road Map 136
- Implementation Costs 137
- How to Be Extremely Successful in the WMS Software Project 138
- The Human Side of WMS Implementations 142
- WMS Software: The Importance of Testing 147

APPENDIX 152

A... WMS SOFTWARE PROVIDERS 152

B... ERP SOFTWARE WITH A WAREHOUSE MODULE 172

C... SHIPMENT MANIFESTING SYSTEMS 176

D... LOAD BUILDING SOFTWARE 179

E... WAREHOUSE SIMULATION SOFTWARE 181

F... SLOTTING OPTIMIZATION SOFTWARE 183

G... LABOR MANAGEMENT SYSTEMS 185

H... YARD MANAGEMENT SYSTEMS (YMS) 188

INDEX 191

GLOSSARY 195

Introduction

Mission & Goals

*The mission of this report is to **substantially reduce the cost of the Warehouse software search while locating the best software.*** Searching for warehousing software is an expensive and time-consuming project. This report is designed to assist in finding the best package by focusing on five goal areas.

Our first goal is to list base line functionality that all software packages have. This is done to assist the selection team members to avoid spending valuable time on the basics. Just perform simple "litmus testing" on these basics – then expend your energies on the tougher & missing functionalities! Chapter 1 covers Expected Base Line Functionality in a rapid manner.

Warehousing software solutions are NOT created equal. Our second goal is to delineate the key differentiators among packages. This is what separates the "contenders" from the "pretenders". There is a wide variety of functionality in warehouse management systems. When a software vendor says he does a specific function, such as Volumetric aka Cubic, does he do it properly and completely? Chapter 2 covers differentiators in detail.

Pointing out the common deficiencies in WMS & ERP software is our third goal. This has happened because the warehousing software packages have focused primarily on inventory movement within the warehouse. Even the better warehousing packages will have deficiencies, missing some items as error analysis, labor productivity standard reporting, hazardous material, trailer tracking, etc. Chapter 3 covers common deficiencies in detail.

Best of Breed WMS versus ERP Warehouse Module. Our fourth goal is to educate everyone on the common differences & strengths of a WMS versus an ERP (Enterprise Resource Planning). Some ERP solutions now have a warehouse module and there are a few ERP vendors that should now be included in a software evaluation project. See Chapter 4 for WMS to ERP differences.

Building the RFP. The fifth purpose of this research report is to encourage one to develop a Request For Proposal (RFP). With minimal expense, one may send an RFP to the software vendors and get detailed responses as to what their warehousing software product does and does not do.

As one reviews each differentiator and deficiency, ask the questions:
- Is this a "must have" function?
- Is this a "nice to have" function?
- Is this function not applicable to our company?

It is extremely important to decide on each function desired and whether it is a required or a preferred function. A simplistic RFP including all differentiators and deficiencies is found in Chapter 5.

Send the RFP out. Once the RFP responses have been analyzed, then one may eliminate all vendors that miss any one of the *required* functions. This results in the short list of vendors with whom to go into a more expensive evaluation process of demonstrations, site visits, detailed functionality reviews, negotiations, and contracts.

Having the knowledge found in this research report and using a RFP for quickly getting to a short list of possible warehousing solutions for in-depth reviews, does accomplish our mission of assisting in finding the best package. In addition, *by eliminating the weaker solutions **early on** in the process via a strong RFP, one has saved significant expenses (and those software vendors have saved expenses as well).*

Additional Help is Available

IDII provides

(1) **Software selection and implementation consulting services**. IDII provides project management to lead the team during selection and provides implementation auditing.
(2) **WMS Training Classes** for the selection team. Raises their knowledge level on what to expect (base line functionality, common differences to look for in warehousing software, missing functionality, advanced WMS functionality). Project failure & success factors are also covered, in order to be successful during the implementation of new software.
(3) **Professional WMS RFP Service** that results in a complete WMS RFP that is tailored to the company's expectations, operation requirements, and future needs.
(4) **Research reports on WMS Software**. IDII produces research reports on Private and Third Party Logistics warehousing software solutions.
(5) **The Glossary of Supply Chain Terminology** is a robust and extensive glossary covering standards, warehousing, transportation, business, computer, and other terminology - available from Amazon.com. Or access this glossary online at http://www.scglossary.com

Due Diligence in New Warehousing Software Selection

Wake-Up Call

Many small to mid-size companies are guilty. So are the larger companies. What are they guilty of? They are guilty of making a **quick decision** on acquiring new warehouse software, by taking a quick look at a few solutions and landing on the one that "feels good". This short sightedness leads to (1) spending too much money, (2) missing out on stronger solutions, and (3) failure to leverage by implementing new technology.

Common Reasons for Failure in Doing a Proper Search

We have witnessed a number of companies that fail to do a proper software search. Here are the reasons for lack of due diligence:

1. A quick short list of software based on the horse racing "blinders" syndrome.
2. Treating it as a warehouse project, rather than a technical, complicated, and expensive project.
3. Full delegation to a vendor. Being too quick in finding a vendor that one can completely trust to do everything.
4. Ignoring goals to be achieved and only focusing on the immediate needs.

Quick Short List Failure

Let's get specific on these four points above. First, ask the question, *"How did you get to your short list of vendors?"* Answers such as "looked at the trade magazines" and "went to a trade show" are too common. Let me ask the questions now – Do ALL companies advertise in ALL issues? No, they do not. Do ALL companies show their products at ALL trade shows? No, they do not. Especially the smaller and mid-size software vendors do not. Conclusion – a quick short list is an injustice to your company.

Warehouse Project or Complex Software System?

Second, recognize the complexity of the warehousing as it is highly interfaced to other software solutions. A WMS can be interfaced to work with an accounting (ERP) solution, shipping software, transportation management system (TMS), material handling equipment, optimization software, and EDI.

Cure Immediate Problems Only vs. Accomplishment of Goals

Lastly, look forward to accomplishing more that just what is needed today. Make a list of short term and long-term goals. Why not require that the new software have these features today? One may implement the new software with some features turned off. Later, the desired features are turned on. By doing such, one may avoid weaker solutions and make your initial software investment last longer. In addition, you will wait less on the software vendor to deliver the functionality that you need.

Due Diligence – Look at ALL of your Options

Only 41% of new customer WMS installations are satisfied, according to WERC and the Anderson study. When one realizes that *new software will impact the company*, becoming better informed becomes more important. How large an impact is a new WMS or new ERP system on your organization? **The impact is tremendous.** A poor installation could end up with major delays in outbound shipments or even stoppages. On the other hand, an excellent installation is a major blessing.

Ask yourself, is our company going to leverage that new bazooka or just use it like a machete? In order to leverage technology to your advantage, you must validate that the product has the desired **advanced** functionality.

Due Diligence – Learn about Technology & Warehousing Software

The better installations are focused on learning about technology and warehouse software functionality. Information is available from IDII, AMR, Gartner Group, Forrester Research, and others that provide information on technology. This book covers WMS technology in detail.

To really leverage the warehousing software's technology, one must understand the details of it well. The operations and warehouse management should be trained in the following areas: report writer, basics of SQL, intelligent alert software, RF equipment, basics of network, barcode symbology, RF/ID, basics of XML, and any application software utilized (I.E., WMS, shipping system, TMS*)*.

Remember that one is investing in a product
for the long term.

A Second Time Buyer's Focus is Quality First,
then the Price.

It's a long-term relationship!

How to Be Extremely Successful in the WMS Software Project

Executive Commitment

Executives must commit money, momentum, and a strong mindset that "we will make this happen". It's much more than just a money commitment. Executives must keep management & staff on course – especially during challenging times!

IT hand-in-hand with Operations

Operations, Traffic, and Information Technology groups *working together is critical* for success! Why not partner with the IT manager on selecting a new WMS? This is not the time to do it on your own. The IT experts (or consultants) should understand all of the technology available (UNIX, NT, Linux, iSeries, TCP/IP, XML, X12, OAGIS, RF/DC, and RF/ID). Implementing a new WMS is *both* a technology and a logistics project! You need to have both types of expertise on this project, which can be trusted to select the right solution & technologies.

Consider your long-term company and IT strategies!

- What is the long-term goal for database of choice?
- What is the long-term goal for operating system(s) of choice?
- Are we moving to a new ERP system?
- Does that ERP system have a solid WMS module?

Proper Software Selection Process

Leverage our seven-step process for software selection. Skipping a step increases your risk of project dissatisfaction. It's best to verify *all* the pricing, modules, and functionality early on. In this manner, some of the pre-sales (no-cost) discussions with the vendors can cover business processing re-engineering.

Ignorance of technology, whether willful or not, is not acceptable today. It just leads to poor results.

Training personnel in the warehousing solution is critical – as many packages have tremendously powerful options to configure per part and per customer. One must consider how to train new personnel on an ongoing basis.

Who Are You? – Start There – What is the Big Picture?

Start a search by identifying the easy items, the "Who am I?" and "Where am I going?" questions. Identify the *scope* of the software search by listing what modules are desired.

If you are a food wholesaler, are you looking just for a solution for the four walls of the warehouse, or an enterprise wide solution that is strong in warehouse functionality? If you are a 3PL looking for new software, ask yourself, "Are we looking just for a solution for the four walls of the warehouse, or an enterprise wide solution that is strong in warehouse functionality?"

When a 3PL says they need a "warehouse management system", they need to be more detailed on what that means. Literally, what that means is they need the following nine modules:

- WMS
- Accounts Receivable (AR)
- Billing
- Order Management (OMS)
- Sales Analysis (SA) = 3PL Profit & Loss Analysis
- Electronic Data Interchange (EDI)
- Transportation Management System (TMS)
    - Multiple Modules in Freight, Planning, Manifesting
- Web Visibility
- Data Mapping Tool

Therefore – One needs to be very specific and precise on what one is shopping for – in order to get **ALL** of the groceries in one's shopping cart.

Start an Initial Scope Document

By identifying these issues, we have limited our scope of what we need and have also limited the possible software solutions. Here is a recap of our *first cut* on what we are searching for:

Initial Scope Document Items

- Solutions for our vertical (food, 3PL, consumer goods, apparel...). What vertical(s) are you involved in? List them.
- What modules are we looking for? List them out.
- What are our objectives? List them out in *detail*.
- What is the big picture? List out your expectations – *all of them*.
- What databases & operating systems do we have expertise for? What will the information technology (IT) department agree to and what is the long-term plan? List them.
- Will we limit the search to specific operating systems?   Yes No
    If yes, then UNIX? Linux? Windows XP? iSeries?
- Will we limit the search to specific databases?   Yes No
    If yes, then Oracle? Sql Server? DB2? Informix? Sybase? Progress?
- Are we planning on replacing other software applications within the next 5 years? Which ones?

Use the initial scope document as a basis to gather consensus with management in the company. Both goals and expectations are clearly stated and agreed upon – which increases implementation success rates. Later, this initial scope document becomes part of the RFP document.

Search Techniques

A strong RFP can be utilized as a "litmus test" to eliminate the weak solutions. A strong RFP has questions that are accurate and leave no room for inference. IDII provides an advanced WMS RFP question set. One may build upon this set, develop their own set of questions, or use a consulting firm to do a need analysis, build the RFP, and guide the software selection process. In addition, a solid RFP has company & warehouse information, plus the goals & expectations of the new system installation.

How To Select WMS Software - Diagram 1

1 - LEARN
Understand the expected, different, and missing functionality. **Use this book!** Tap into consultants as needed. Build the Initial Scope Document.

← - - - - - - - - - - - - - - Start Here

2 - BUILD RFP
Based on WMS knowledge and company practices, build a well thought out RFP and send it to all vendors. **Basic RFP is in this book!**

3 - GATHER RESULTS
Enter RFP results into spreadsheet. Challenge vendors on unusual responses to make fair "apples to apples" comparison. One now has a valuable functionality comparison and cost comparison.

4 - DETERMINE FINALISTS
Eliminate all software solutions that do NOT have "must have" functionality. Others may be eliminated on company specific requirements. Call finalists for on-site demonstrations.

Major costs incurred in this step for travel, expenses, and time spent.

5 - DEMO'S & SITE VISITS
Arrange demonstration of software solution with your inventory items. Indicate important areas that must be demonstrated. After demonstration, go to 2 or 3 sites that are using the software. Insist on sites that are similar in operation, volumes, and size to your operation.

6 - RECALCULATE FINAL COSTS
Have vendors refine cost proposals.
Make sure **all costs are included** and updated in the cost comparison.
Decide which software vendor is #1 and #2.
Make written offer to #1. Negotiate.
Fall back to #2 choice, if necessary.

7 - Sign Contacts - Start Installation
With all large computer installations, it takes dedicated staff and a key individual to drive it to successful implementation.

It is a wise idea to do a pilot project, so that the expected and agreed upon procedures can be modeled & changed repetitively before "going live" with the full warehouse.

What is a Warehouse Management System?

A WMS is a set of computer software programs designed to automate the flow of material throughout the entire warehouse premises. It will direct and control all movement of inventory within the warehouse. The WMS must interface with a multitude of other computerized systems, such as the host computer system and various computerized systems in the warehouse. The WMS is occasionally called a warehouse module by ERP vendors. SAP calls their warehouse module WM. For readability and expediency, both warehouse modules and warehouse management systems will be called WMS in this book.

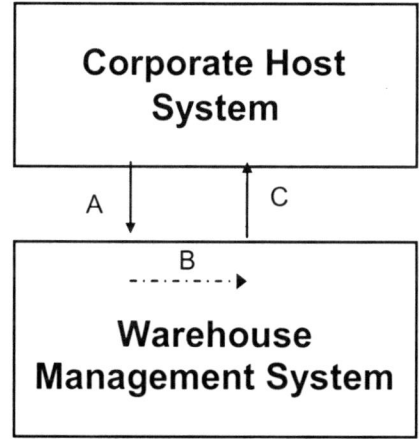

Diagram 2 - Basic WMS Diagram for Outbound Sales Orders

Diagram 2 shows the corporate host system interacting with the warehouse management system. In step A, the corporate sends sales order to the WMS. The WMS directs warehouse activities (plan, release, pick, pack, repack, ship) in step B. In step C the WMS sends the host the actual shipment quantities that were shipped out.

The major concept to learn here is that the host and WMS are pushing and pulling many types of information between them such as product management information, unexpected receipts, returns, transfer orders, purchase orders, inventory counts, inventory adjustments, and more.

Warehouse Management Systems are much, much more complex than they appear! Diagram 2 above is NOT a realistic picture! WMS are complicated on a technical computer level, especially with the WMS interfacing to material handling equipment, AS/RS, carousels, shipment manifesting system, Cubiscan, and other computerized systems. From many years of the author's software experience, the WMS is one of the most highly interfaced computer software systems in the software market place. Do not let this intimidate you! *Press on and learn!*

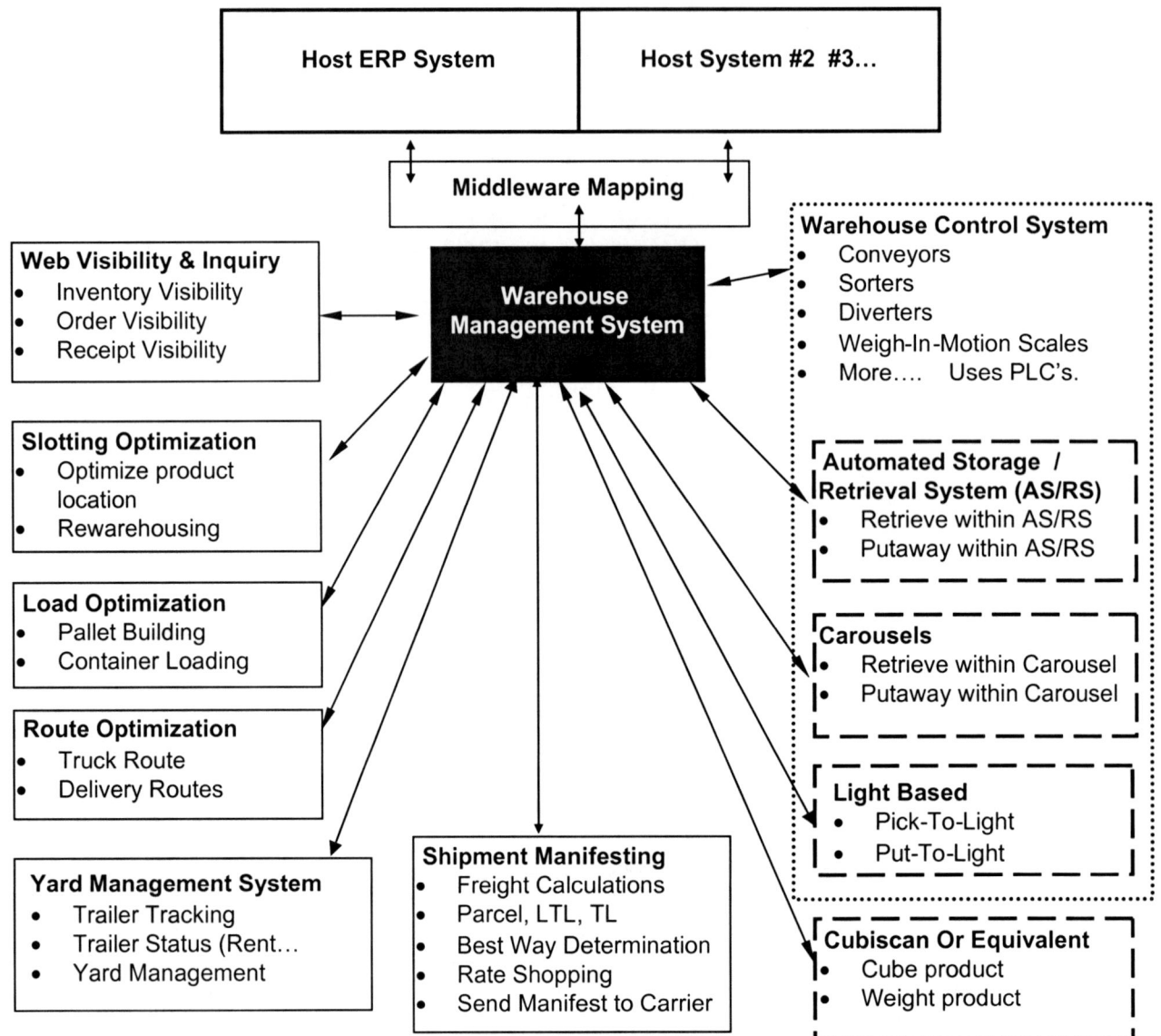

Diagram 3 - WMS Interfaced to Other Computerized Equipment & Computers

The WMS is the brains and backbone that ties the computerized equipment in the warehouse together. It is the brains, as it directs material handling equipment, AS/RS, and Carousel by giving them work to be processed and getting instruction back when it is done. The WMS is the backbone, like your spinal column. Therefore if it gets cut ("is down"), the other computerized equipment may be down, since no data can be pushed & pulled from the WMS.

It is imperative to note three items from Diagram 3 above.

First, *learn and master the WMS well*   The WMS interfaces heavily to other systems. By understanding Diagram 3, it will help you talk intelligently to many technical vendors, who provide the various material handling equipment and application software systems.

Second, the box between the Host and the WMS that is labeled **"Middleware Mapping" represents Middleware Software** that permits data to be reformatted and remapped on-demand. Many Middleware Software solutions exist, such as Mercator and Boomi. Find out which Middleware Software solution the WMS vendor is using and get a thorough understanding of its power and its limitations. E.G., can the Middleware Software receive any format and send out any format (XML, EDI, Fixed Column, CSV, and Delimited). Find out if there is a ready-to-use "adapter set" established for the WMS software product by this middleware vendor. The adapter set has the data formats (AKA API formats) already defined, which equals to less time & effort needed in building the interface (the bridge) between the WMS and the Host system.

Third, *realize that **every software vendor will have its own version of Diagram 3 and you should obtain their version of it.*** *Obtain this important diagram from each software vendor - especially if they are one of your finalists or your vendor of choice.* Study the above diagram as it shows what is possible with today's technology. Scrutinize the WMS packages to see what reality is.

Very few vendors have interfaces built in into their WMS products for Slotting Optimization, Route Optimization, Load Optimization, Yard Management, or a Cubiscan.

A WMS or ERP that interfaces to a Warehouse Control System (WCS) is for high volume warehousing. The WCS handles the material handling equipment as illustrated in the diagram above.   Only a small number of WMS & ERP solution providers offer a WCS; therefore, a number of WCS products are now available from consulting firms and integrators that support multiple MHE manufacturers.

High Level View - What is a Warehouse Management System?

Standard Definition

The standard & old definition of a WMS is software system capable of handling the four walls of the warehouse and everything contained therein (inventory, storage devices, equipment, workers, supervisors) and slight management of entities outside these four walls. Basically, this leads one to perceive a warehouse operation that is doing distribution only, no manufacturing, and a few simple value added services.

3PLs need much more software functionality than the standard WMS (defined above). The additional logic & coding for 3PL WMS is *twice as complex* as a private warehouse WMS solution. Issues such as inventory ownership, customer contracts, rates, item setup, preferences for inventory allocation – picking allocation – task workflows – exception & normal processing procedures, billing, manual billing of accessorial charges, client reporting (data, reports, charts), and profit vs. loss reporting is expected by most 3PLs. If you need more information on specific 3PL warehousing solutions, obtain IDII's research report on "Third Party Logistics WMS Software".

On the other hand, many manufacturers have had an early impact on the WMS software community and IDII knows that many of the WMS solutions can **perform light manufacturing.** This includes work orders that direct warehouse components to be delivered to a work center, dictated by a BOM. The work center assembles and performs various operations on the components to deliver finished goods, which are stored in the warehouse, transferred, or shipped per customers' requirements. Many WMS have advanced kitting options that mimic light manufacturing concepts, to track labor utilized.

What is Your Definition & Need from a WMS?

Out of these areas described - which ones do you require? It is important to identify your overall "definition of a WMS" as the majority WMS providers, system integrators, and logistics professionals still use the "standard definition".

The good point about this discussion is that many WMS have significant depth & breadth. Still - one needs to be focused on defining and iterating your requirements over & over again!

Dashboard - Metrics - KPIs - ScoreCards

Labor Standards - Work Planning

Mindset of a Conductor & Orchestra

When you go to the symphony, you expect skilled, accomplished players to perform and to hear wonderful music. The players are professionals, understanding their instruments, arrangements, and have enough self-discipline to not get out of order. The conductor is the mastermind, conducting the current pieces of music, planning the next set of arrangements, and leading the orchestra in practice and improvements. Bach, Mozart, and Beethoven composed complicated pieces of music.

When your customers come to tour the warehouse, they expect automation, efficient & knowledgeable employees, organization, and well thought-out design. Warehouse Management Systems are complex; therefore one should contrast the two:

- Your Warehouse Manager & His Supervisors are the Conductors
- Your Warehouse workers are the Orchestra
- Both Are Highly Skilled (Trained) in their Instruments
- Excellent Planning = Good Implementation and improvement of the WMS. The WMS are the instruments.
- Spend the Training Dollars = Skillful Conductors and Players!

After a WMS is implemented, it is wonderful when the trained workers can recommend a potential remedy to eliminate future errors! Before this can happen, there must be acceptance of the WMS, training, and individuals understanding their parts of the WMS. Raising the knowledge level, giving the conductors the most intensive training, and setting expectations of everyone being involved is essential. Being involved (even in small ways) is a way for people to take on ownership of what they do.

Importance of Software Selection Steps

When one short cuts any of the seven selection steps, the risk for selecting an inferior solution is greatly increased. Since WMS systems are complex, one needs a best practice of selecting software. Our steps 1 to 7 in Diagram 1 are a proven process in software procurement. One must fully understand the requirements & needs *and only then* acquire the solution that meets the current & short-term needs.

One can be thorough by having an exhaustive set of detailed functionality questions and a thorough list of WMS solutions. Some companies will short cut the process with a 20 to 60 question set and develop a list of WMS solutions from their favorite trade magazine. This is a mistake – as one will probably compromise on a "less than the best" solution.

Spend the time and develop a solid list of detailed questions in your RFP and research what solutions are in the industry. It is well worth the time & effort! IDII has an exhaustive set of WMS questions to assist the search. See our website for details.

What is a Differentiator?

A differentiator is a distinguishing feature one WMS can perform well, but that does not exist in another WMS. For example, does the WMS have the ability to avoid directing a forklift into a narrow Mezzanine aisle? Some WMS solutions do and some do not. For more information on this example, see the Equipment Table section in Chapter 2. Chapter 2 Differentiators has a focus on the critical software differences.

What is a Common Deficiency?

When the majority of WMS products are lacking in a certain area, this is called a common deficiency. For example, almost all WMS do not have a standard interface to a document imaging system. For those having engineering diagrams, MSDS, or other documents that need to go with the product, it is important to understand that *most* WMS do not have an established relationship with a document-imaging vendor. In such cases, the WMS vendor is not providing a standard interface bridge. There are many other common deficiencies across the WMS products available today. These are discussed in detail in Chapter 3, Common Deficiencies.

Filling in the GAP – Custom – Next Release Enhancement?

As one comprehends the differentiators and the deficiencies, one should realize that WMS vendors are often willing to add missing functionality to their WMS product at a price. *It is imperative to make sure that any missing functionality goes into the standard WMS product* in the current release or a future release. Get this in writing. Otherwise, when one pays for missing functionality to be added, it will be considered "custom" and one pays extra as each new WMS release comes out year after year. *Have the vendor add missing functionality in a manner that you and the installed customer base may benefit from it.*

To help distinguish between costly and difficult functionality, after each differentiator and common deficiency there is a cost level and difficulty level. Cost level is from 1 to 10, where 1 is very low cost to 10 being very expensive. Difficulty level is from 1 to 10, where 1 is simple modification to 10 being very difficult. Our difficulty rating is how challenging it is to the architects and programmers to add this function to the WMS. *Both the cost level rating and the difficulty level rating assume that the WMS does **not** have this function.* These ratings are here to help you in the negotiation phase and to prepare you mentally for what will be expensive functions to add.

Warehouse Management Systems Will Work Best If You Have:

- **Full commitment** from upper management on the WMS Project.
- **Involvement & commitment of key warehouse & IT people.**

- **Clean and complete product data.**
- Capture the weight for proper "bin locator" operation. Consider a Cubiscan at the receiving dock.
- Decide whether to capture volumetric (Height, Width, Depth) on all product packaging sizes for proper "bin locator" operation.
- Bar-code every bin and product for verification of product movement.
- An acceptance of license plate number (LPN) on containers (pallets, cartons, totes…).

- A warehouse site survey by Radio Frequency (RF) Hardware Vendor of choice
- An understanding that today's WMS packages are designed primarily for RF.
- A full RF installation. Consider paper for unusual circumstances.

- **Openness to cost saving and "best practices" recommendations** made by software vendors & consultants.
- A drive to improve process for optimal material flow.
- **Technical computer personnel** that know WMS and the technology.

- Voice technology for productivity gains, especially in picking, counting, and putaway.
- Consider & evaluate voice picking (piece picking and case picking) over costly pick-to-light investment.

- **Understand your customer & internal requirements for RFID tags.**
- Access to an RFID testing lab, so that one may test multiple RFID tags under various conditions and distances.

Chapter 1

Expected Base Line Functionality

Items That Exist In Warehousing Software

Common Expectations Today in Warehousing Software

There is a common level of functionality that is in the market place. Therefore, we advise the selection team members to look beyond the basics of inventory control & management and to focus on the advance functionality that is needed for business process optimization. The following listed areas should be solid in every solution. It is unwise to spend significant time of a demonstration on the basics, but rather focus on the more difficult functionality, as explained in the chapters on differentiators and differences. Basics to expect from all solutions are explained below.

Core Functionality to Expect

- **Strong inventory control & management.** The four-wall inventory functionality for highly accurate inventory tracking & control is to be fully expected. For many years, warehousing software solutions have fully supported Radio Frequency (RF) equipment and License Plate Number (LPN) schemes. The combination of these two provides a solid base for good inventory control.

- **RF & Paper in the Same Warehouse.** There are occasions when paper is proper for certain zones within a warehouse, while the other zones are RF. Likewise, paper can be used as a fall back if RF units have failed for a significant time period. Most software solutions can handle both RF and paper on *a zone-by-zone configuration basis*.

- **Directed RF tasks that are real-time.** The software solution should direct the warehouse worker. Real-time transactions mean that the database is updated instantly as the warehouse task is performed. If a manager queries the status of a receipt (just received 1 second ago), it will show received and inventory on-hand reflects such.

- **Manual RF task set.** In addition to a directed RF task, the software should have a RF manual version. For example, Directed RF Putaway will have a Manual RF Putaway, where the worker selects which pallet to putaway, instead of being directed to a specific pallet. Every directed RF task type (pick, move, receive, putaway, count...) should have a manual RF version.

- **Basic Inventory Allocation Methods.** Allocation methods such as Last In First Out (LIFO) and First In First Out (FIFO) are common. One still needs to investigate First Expired First Out (FEFO) and LIFO with N day window.

- **Lot control with lot tracking.** Inventory lot control is in place. See section on Lot Masking in Common Differences chapter.

- **Outbound serial number tracking.** Outbound serial tracking is found in every package that we have seen – but *inbound* serial tracking is commonly a weak area.

- **Kits with a single level Bill of Material (BOM).** For simplistic kits, the majority of software solutions have a BOM. For advance BOM, see section "Work Orders & Manufacturing" in the Common Difference chapter that discusses scrap, labor, and subcontractors.

- **Advanced Shipping Notice.** Expect the software to be able to receive and send an Advanced Shipping Notice via EDI X12 or EDIFACT. The Advanced Shipping Notice (ASN) EDI transmission is sent prior to the receiving of goods and contains the exact details of what is in a pallet, box, or container. Each container is uniquely bar-coded which ties into the ASN previously received. The WMS can thereby receive an entire container, pallet, or box - without having to scan each product. Receiving is simplified and cost savings are obtained.

- **GUI and Web enabled screens.** The majority of WMS & ERP solutions are a combination of GUI PC Windows based interface with *some* functionality that is web browser enabled. *Web enabled* means that the vendor took some of their GUI functionality and made a web version of it. Only a few of the software solutions are 100% *web based*, which means the software solution was originally designed for the web and there is not a GUI version for it.

- **Web Enabled Customer Inquiries.** All solutions have the basic inquiries that require the customer to first log into the Web Enabled software. Inquiries such as inventory availability and outbound order inquiry are common. For a 3PL – their customer may view their expected receipts, outbound shipments, and download current inventory onhand quantities.

Built-In Utility Software to Expect

It is common to expect the software solution to have some utility type (tools built into the package). These tools are from other software companies or may have been a tool the solution provider has built.

- **Supply Chain Event Management (SCEM)** in the WMS or ERP software. Provides capabilities to ***automatically*** send intelligent alerts via email, page, fax, and data file to the right people (subscribers to that event). Intelligent events are business events, application software events, and system events. For example, when an outbound order shipment is complete, then messages are sent to subscribers (customers).

    Note that a few vendors deliver a 3rd party SCEM tool such as Categoric. This approach (1) raises the overall cost of the solution slightly and (2) provides sophisticated SCEM functionality where business events have been defined.

- **GUI Screen configuration ability** for column-type inquiries and lookups. Permits client configuration and user configuration to hide columns, move columns, and resize columns. Settings would be saved, so that the next time the inquiry or lookup was executed, it would have the user's preferences.

- **Security rules by user group and function.** The solutions have very good application security. The majority of them have the ability to define security for a function to a list of users and a list of user groups. A user group is a self-defined list of users that are in a common department such as receiving or a common work task like picking. Unless you have extreme & difficult security requirements, spend your time on other functional areas to make your operation more efficient.

Expect Leveraging of 3rd Party Software Products

Middleware Data Mapping Software

- Middleware mapping package such as Boomi or Mercator that will take data files and transform them into the proper format, for both input and output from the SCM database. A wide variety of data formats & data transmission types are supported. A few WMS vendors have built a sophisticated mapping package as part of their offerings. E.G., Red Prairie.

- Adaptor sets are available from these middleware mapping solution providers. These adaptors are certified business transaction definitions for SAP, PeopleSoft, Oracle Applications, Lawson, and other major software vendors. By leveraging middleware data mapping package with an adaptor set, one may rapidly build the "data bridge" between the warehouse software and host system.

Shipping Manifest System Software

- **Shipping Manifest System (SMS)** is a package for handling multiple carriers, freight rating, carrier shipping label, freight manifest, and bill of lading for LTL & TL. SMS packages such as Clippership, ConnectShip, Aristo, and others handle all parcel carriers, LTL, and TL. SMS is also known as Parcel Manifesting (PM) software.

  By leveraging a SMS solution, this reduces the ongoing maintenance issues out of the WMS software – including ongoing rate changes and occasional new charge functionality. The SMS package provider will provide rate updates for most carriers. In addition, many SMS vendors now make their SMS rating engine available for dynamic freight rating, which can be invoked seamlessly by the WMS software.

Barcode Label Printing Software

- **Barcode label printing software** such as Loftware, BarTender, and many others. Printing of barcode labels (product, carton, and UCC128 labels) must adhere to specifications from vendors, which is known as compliance requirements. Compliance labeling is critical in the WMS / ERP / SCM environment and heavy fines are allocated against non-compliant shipments. Wal-Mart, Target, JC Penney's, K-Mart, and many others require & specify the format of the product and carton labels. Loftware, BarTender, and others have sets of 'ready to use' compliance label formats' for major retailers, and new labels are easy to configure with a GUI drag & drop environment. These label printing software vendors supports a multitude of bar code printers from all major bar code printer manufacturers, such as Intermec and Zebra printers.

Report Writer Software

- WMS solutions utilize a database that SQL can be performed. Therefore, users commonly use report writers such as Crystal Reports in most WMS solutions for creation of new reports.

- Many WMS solutions use Crystal to create their **standard** reports. This helps the customer base to adapt standard reports via Crystal and to have one "look and feel" format. Older WMS solutions have their reports written in their programming language and encourage the customer base to either (1) pay for custom reports or (2) use Crystal for new & desired report changes. This results in two "look & feel" for reports. WMS vendors that use Crystal for standard reports will deploy the WMS with 1 to 4 Crystal developer license and an unlimited Crystal run time license.

Chapter 2

Differentiators

Items That Fluctuate In Warehousing Software

Summary of Differentiators

Subject Area	Cost Level 1 to 10	Difficulty Level 1 to 10	Brief Description
Equipment Table	6	6	Login procedure must be improved to ask for equipment ID#, plus any process where equipment is utilized.
Unique Paths for Pick, Putaway, Replenishment	3	3	Paths may be purposely different for material handling equipment, flow racks, or other reasons.
Sub-Part Number	5	5	Part number is insufficient for uniquely identifying inventory. Part number plus a sub-part number will identify an inventory item.
Automatic Release to Picking for Emergency Orders	3	3	Host can mark which outbound orders are emergency/walk-in orders, or the WMS can have a rule-based system to know what an emergency order is. Either way, the order is automatically released.
Automatic Grouping & Release to Picking	4	5	WMS must have a rule-based system that is evaluated over and over again on a timed basis. When a group of outbound orders is found, then release them.
Wave Selection	4	5	WMS must have robust set of selection criteria so that waves can be custom designed – including a limiting maximum weight and volume of the wave.
Carton Selection	4	5	Insist that carton selection have the ability to not put certain items together and limit what items can go into a carton based on the carrier's service.
Pick To Carton	4	4	Print carton bar codes and create picking tasks. Instruct picker to close carton when completed.
Pick To Carrier Shipping Label	4	5	Print and utilize the carrier's shipping label as the LPN for the carton. Leverage pick to carton logic.
Weigh-In-Motion	4	5	Conveyor system for outbound shipments to include a weigh-in-motion scale and ability to handle rejects that is over a specified weight variance.
Repack Function	5	6	Repack product based on customer demands.
Inbound			**Inbound Considerations**
Cubics Per Uom	5	5	Impacts multiple places (carton selection, putaway, move, replenishment, pallet building).

Subject Area	Cost Level 1 to 10	Difficulty Level 1 to 10	Brief Description
Bin Locator System	7	8	Selecting the right bin is NOT trivial. Try doing it on paper, once you have identified all the parameters and all possible bins that could meet the criteria.
ABC Classification	2	2	A velocity code calculated by the WMS. Handy and can be utilized for slotting optimization (bin locator system).
Affinity Code	2	2	So similar items are not slotted next to each other.
Nesting Factor	2	2	To correctly compute the cube on nestable items, such as buckets.
Maximum Height	2	2	To avoid slotting heavy or expensive items at a high height when damage minimization is important.
Maximum Stack	2	2	To avoid crushing & spoilage.
Lot Control – Date Code Masking	4	5	Date Code Masking assists the warehouse worker in receiving, to automatically calculate and auto-fill the expiration date & date of manufacture.
Overall			**Overall Considerations**
Catch Weight and Dual Qty Capture	4	4	Some verticals require catch weight processing and other verticals require dual quantity ability.
Part Condition – Item Condition Code	5	5	Spare part facilities that perform MRO require inventory condition tracking, so that critical parts are categorized (repairable, dispose, good stock). Proper action can be taken, based on that inventory condition.
RFID Tag Function	5	5	WMS must have the ability to read RFID tags on pallets and cartons. The WMS must have the ability to create a new RFID tag.
Interleaving of Multiple Tasks	8	8	Warehouse worker assigned multiple types of functions to do in one trip. I.e., putaway person can do a putaway, cycle count, and replenishment for his designated zone(s).
Cross Docking	5	5	Ability to take received product directly to outbound shipping, without putting product away at normal stocking locations.
Work Orders & Manufacturing	9	9	Work orders take components and result in finished goods to be shipped out or stocked in the warehouse. Solid work orders have a complex BOM, back flush, account for labor utilized, and scrapping of components.
User Configurable System	8	9	Basic design of the WMS. Can the user easily change WMS processes? Must vendor get heavily involved every time some change is required? A few WMS systems are designed as true "user configurable systems".

Subject Area	Cost Level 1 to 10	Difficulty Level 1 to 10	Brief Description
Configuration of the Client's Customer Level	4	4	The customer of the client has specific preferences in shipping, packaging, and hours of service. This consignee information must be stored and utilized by the WMS.
Labor Productivity Information	3	1	Simply use a Report Writer against completed task information.
Labor Productivity Reporting	4	5	Reports and charts to show labor productivity by warehouse, task type, date, zone, employee.
Labor Productivity Standards	7	8	Standards to measure labor productivity and to estimated needed labor for current & future workloads.
Supply Chain Event Management (SCEM)	3	1	Business event messaging that notifies appropriate subscribers about that event.
SCEM – KPI & Non-Compliance Reporting	4	5	Tracking non-compliance and KPI is important. If the SCEM engine has a thorough set of business events, one may extend the SCEM to have summarized tables for non-compliance and KPI reporting.
Metrics, KPIs, and Dashboards	7	6	Operational metrics so that each supervisor and manager can view & evaluate their department's operational in real time via a dashboard with their selected metrics.
Scorecards	4	4	Supplier and Carrier scorecards to evaluate the performance of our partners.
Standard XML Transactions	4	5	OAGIS, RosettaNet, and BizTalk are XML standards for business transactions. How many standard XML transactions are currently supported are the key items.
Standard Interface to Material Handling Equipment	6	6	WMS has interface to PLC's and leading material handling equipment. Interface is standard part of WMS product.
Standard Interface to Shipment Manifesting System	5	4	WMS has interface to one or more leading SMS vendors. Interface is standard part of WMS product.
Voice Enablement	7	8	Productivity gains are reached with "hands free" voice picking. See what other tasks that the vendor has voice enabled.

Table 1 - Summary of Differentiators

Fill In The Gap Explanation

If a WMS solution is missing functionality, then one could "fill in the gap" by paying to have the missing functionality be put in the WMS. This table gives an approximate cost and difficulty levels. *Estimated* costs and hours are not given since vendors vary in time & material rates.

Cost Level	Cost Description	Difficulty Level	Difficulty Description
8 - 9	Very High Cost (Expensive)	8 – 9	Very Difficult Modification
6 - 7	High Cost	6 – 7	Difficult Modification
4 - 5	Medium Cost	4 – 5	Medium Modification
2 - 3	Low Cost	2 - 3	Simple Modification
1	Very Low Cost	1	Very Simple Modification

Table 2 - Cost Level Rating & Difficulty Rating Level

Equipment Table

Material handling equipment that warehouse personnel utilize to move material is very important and often overlooked in the search for a WMS. Ask yourself these questions:

1. Can a forklift go through narrow mezzanine aisles?
2. For bins that are double deep, can a regular forklift get the deep pallet in a double-deep bin?
3. For bins that are located extremely high, can that puller get to it on his normal piece of equipment?

The answer to these three questions is normally **NO**.

Watch Out. There are some WMS that do not limit the equipment in any of the above examples. Ask the WMS vendors how the right person on the right equipment will be assigned to each of these tasks.

Since the WMS directs all movement of inventory in the warehouse, it must analyze the material to move AND correctly correspond that to the abilities and limitations of the equipment that each warehouse personnel are using. The WMS are real-time systems, which means that the current personnel with the current equipment must be matched correctly **every time** by the WMS

The WMS must utilize an equipment information table that uniquely identifies the type of equipment, equipment abilities, and equipment limitations.

Abilities should include:
- Equipment width
- Equipment height (not extended)
- Maximum weight load
- Maximum volume load
- Maximum extended height (for access to bins at this level)
- Maximum depth reachable (for double-deep, triple-deep bins).

Limitations should restrict the what, where, and who.
- What types of warehousing tasks are permitted for this equipment type?
- Zone(s) and/or aisle(s) can limit where this equipment is allowed.
- Who can use the equipment is another WMS limitation to be preferred, as not all workers may be approved for that piece of equipment.

⚑ Differentiator Alert!

A mark of a better warehouse management system is quickly identified, when the warehouse person logs onto the WMS using a RF terminal. It should prompt for their user ID, password, and *equipment type*. Now the WMS knows what tasks that it can *properly* assign to this person.

FILL IN THE GAP: COST LEVEL 6 (Medium)   DIFFICULTY LEVEL 6 (Medium)

Unique Paths

WMS must provide unique user-definable paths for putaway, picking, and replenishment activities. These paths are the preferred travel paths for equipment & personnel to take. For example, with flow-through racks, the replenishment path will be different than the picking path. *Some WMS do not have unique paths that are configurable for each type of task.* Some have a pick path sequence number stored on each product by distribution center, but are missing the putaway & replenishment path sequence numberings.

FILL IN THE GAP: COST LEVEL 3 (Low)   DIFFICULTY LEVEL 3 (Simple)

Sub-Part Number

Test your knowledge... Answer these questions –

Is the part number alone is enough to select a unique inventory item?

Does a UPC code always point to a unique inventory item?

The Answer to both of these questions is no.

Once we realize that the part number *by itself* is not unique, we understand a sub-part number is necessary at times. The combination of part number plus the sub-part number gives us the uniqueness to specifically identify a specific item. For example, a company decides to leverage the UPC code as the part number in the database. Unfortunately, the UPC code points to one shirt, which has multiple colors and sizes. By adding a sub-part number, the WMS can now manage inventory for the specific shirt by size, color, and style.

Many ERP and WMS solutions are built assuming the part number is unique. This faulty assumption is problematic in certain verticals, such as Apparel. Only a few solutions have the sub-part number or a list of user-defined categories to uniquely identify the correct inventory to be picked & shipped out. This sub-part number must be part of the table key structure for fast data retrieval.

With the EPC numbering system that most WMS solutions have, this problem is minimized as EPC numbers uniquely point to a specific part and a specific unit of measure (uom). Still one is advised to consider the above information, especially in the Apparel industry.

FILL IN THE GAP: COST LEVEL 5 (Medium)   DIFFICULTY LEVEL 5 (Medium)

Automatic Release to Picking for Emergency Orders

Does your company have emergency orders that need to be picked immediately? Do your overnight shipments need to be picked immediately? If so, then make sure that the WMS can do an *automatic* release of an emergency order to be picked. Do not settle for waiting on a person to manually release the order into picking.

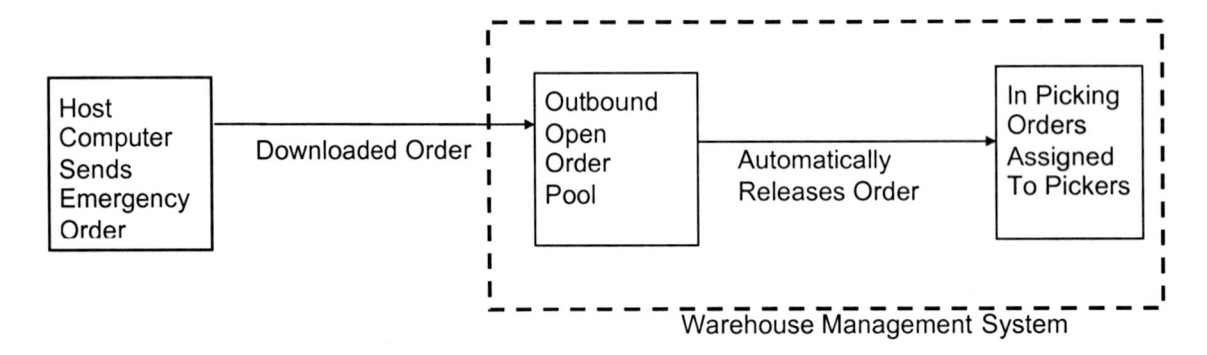

Diagram 4 - Emergency Order Being Released for Picking

In Diagram 4 above, there are two places where the new downloaded emergency order might stop along the way. First the order is created in the WMS and is placed in the Outbound Open Order Pool. Then the wave planner may manually release the order, which takes the order from the pool into a picking assignment. Manually releasing the orders into picking is standard in all WMS and requires two steps (create order into the pool and later release the order).

Now here is the million dollar question: when the order is created initially in the WMS, is it interrogated by the WMS to see if it needs to be *automatically* released and released into picking when appropriate? This is done in one step (create order into pool and right away release the order). This one-step, *automatic release* process is much faster and does *not* require a human to be monitoring & releasing these ASAP orders. Some WMS do this and some do not.

FILL IN THE GAP: COST LEVEL 3 (Low)   DIFFICULTY LEVEL 3 (Simple)

Automatic Grouping & Release to Picking

One way to optimize picking is to group a number of outbound orders in a pick wave, also known as a wave or pick batch. The picker is directed to pull for all stock in the wave, and the stock is then divided per order (if necessary). Since there are various strategies in developing the wave of orders, the WMS must have a rule table that the planner can configure and save these repetitive waves to re-run often. Once the wave is defined and put on a timer, the WMS will automatically run the following process as illustrated in Diagram 5.

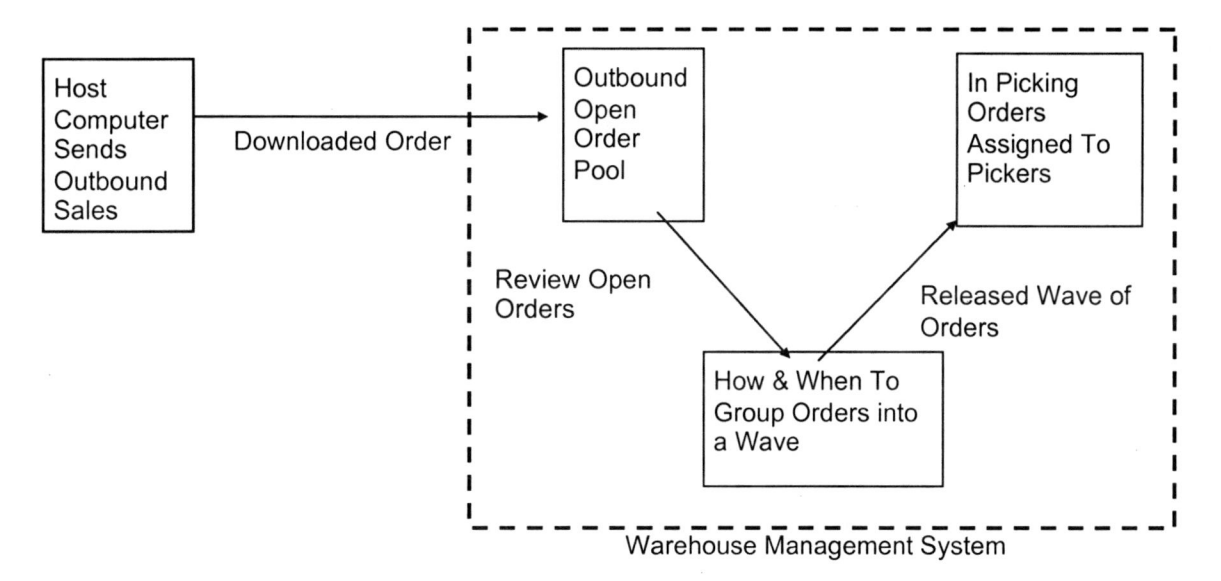

Diagram 5 - Automatically Scan All Open Orders and Release a Wave of Orders

The outbound shipments within a wave are determined by a set of selection criteria. This wave has a goal in mind, such as release all outbound shipments for UPS to picking hourly from 6:00 AM to 6:00 PM on MTWTF.

FILL IN THE GAP: COST LEVEL 4 (Medium)   DIFFICULTY LEVEL 5 (Medium)

Wave Selection Criteria

Variance with wave selection criteria is significant, regardless of the price of the software.

Many times, the maximum weight and maximum volume is missing in the selection criteria. For example - the wave planner wants to max out a trailer, with a maximum of 40,000 lbs to destination New York. The wave planning software should initially plan just over this maximum of 40,000 lbs. Next, automatically reduce the wave to just under the target weight. This can be done - by dropping the orders in lowest order weight first – until the target is reached (just slightly **less than** 40,000 lbs).

The following list is our expected *minimum* expectations.

- Type of shipment (sales order, transfer order, vendor return...)
- Carrier
- Carrier service (shipvia)
- Pick Up Time
- Route Number
- Customer Number, Shipto Number
- Order Classification - (stock order, special processing...)
- Priority Code
- Minimum and maximum dollar amount for the wave
- Minimum and maximum # of line items for the wave
- Minimum and maximum # of orders for the wave
- Minimum and maximum weight amount for the wave
- Minimum and maximum volume amount for the wave
- Warehouse ID
- Warehouse Zone
- Wave schedule: time, date, day of week pattern, day of month pattern, run on holidays
- Is this a one-time wave or a repetitive wave that is to re-occur based on the schedule?

FILL IN THE GAP: COST LEVEL **4 (Medium)**   DIFFICULTY LEVEL **5 (Medium)**

Carton Selection & Pick To Carton

Does your company break have a significant amount of piece picks? Does your company spend a large amount of labor packing a shipment? The better WMS systems support carton selection and "pick to carton" for the warehouse or a zone within the warehouse.

When piece picking is frequent for a site, then one may prefer to have the WMS direct the picker on what cartons are needed and what products will be placed into each carton, tub, or other suitable container. The WMS will also instruct the picker to release a carton when full. This is complex! Remember the WMS has made the decisions and the picker is following pre-determined instructions.

The benefits of starting "picking to carton" are very good. First, packers and packing stations are eliminated – resulting in significant savings.

Second, errors are reduced, since the elimination of the human packer means less error with that carton and it's contents. Accuracy can be even higher, since a marriage between the carton and the product is easily done by scanning both product and carton barcodes. The picker is WMS directed to do these scans and verify that the correct product has been placed in the correct carton!

For Proper Calculations

In order for the WMS to calculate the correct carton in "carton selection", the dimensions of the part and the dimensions of the carton must be properly defined. This is covered in "Dimensions per Product UOM" section later in this chapter.

The carton should be defined in a table within the WMS with the carton's height, width, and length. With a carton table and uom cube calculations, a 24" pipe wrench would *never* be attempted to be forced into a 10" x 8" x 12" box.

Critical Factors Involved In Pick-To-Carton

- Total weight of the products in the carton must be checked against the maximum weight allowed in the carton and the maximum weight that the carrier will allow for that service.
- WMS to continue to optimize picking task for this picker, items, bins, and carton sizes. In other words, the WMS determines the carton size and what items will be picked into it. The WMS will also determine the pick path.
- There are some hazardous products that may not be shipped together in the same carton.

⚑ Differentiator Alert!

Be aware, that some WMS vendors claim to do "pick to carton" but do a mediocre job in carton selection. These vendors usually do not have *uom cube* solutions.

Also, ask whether a carton table exists in the WMS. This is where all carton sizes utilized in the warehouse are defined. The carton table should have the following information: carton height, carton width, carton depth, carton weight, maximum content weight, and maximum carton volume fill percentage.

FILL IN THE GAP: COST LEVEL **4 (Low)**   DIFFICULTY LEVEL **5 (Medium)**

Pick To Carrier Shipping Label – Optimized Pick To Carton Method

Pick to Carrier Shipping Label is an optimal time saving version of pick-to-carton. The software is configured to print the carrier's shipping label and the carrier's tracking number is utilized as the unique license plate number.

The shipping label is applied to the carton and picking into the carton begins. Once the carton is completed, it can be closed (sealed). It is placed on the take-away conveyor to be loaded into the carrier's trailer.

This is a valuable time saving method, which bypasses the printing & application of a LPN to the carton and skips the involvement of a second person applying the carrier's shipping label.

Obviously, the software must perform the regular "Pick To Carton" methodology, in order to support this optimized version of pick to carton.

Helpful Information - Anatomy of a UPS Shipping Label

Overview of the UPS shipping label:

1. **Routing Code:** This code tells UPS how to route a package within a UPS building & system.
2. **Postal Bar Code:** The linear version features the zip code for the package's destination.
3. **Service Icon:** This symbol indicates the package level of service (1DA, 2DA etc.) without reading any other text on the label.
4. **MaxiCode:** This machine-readable code can be understood regardless of its direction. It uses 2D symbology for such information as postal code, country code, service class (1DA etc), tracking number, Julian date, package quantity and weight, address validation, and ship street, city and state.
5. **1Z tracking number:** The tracking number that a customer and recipient can use to trace a package through the UPS system. A 1Z tracking number identifies the customer shipper number, package service level, and customer reference number.

UPS Shipping Label Image and Anatomy from UPS. www.ups.com

Weigh-In-Motion Conveyor

Why should the outbound shipment stop *to be processed at the shipping station for weighing, dimensioning, rate calculations, and label applications?* This can be fully automated, so that the outbound shipments stay moving on the conveyor while it is weighed in motion, rated automatically, and shipping labels applied - all done in motion and no personnel needed at the shipping station!

With bar-coded license plates on every shippable unit on the conveyor system, the WMS should interface to a weigh-in-motion scale. The WMS should divert a shippable unit that is not within tolerance to be inspected and corrected if necessary. It should allow configuration by a weight tolerance expressed either as a maximum deviation percentage or a maximum under/over weight allowance.

In addition, the WMS should take the actual weight of the outbound shippable unit and access the shipment manifesting system for actual freight charges, which can trigger additional event logic to happen. Printers are available that will automatically apply labels to the moving carton while it is on the conveyor system. The shipment manifesting system or WMS should drive content & compliance on the shipping labels.

If your operation does outbound cartons, pallets, and other large & odd shaped items, then focus on what is practical. Large & odd shaped items, like extension ladders, are to be coded in the WMS as items that are not conveyorable. The strategy is that outbound processing can have "weigh-in-motion" & the rest will stop at a manned shipping station.

FILL IN THE GAP: COST LEVEL **4 (Low)**   DIFFICULTY LEVEL **5 (Medium)**

Repack Function

In order to make an item "shelf ready" for the customer, it will often require value-added steps at the warehouse to correct label and repack the product. A common difference among WMS packages is that only some will have a repack function.

This repack function is quite different from other WMS functions (receive, putaway, move, pick, pack, ship, count) since the product in a case pick is repacked to the customer's preferred case equivalent. While this operation is happening, the repacker may also apply customer specific pricing labels and prepare the product for sale. Once the repacker has finished this operation, the new "floor ready" case is closed.

All of this is customer specific; therefore the WMS must support a rule-based system, which can match customer requirements to individual SKU numbers. For example, retailer A-Mart requires that 12oz aerosol cans of WD-40 be priced at $4.95 (with retailer A's label) and is packed 8 per case. But, competitor retailer B-Mart requires that 12oz aerosol cans of WD-40 be priced at $4.90 (with retailer B's label) and be repacked at 10 per case. The WMS would direct the picker to drop off the WD-40 at the repack station, and then when the repack is completed the WMS would direct a move out of the repack station to the outbound shipping lane.

A second example: An Industrial Wholesaler also orders WD-40 but has no repackaging requirements. The WMS would directs the picker to the outbound shipping lane and totally avoid the repack station. This is why *the WMS repack function must be extremely specific in regards to who it is being shipped to, what product packaging profile is needed, and what are the customer's preferences.*

The point is **"To Repack or Not To Repack – that is the question"** – let the WMS determine it on each shipment and the shipment's destination.

Large to middle size retailers are now requesting these types of value-added steps. If your customer requires it, then make sure the WMS has the repack function.

FILL IN THE GAP: COST LEVEL **5 (Medium)**   DIFFICULTY LEVEL **5 (Medium)**

Dimensions per Product UOM

Do you stock, buy, or sell products in more than one unit of measure? If so, having defined dimensions per packaging unit of measure is important in your operation. But be alert - some WMS use only a *single cube method* and the better WMS use a *uom (unit of measure) cube method.*

The single cube WMS method will "calculate" the total volume for the case and pallet. These "calculated" volumes are close, as a factor is utilized to estimate packaging. *But the exact total volume, exact height, exact width, and exact depth of the case and master pack are never known to the single cube system.* This presents a serious problem for random bin selection (wrong bin occasionally selected), pick to carton (wrong carton size occasionally selected), load optimization (compromised), and any bin movement functions.

Placing N pieces of a SKU into a carton packaging unit, one must realize that the carton has specific dimensions. This Height, Width, and Length (HWL) vary – some cartons are either elongated rectangles, rectangles, or a square. **This poses a problem** as the distribution center will store cases and pallets that do vary in dimensions. Manufacturers will ship various case sizes and pallet sizes to your facility.

Best practices dictate that dimensions for each product's packaging units must be recorded in the WMS to have accurate slotting in putaway and moves through the 'bin locator' sub-system of the WMS. Here's why...

	Single Cube EA unit	Single Cube CS unit	Single Cube MP unit	Uom Cube EA unit	Uom Cube CS unit	Uom Cube MP unit
Height	1"	Missing	Missing	1"	4.25"	13.00"
Width	2"	Missing	Missing	2"	6.25"	12.75"
Depth	6"	Missing	Missing	6"	6.25"	12.75"
Qty Per EA	1	12	144	1	12	144
Factor	1.0000	1.0000	1.0000	1.0000	1.0000	1.0000
Volume	12 CU IN	144 CU IN	1728 CU IN	12 CU IN	166.0156 CU IN	2113.313 CU IN
Error Rate on Volume	0 %	13.26%	18.23 %	0 %	0 %	0 %
Notes	Accurate	NOT Accurate in volume, height, width, or depth! Be wary on WMS slotting.	NOT Accurate in volume, height, width, or depth! Be wary on WMS slotting.	Accurate	Accurate	Accurate

Table 3 - Comparison of single cube vs. uom cube methods to compute volume for the same part number ABC-123.

In Table 3 above, product ABC-123 is stocked and sold by the each, case, and pallet. There are 12 each/case and 144 each/pallet. The single cube method computes the volume on one case (CS) to 144 CU IN. The 144 CU IN is calculated by first computing the EA's cube by taking the EA's Height, Width, Depth and factor. Then the EA's cube is multiplied by the CS's quantity and factor. 144 = ((1x2x6) x 1.00 factor) x 12 x 1.00 factor). This volume calculated by the single cube is too low!

The better calculation, the packaging uom cube method, computes a realistic 166.0156 CU IN. A simple calculation is done, by taking the cases' actual height, width, and depth. 166.0156 CU IN = 4.25 x 6.25 x 6.25. As one may observe in Table 3, the WMS systems that have the ability to setup cubics per uom are more accurate. As packaging changes from uom to uom, the gross weight will also change. *Make sure the weight is definable per uom as well. The same problem can occur with the weight!*

Accuracy is important. With a large number of Stock Keeping Units (SKUs), invest in a Cubiscan (or equivalent) to minimize the time it takes to get dimensions & weights. **The "bin locator" subsystem needs dimensions for optimal slotting!**

FILL IN THE GAP: COST LEVEL 5 (Medium)   DIFFICULTY LEVEL 5 (Medium)

Bin Locator System

The WMS will "computer direct" the putaway person on every putaway and directed inventory moves. Take the time to fully understand what steps the bin locator system will utilize to suggest a location for a putaway or move. A bin locator system will *commonly* evaluate 50 to 200 data fields for the following areas:

- **Warehouse Limitations** - Quite a few items here
- **Zone Limitations** - hazardous, refrigerated, freezer, security ...
- **Bin Limitations** – max weight for bin, dimensions, OK for hazardous items? ...
- **Bin Availability** - Is bin empty or partially filled?
  Can different products or lots be stored in same bin? ....
- **Product Limitations** - Refrigerate? Freezer? Hazardous? ....
- **Product Attributes** - cubics of the product, weight, dimensions ...
- **Preferred Product Slotting** - primary bin, designated overflow bin ...

Differences in warehousing locator software are normally found in:

- **ABC Class Changes** - Limit this product to bins that have been assigned with the same ABC Class. When ABC Class changes on the product, the new receipts will be slotted correctly. Using a picking strategy such as PICK ON OLDEST or a PICK TO CLEAN method may eliminate inventory in the desired bins.

  PICK ON OLDEST is a picking strategy to always pick the oldest stock first.
  PICK TO CLEAN is a picking strategy to empty bins for re-use by picking the bin with the smallest quantity of this product. This bin is emptied. The next bin with the smallest quantity of this product is picked, and so forth until the total pick quantity requested is fulfilled.

- **Affinity Code** - Not to slot similar items next to each other. Avoid this type of picking errors. For example, to a puller in a hurry, a 12" adjustable wrench is visually the same as a 10" adjustable wrench. Set an affinity code on similar items, so they will not be located next to each other.

- **Nesting Factor** – To determine cube on items that fit within each other, i.e., pails, buckets, cups. First item takes full volume and the 2nd, 3rd, 4th... are computed with a lower volume by this nesting factor. Used in Carton Selection & Picking Release.

- **Maximum Height** - The maximum height allowed for this valuable or heavy item. This can be compared to the bin information and the bin locator will consider only bins at or below this maximum height.

- **Maximum Stack** - The maximum quantity of the product that can be stacked on top of one another. This helps in avoiding product being crushed or damaged.

FILL IN THE GAP: COST LEVEL **7** (High) DIFFICULTY LEVEL **8** (Very Difficult)

Lot Control - Date Code Masking

Scanning the barcode for date code requires a mask in order to *automatically* populate the lot number, manufacture date, and the expiration date. If we obtain the manufacturer date, the expiration date is the simple calculation of manufacturer date plus the shelf life days. The following are examples of date code with the relevant masking pattern underneath:

09 RBSET1122 Results in 11/22/2009 manufacturer date
yyAAAAmmdd Expiration date is 11/22/2008 as shelf life is 2 years
                Shelf life is located in the product table.

364CBA08 Results in 12/30/2008 as the expiration date
DDDAAAyy 364 is the Julian date for December 30th.

CHICE2109 Results in 05/21/2009 manufacturer date
PPPPCddyy If we have shelf life, then we can calculate expiration date.
           C = Code conversion was invoked for this manufacturer...
           May is the 5th month (A=January.... E=May....)
           The plant was CHIC for Chicago, Illinois, USA.

Masking Code Explanations:
    mm is 2-digit month (01 = January ... 12 = December)
    dd is 2-digit day of month (01 to 31)
    yy is 2-digit year with current century.
    DDD is the Julian day of the year. (001 to 365)
    A is an alphanumeric representing lot number.
    P is an alphanumeric representing the manufacturing plant.
    X indicates to skip this alphanumeric position.
    C is an alphanumeric representing a manufacturer code to crossover.
        And the list goes on...

⚑ Differentiator Alert!

Many times the WMS only has one simple mask for a selected SKU. Masking needs to be per product and plant –or– product and product group basis. Masking needs to handle crossover code tables provided by the manufacturer, therefore the WMS needs supporting **mask-mapping tables** for code conversion.

- For the same item number, there are five manufacturing plants providing the same DC the product. Each manufacturing has a different code date strategy – requiring multiple code date masks for the same item number.

- "A" represents 01; "B" represents 02... for the month of the year. *The manufacturer provides these* **crossover codes**. Manufacturers are very creative in codes - *much more* than our simplistic example here.

    FILL IN THE GAP: COST LEVEL **4 (Low)**   DIFFICULTY LEVEL **5 (Medium)**

Catch Weight and Dual Quantity Capture

For the food, building, metal pipe, and other industries – the ability to capture two quantities are important. In some verticals, catching the weight (catch weight) in addition to the quantity is critical for proper order fulfillment and billing.

For example, in the food industry, a cake of cheese is 1 cake but the weight varies by cake. Besides individual item weight differences, *some products will gain or lose weight during their warehouse storage.* It is important to "catch" their weight on the outbound, while leaving the DC, as the resulting invoice cost is based upon the weight, not the number of cheese cakes. It is also important to track dual quantities for lumber and random pipe.

Many ERP and WMS solutions are weak in this area and it is a significant enhancement to properly add dual quantity capture or catch weight capture.

⚑ Differentiator Alert!

Catch Weight Processing - If one needs this functionality – determine if it is only on the outbound, or if it is also needed on incoming receipts. More companies require outbound catch weight processing only and not on the inbound catch weight processing. Therefore, a warehousing software solution performing outbound may *not* have the *inbound* catch weight functionality.

FILL IN THE GAP: COST LEVEL **4 (Medium)** DIFFICULTY LEVEL **4 (Medium)**

Part Condition - Item Condition Code

A major differentiator between software solutions is in the tracking the condition of the inventory. In spare part facilities, repair facilities, and MRO (Maintenance and Repair Operations), there is a definite need to segregate inventory based on the received inventory *condition*. The following table shows a single SKU representing a circuit board.

Part Number	Part Condition	Uom	Qty	Can Allocate to Sales Orders?	Can Allocate to Work Orders?	DC Storage Zones
010-B567890	Finish	Each	45	Yes	No*	A,B,C,D
010-B567890	Repair	Each	120	No	Yes	E
010-B567890	Dispose	Each	70	No	No	F

Table 4 - Part Condition Example
* This example part is a finished goods product and **not** used as a component in a BOM.

Allocating inventory to new outbound orders for SKU 010-B567890 will be limited to 45 circuit boards. If additional demand occurs, the software should create a work order to direct REPAIRable inventory to be directed to a work center. When the work center is finished, it will (1) return to stock the upgraded/repaired circuit boards into finished goods inventory as "Finish" condition, (2) return to stock the circuit boards that were not repaired as "Repair" condition, and/or (3) mark a few circuit boards for disposal with a part condition "Dispose" and these are returned to stock.

The part condition should drive the bin locator system, so that inventory to be disposed of, is located in specified zone(s) of the warehouse and not mixed with the inventory for repair and finished goods. If warehouse space permits, the inventory with part condition "Repair" should be segmented in separate bins from the "Finish" condition inventory.

⚑ Differentiator Alert!

Workarounds exist on this differentiator, which may combine hold, Quality Assurance (QA), part status, and part condition logic together. This gets convoluted rapidly and IDII prefers software solutions to have separate hold, QA, part status, and part condition logic. If your organization requires the condition of the part as described here, then carefully explore in detail the workarounds that some software providers are suggesting.

Ask the software vendor very specific & detailed questions. For example, if the only inventory left for a designated SKU is in "repairable" condition (and is not on QA hold), will new outbound orders allocate this inventory and ship it? If the vendor says yes or gives a positive response – then this is a problem, as "repairable" inventory needs to be repaired or upgraded! Only good, serviceable, finished goods can be allocated to outbound orders to be shipped out. Have the software vendor demonstrate this functionality in detail.

FILL IN THE GAP: COST LEVEL **5** (**Medium**) DIFFICULTY LEVEL **5** (**Medium**)

RFID Tag Function

Wal-Mart, the US Department of Defense (DOD), and many retailers are requiring that RFID tags be on pallets and cartons. This is to **expedite** their warehousing & retail/field operations.

Software vendors vary on their approach to RFID tags. A few created a new utility module (middleware), while others imbedded the read/write to the RFID tag as part of the WMS. Previously, a license plate number (LPN) was printed on a barcode label and attached to the carton or pallet. **Upgrading this barcode label to a RFID label** keeps the LPN purpose the same, to uniquely identify the container, and to know what inventory is in the pallet or carton. Note that the RFID label can still have a printed barcode on it, if one is desired.

The RFID tag is read-writeable – unlike the one-time bar-code label print. Information on the RFID tag can be updated, when needed.

Key Items for RFID Usage

Level 1 – SLAP AND STICK. Most WMS vendors are supporting only "slap and stick" RFID tag application.

Level 2 – RFID ENABLED TASKS. A few WMS vendors are optimizing warehouse labor by using RFID readers on the forklift and eliminating the RF barcode scans.

RFID tags with sensors. Pay attention to the many lot-controlled items that could need RFID tags with sensors and serialized items. Explore support for RFID sensor options (temperature, humidity...).

LEVEL 1 - **FILL IN THE GAP**: COST LEVEL 5 **(Medium)**   DIFFICULTY LEVEL 5 **(Medium)**
LEVEL 2 - **FILL IN THE GAP**: COST LEVEL 7 **(High)**   DIFFICULTY LEVEL 7 **(High)**

Interleaving of Multiple Tasks

Interleaving or "multi-tasking" is the ability for the WMS to direct a warehouse worker to perform multiple tasks in one trip. For example, an employee is directed to pick and cycle count in an optimal manner. Based on the optimal picking route determined by the WMS, any bins needing a cycle count are added to this route. In this manner, the picker is multi-tasking or "interleaving".

The better WMS will allow configuration of what types of tasks this worker can be assigned. *The better WMS will allow all types of tasks to be interleaved.* This is the differentiator - that there are limited WMS that only allow certain combinations of tasks and other WMS that do not do any interleaving. Ask if the WMS can interleave this scenario - On a warehouse worker doing a putaway in a narrow aisle, how about count and putaway on the way in, and pick and let-down (replenishment) on the way out?

Here is tremendous opportunity to avoid deadheading! Deadheading is a warehouse worker making a round trip, but doing nothing productive while either getting there or coming back. Studies show that warehouse workers spend 60% of their time deadheading. Your potential ROI is high in avoiding deadheading and there is just one thing that could stop progress - the selected WMS. Grab your Albert Einstein and strategize about how to capitalize on interleaving.

Differentiator & Time Waster Alert!

When software vendors feel inadequate (from a functionality view), it is quite amazing on how many of them will flip the tables on interleaving questions and ask *"A lot of people want interleaving, but how many of them have implemented it?"*

Good vendor question – but let's stay on track with a 1 – 2 punch.
One – Dig to find out what is the full range of this vendor's interleaving capabilities? Two – Focus on best practices and redeem the time on "your operations".

Expect this question and turn the conversation by asking, *"How can I effectively implement interleaving on the inbound, outbound, and other tasks like cycle counting?"* Have them suggest some business re-engineering. Much better & wiser use of time!

FILL IN THE GAP: COST LEVEL **8 (Very High)** DIFFICULTY LEVEL **8 (Very Difficult)**

Cross Docking

In order for the WMS to perform cross-docks, the unfulfilled outbound shipment demand must reside in the WMS. In this manner when a backordered item has been received, the WMS may detect and initiate a cross-dock task. Some WMS are not designed to retain the backordered (unfulfilled) items and therefore does not support cross docking.

The WMS that do support cross docking vary in their approaches. The WMS will direct either the putaway or the picker to move the cross docked inventory. Note that the cross dock is done as part of the putaway task or picking task, with other normal inventory movement in a putaway or pick. A few WMS will have a setup indicating whether to do cross docking as part of the pick task or the putaway task.

Backorders

Once the original shipment leaves the warehouse, does the WMS retain the order for future shipments or mark it closed? Some WMS retain the backorders and some do not. For WMS that do not retain the backorders, the Corporate Host Computer must resend the outbound backordered items back to the WMS in order to repopulate the WMS. This is only a design issue when building the data bridge between the Corporate Host Computer and the WMS. The WMS that do retain the backordered items must also be provided with the customer's preferences, such as "line complete" shipments only, backorders not allowed, and so on. Customer preferences may be downloaded from the Corporate Host Computer to the WMS either on each order, shipto, or customer.

FILL IN THE GAP: COST LEVEL 5 **(Medium)** DIFFICULTY LEVEL 1 **(Very Simple)**

Work Orders & Manufacturing

About half of the warehousing software providers have a history with the manufacturing industry. This has provided solid functionality for Work Orders, where components & labor are applied to build finished and semi-finished goods. The Bill of Materials (BOM) should be sophisticated, with support for Work Centers.

Examine the BOM setup and work center capabilities carefully, as functionality will vary from vendor to vendor.

- Investigate BOM setup for sequencing the flow between work centers.
- Ask how scrap and labor is accounted for – it can vary significantly.
- See if one can post *partial* work orders to finished goods.
- Most do *not* allow the work order to be sent out to a subcontractor and received later at the dock, with scrap considerations.

FILL IN THE GAP: COST LEVEL **9 (High)**   DIFFICULTY LEVEL **9 (High)**

User Configurable System

Most WMS on the market are vendor configurable and just a few are user configurable. Having a user configurable system is the ability for one to re-engineer the rules, processes, flows, and setup without having to involve the WMS vendor.

One can make changes as to how the WMS is to perform without programming and without vendor involvement. This is important to companies that want to reduce the TCO (total cost of ownership) of the system.

Configurability includes the following:

- **Rule-based Evaluations** for deciding on major issues (E.G., where is this inventory item to be slotted during the putaway). Having table based (rule-based) logic is better than the limited old-fashioned parameters.

- **Screen Configuration** for column-type inquiries and lookups. The user can hide columns, move columns, and resize columns. Settings would be saved, so that the next time the screen was executed, it would show the user's settings.

- **Reports** to be saved as delimited files and Excel spreadsheets.

- **Extensive Alerts** that one can subscribe to. Configurability includes a strong Supply Chain Event Management (SCEM) offering that allows the end user to create their own events and specify SQL statements. SCEM provides the capabilities to ***automatically*** send intelligent alerts via email, page, fax, and data file to the right people (subscribers to that event). Intelligent events are business events, application software events, and system events. For example, outbound order shipment is complete and a message is sent. Other business events can assist in Key Performance Indicator calculation and non-compliance reporting, as they would log each time a KPI or non-compliance event occurred. For example, late carrier arrival is logged and later a report or inquiry shows a monthly snapshot on how many times the carrier was late. See the SCEM sections in this chapter.

- **RF Screen Configurability** where one can change the RF Task Workflow by dropping prompts, adding prompts, changing the labels, setting default values, and requiring/not requiring validation of prompted fields. Surprising – This RF Task Workflow configurability is not found in half of the software solutions. If the WMS vendor does not have this configurability, then one will pay time & material to customize the RF tasks.

- **User Definable Tasks & Workflow** is a rare commodity. The software permits one to create new tasks *and* allow a user to change the workflow of inbound & outbound tasks. E.G., for a selected product & vendor combination – our inbound workflow would be "receive then repack then putaway".

FILL IN THE GAP: COST LEVEL 8 (Very High)   DIFFICULTY LEVEL 9 (Very Difficult)

Configuration of the Client's Customer Level

The ability to configure two or three levels deep into all the customer preferences, restrictions, rules, & requirements are now a vital request in supply chain software. For example, a 3PL running a WMS who has multiple clients with inventory in the distribution center (DC) has many client & consignee requirements. One of those clients has hundreds of customers with requirements. Another example would be a wholesaler that is shipping to his client's customer DC #2, which has delivery time windows, carrier restrictions, & carrier preferences. See Diagram 6.

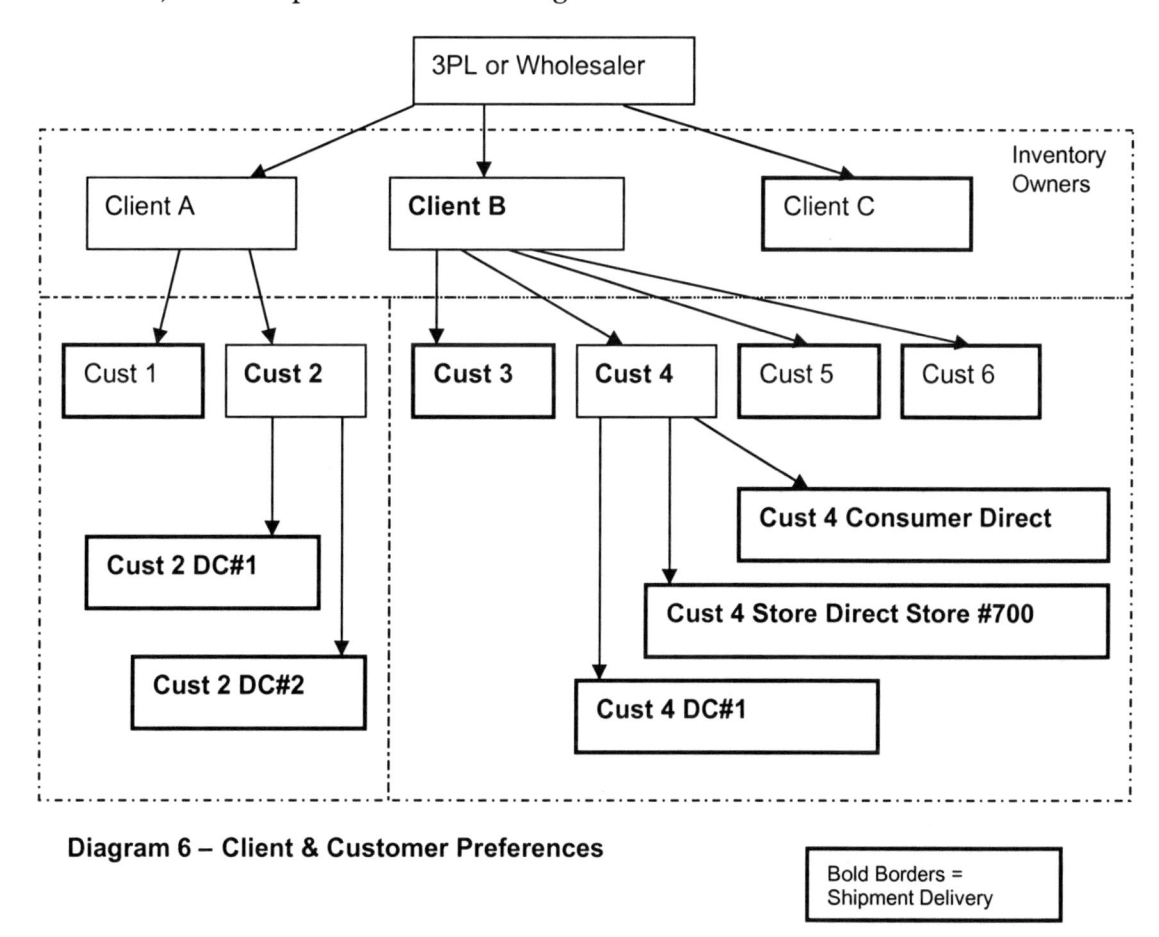

Diagram 6 – Client & Customer Preferences

Bold Borders = Shipment Delivery

The above diagram illustrates normal shipments that our 3PL (or wholesaler) is servicing on a daily basis. These shipments are repetitive, meaning that all customers & clients illustrated above, order on a regular basis – therefore each on them imposes their individual preferences, restrictions, rules, & requirements upon our 3PL.

The software must be able to store **customer destination rules for our clients** that we service. His customers may provide a list of preferred carriers, a list of carriers that are not to be utilized, days & times of operations, compliance labeling requirements, shipment packaging preferences that impact inventory allocation methodology (E.G., for a 10 pallet delivery, all of the same SKU should be on the same pallet to make receiving efficient and NOT scattered on multiple pallets), and more.

FILL IN THE GAP: COST LEVEL **4 (Medium)** DIFFICULTY LEVEL **4 (Medium)**

Labor Productivity Information

Be very careful in your wording with WMS experts on what you want in regards with Labor Productivity. *There is a difference between "getting reports on Labor Productivity via a Report Writer", "Labor Productivity Reporting", and "Labor Productivity Standards".* **Let us explain what this means.**

Getting Reports via a Report Writer

Firstly, almost all WMS packages carry an activity log indicating information on a performed task. The information usually contains task type, date done, time started, time ended, employee ID. Therefore, almost every WMS vendor can honestly and precisely say "Yes, you can get Labor Productivity reports from the database." What this means is that one must have a REPORT WRITER product and an adept individual to develop a report from scratch. The WMS does not have any standard, built-in reports. Many WMS vendors are in this boat and recommend that one just use a Report Writer to get the information into the "presentation" that best fits the company.

> **FILL IN THE GAP:** COST LEVEL 3 **(Low)**   DIFFICULTY LEVEL 1 **(Very Simple)**

Labor Productivity Reporting

Some WMS products have standard, built-in reports that produce statistics on labor in various perspectives. These perspectives include warehouse history, employee history, current vs. pending load, and task history analysis. Charting is popular in these perspectives to see if performance is improving or not. If standard Labor Productivity Reports are available, here are two suggestions for improved operations:

1. Warehouse Manager/Supervisors should have a PC with bar charts showing current tasks, pending tasks, current labor assigned to those tasks, pending labor assigned to tasks. By using red (shortage of labor), yellow (slight shortage of labor but near capacity), and green (labor can accomplish), one may determine if there is an imbalance and personnel needs to be re-assigned. I.e., if receiving has excess labor and picking is going red, then pull two receiving workers into picking. If the warehouse is zoned, the display should toggle between overall warehouse and selected zone.

2. Place monitors in warehouse to show productivity for warehouse for last 30 days in a bar chart format. Show overall warehouse performance and switch display for each task type (picking, putaway, count, replenishment, repack, etc.). The current day should be on the display!

Labor Productivity Reporting is just that -- the WMS will "report" the history of the labor. In this type of WMS solution, the labor standards are entered at installation of the WMS and then infrequently re-entered by a warehouse manager or supervisor. In this type of WMS, recalculation of the labor standards is not done! One gets the "reports" and the reports do not feed back into the WMS. Under the chapter of Common Deficiencies, the Labor Productivity Standards are covered. This is the icing on the cake, but is not found in the majority of WMS solutions.

A major differentiator between WMS solutions is Labor Productivity Reporting. Most WMS vendors that do not have built-in reports in the WMS should spend the analysis time to add them. Unfortunately, some are still saying "the data is there, just use a report writer". Why not have some very good built-in reports, which will do the entire customer base a favor?

FILL IN THE GAP: COST LEVEL 4 **(Medium)**   DIFFICULTY LEVEL 5 **(Medium)**

Labor Productivity Standards – Engineered Labor Standards

Labor productivity standards are the ability of the WMS to recalculate on a regular basis labor statistics and even use those labor statistics for task balancing. **Many WMS do not have labor productivity *standards*, but rather have labor productivity *reporting*.** IDII is starting to see a trend that some software providers are now adding engineered standards into their software. Have the software vendor prove to you, that the software has "engineered" labor standards.

Labor standards must be configurable and extremely well defined. This can be complex, as every labor component is measured and standards are at multiple levels. For example, the warehouse picking standard rate is 35 pick stops per person per hour, for those assigned to picking tasks. In addition, the zone and each individual picker have standard picking rates as well.

The standard labor rates should include factors such as (1) aggregate quantity, (2) total weight, (3) total volume, and (4) number of stops. In addition, standard labor rates must be re-computed on a regular basis. Automating the integration of the levels (warehouse level to employee level) and factors into task generation for labor load balancing is no easy task.

FILL IN THE GAP: COST LEVEL 7 **(High)**   DIFFICULTY LEVEL 8 **(Very Difficult)**

Supply Chain Event Management (SCEM) - Go Past Fax, Pager, & Email

Messaging can be automatically initiated by designated events that are sent to select personnel, customers, and/or vendors. Set it up once and let the software produce & send the messages and reports – without human intervention and overhead. Events can be warehouse related, such as a stock out, late arrival, picking shortage, outbound shipment completed. See the following Diagram.

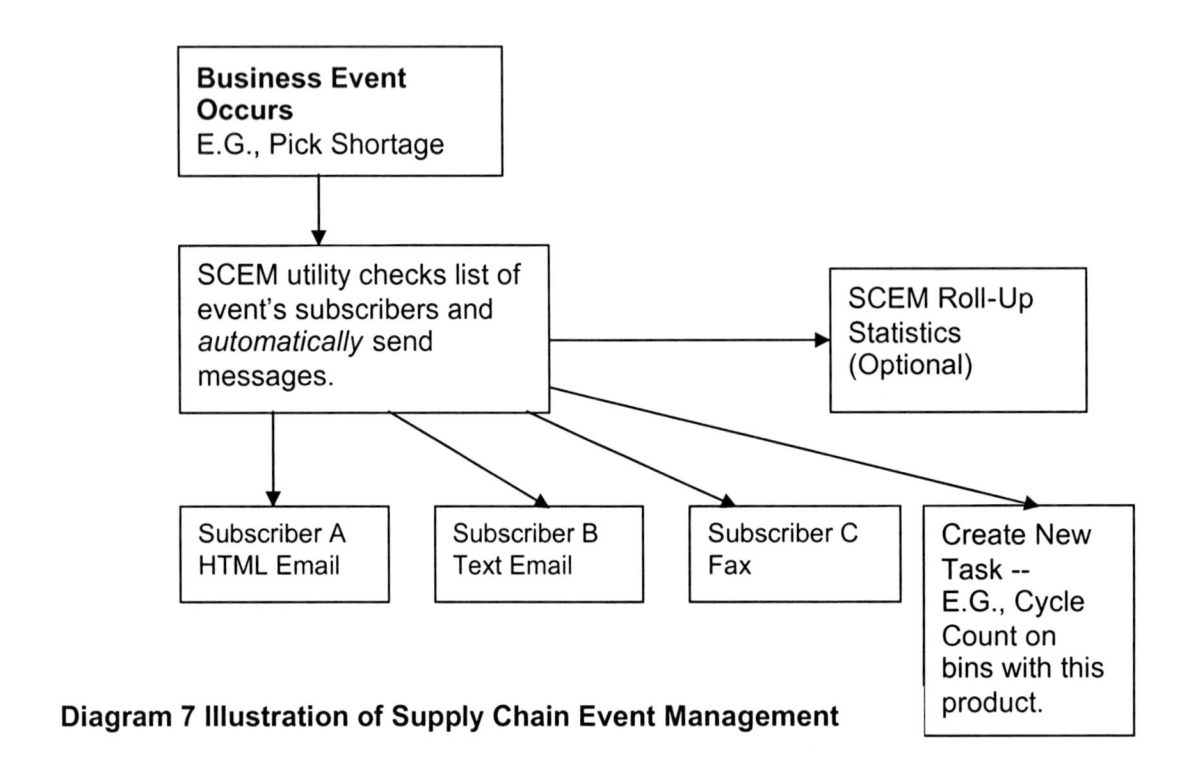

Diagram 7 Illustration of Supply Chain Event Management

For each event, one must ask - what needs to occur automatically? When the outbound shipment is completed, the event starts checking the alert subscribers for that customer, warehouse, and carrier combination. As each subscriber is checked, the message text is created automatically and then transmitted as directed. Transmission may be e-mail, fax, pager, text email, HTML email, EDI, XML, ASCII, EBCDIC, or another data format. These steps re-occur automatically for every outbound shipment.

WMS solutions vary greatly from a basic 20 events to over 500 events. Ask for a list of transmission modes and a list of the designated business events that will trigger the alert. Most WMS solutions support events via fax, pager, and text email. Some solutions have additional transmission modes (HTML email, EDI, XML, ASCII, CSV, Delimited, EBCDIC) beyond the basics of fax, page, and text emailing.

FILL IN THE GAP: COST LEVEL 3 **(Low)**   DIFFICULTY LEVEL 1 **(Very Simple)**

SCEM – KPI & Non-Compliance Performance Reporting

Only a few of the WMS solutions support event logging for Key Performance Indicators (KPI) and non-compliance event data rollup. In Diagram 7, we have a SCEM Roll-Up Statistics/History table. On each SCEM event, one may configure if the statistics is to be kept and the time period (day, week, month, quarter, yearly).

Keeping tracking on non-compliance and KPI information is important. E.G., How many times has this carrier been late (arriving 15 minutes or more late at their designated time)? Another example would be an on-time shipment's KPI's. Find out if the business event has configuration so that its information can be accumulated in a database, for specialized reporting.

FILL IN THE GAP: COST LEVEL **4 (Medium)**   DIFFICULTY LEVEL **5 (Medium)**

SCEM – Workflow

Only a very few of the WMS solutions support SCEM workflow. As a differentiator, the SCEM functionality should have workflow decision logic with priority escalation. Workflow is the ability to configure a series of steps that an event could trigger and respond to. For example, we send out an event message and have the subscriber decide an action, which triggers further software logic. E.G., A HTML web page is sent to the subscriber and they have to decide - On this backorder item now 30 days old, do you wish to cancel it, wait, or substitute this part number? If the subscriber does not reply within a predetermined amount of time, then priority escalation takes over, and the selected workflow task is initiated (cancel backorder or send another message).

FILL IN THE GAP: COST LEVEL **8 (Very High)**   DIFFICULTY LEVEL **9 (Very Difficult)**

Metrics, KPIs, and Dashboards

Expectations have risen on software and on measuring the operations of all parties involved in it. Ten years ago, many companies were satisfied with an online dashboard in the warehouse, so workers could see their performance on a month-to-date (MTD) basis. Now, each manager wants metrics in a visual dashboard that they can configure. The corporation or division wants a small number of metrics known as Key Performance Indicators (KPIs) to see their standing and take action based on these critical numbers.

Metrics

Software firms must make a decision to go down one of two paths. The first path is to partner with a Business Intelligence (BI) tool vendor, such as Blue Sky Logistics, Cognos, SAS, and others. These BI tools will provider the charting and dashboards to show metrics & KPI's in an online manner. The software vendor must take time to setup "data pulls in SQL" to access that database and acquire the calculated metrics.

The second path is for the software vendor to "build it" and software firms are building modules for metrics and dashboards. Again, the software vendor must define all the metrics that need to be supported, which is a significant undertaking – but necessary to compete.

Smart software vendors will research the metrics needed, tap into multiple resources, including the Supply Chain Operations Reference (SCOR) model created by the Supply-Chain Council (SCC) and the Balanced Scorecard methodology. Executive of supply chain companies should get very familiar to SCOR and the Balanced Scorecard background. Warehousing firms should review the research and publications done by Dr. Manrodt and Kate Vitasek.

⚑ Differentiator Alert!

Can One Configure A New Metric?

Will the business intelligence tool permit one to create a new metric? This is very important as executives, managers, and supervisors are very comfortable with dashboards and measuring. The new logistics graduates coming into management positions and current logistics analysts want to measure and analyze. Therefore, creating a new metric, *without programming*, is needed.

Dashboard

The WMS business intelligence tool needs to allow key individuals to create their own dashboards. One may select the metric and how to display in different types of charts. For example, on outbound orders one may want to view the perfect order statistics:

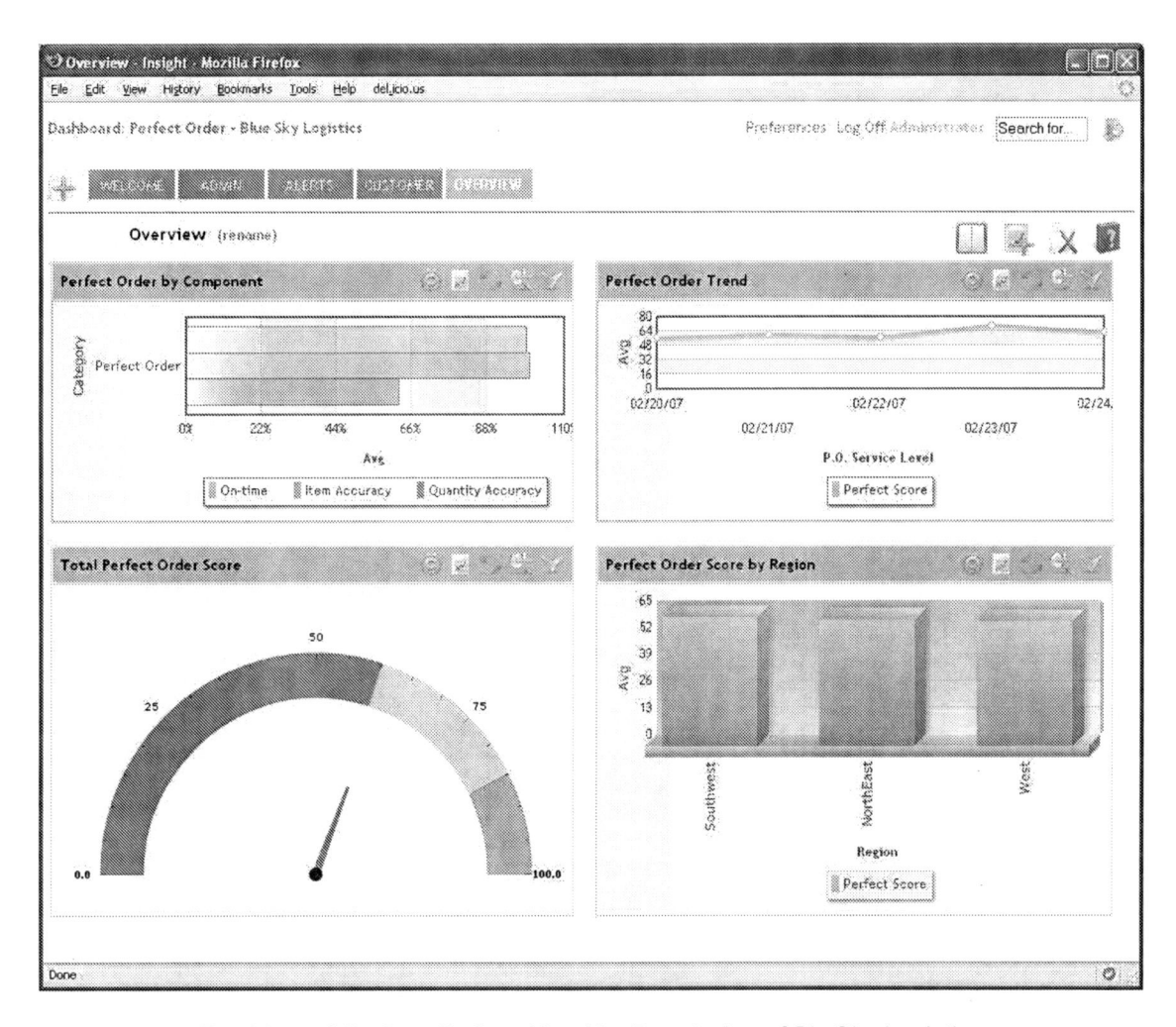

Dashboard Perfect Order. Used by Permission of Bly Sky Logistics.

Blue Sky Logistics, Inc. is a supply chain visibility dashboard software company that provides customers with targeted executive and managerial decision and metrics trending dashboards, such as its flagship product, Insight™, Perfect Order module and Enterprise Inventory Visibility suite of products. The company's solutions are web-based, real-time and configurable to serve the needs of multiple individuals within a company's various levels of supply chain responsibilities. Blue Sky Logistics offers integrated, prepackaged supply-chain software and quality service offerings to clients to enhance their customers' competitive advantage in the marketplace. For more information, visit www.blueskylogistics.com.

Dashboards can have charts and include key alerts. An example of a warehouse manager's dashboard including key alerts is below. This shows the important items that a person in his role needs to know.

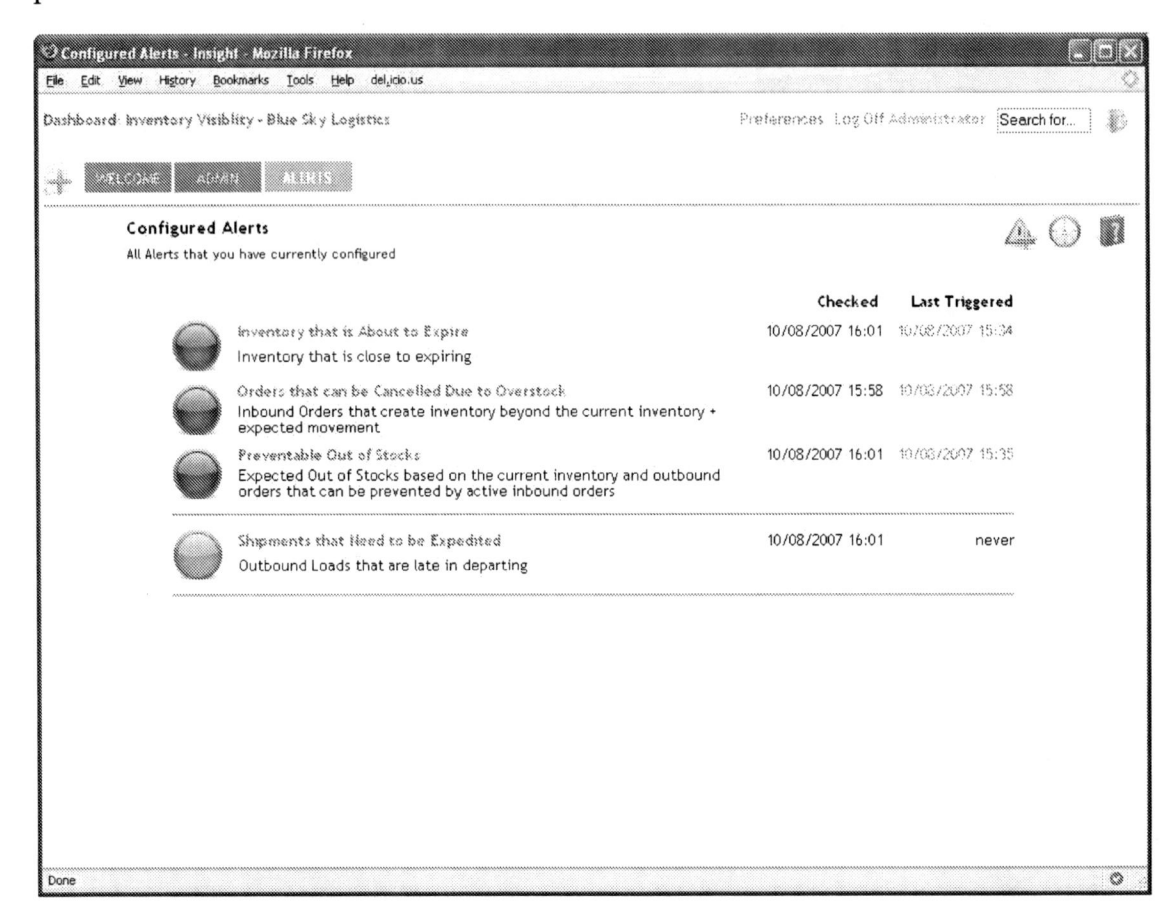

Warehouse Managers Alerts Dashboard – Used by Permission of Blue Sky Logistics

The top three items need immediate attention and by clicking on the alert description a list will appear showing the exact transaction needing to be worked on. This is important to be able to manage the queue (manage one's life) and gives the ability to work the queue. Being browser based, one may access this list from anywhere.

Key Performance Indicators (KPI's)

Key indicators are a small set of critical, must taken action metrics. Ken Ackerman and other experts recommend a small 6 to 8 set of "key" metrics for the entire operation. Sometimes KPI's are mistakenly treated like operational metrics, where **KPIs are really an organization's heartbeat measurement.** Consider the following set of KPI's –

KPI	Standard	Actual
Perfect Delivery	99.8%	99.9%
Dock to Stock	2 Hours	3 Hours
Units Per Hour (UPH) Handled	46	53
Inventory Discrepancies	.5 % of SKUs	1.1 %
Product Availability	98 % of Orders	92 %
Profitable Customers	100%	97%

Source: IDII Presentation on Metrics & KPIs

If any of the above **six** KPI measurements are out of the expected range, investigation is started right away, and the root causes are discovered. Once we understand the root causes, corrective action is decided and taken. This ongoing improvement process continues and is part of the operational culture.

Important Notes

***Did you notice** that there were four KPI's need-to-be-acted-upon in the example above?* See Dock-to-Stock actual, Inventory Discrepancies actual, Product Availability actual, and Profitable Customers actual. The KPI of "Profitable Customers" is for 3PL Organizations and shows that **3% of his clients are costing the 3PL** serious money!

It would be extremely useful for the KPI display to permit one to drill down into the supporting data.

FILL IN THE GAP: COST LEVEL **6 (High)**   DIFFICULTY LEVEL **6 (Difficult)**

Score Cards

Only a few WMS solutions capture inquiries & problems with clients and vendors. This capture and other supplier metrics is the basis for Score Cards. **Does the software have a Client Score Card, Supplier Score Card, or a Carrier Score Card?** These Score Cards are not part of the software solution normally, but medium to large size organizations measure their vendors (suppliers, carriers, and professional service providers) on a regular basis. From Wal-Mart to the Aerospace industry – everyone is grading their suppliers.

When grading the trading partner, the software has to have the ability to capture Non-Conformance events and problem vendors must take "corrective action" which is also captured. Some of the Non-Conformance events are already in the WMS (E.G., carrier arrives late, receive over shipment of an ordered item...). One must define numerically what is late in N minutes and what M percentage is considered an over shipment. Just as in the metric definitions in the prior section, one must perform a "definition" analysis during the BI software installation for Score Cards.

The Score Card and the calculations on how the grades are computed are shared with the scored party. It is only fair to know how one is being graded.

The WMS or ERP software will have to support user definable metrics and formula's in order to "score" multiple items pertaining to the trading partner. These numbers by major area are then shown on the scorecard and can be totaled for an overall grade.

FILL IN THE GAP: COST LEVEL 4 **(Medium)**   DIFFICULTY LEVEL 4 **(Medium)**

Standard XML Transactions

New standard groups have appeared with seriousness, funding, and determination. Their focus is on XML "business" transactions, to make transactions fluid from customer to vendor and vice-versa.

As software solutions are examined, one must ask what 'standards' are being supported? The Open Applications Group (OAG) has a set of standards called OAGIS. One may join the organization at www.openapplications.org and download the standards. Microsoft has assisted (or competed depending upon your view of Microsoft) with a set of standards called BizTalk available at www.biztalk.org. For collaborative planning, forecasting, and replenishment standards (CPFR) between vendor and yourself – see VICS at www.vics.org and the www.cpfr.org websites.

Be aware that other standard bodies exist, both within an industry and other continents. As a buyer of a major software purchase, verify that the vendor is extremely committed to standards by involvement and a list of transactions that are now supported in the current release of their software product.

Differentiator Alert!

The more XML transactions supported, the easier it will be to interface to other systems, especially with the emphasis in collaboration with customers, vendors, and carriers - that heavily involves data sharing. If the vendor has committed to one or more standards (OAGIS, BizTalk, etc.), then this makes it easier to share data, as popular middleware software packages have adapter sets for these.

Each software solution varies in its quantity of XML transactions supported, as each transaction requires code, also known as an Application Programming Interface (API). Again, obtain a list of supported XML transactions. The more XML transactions that are supported by the application software, then the easier it will be to share that data.

Counter Claim: A common argument against this XML transaction set is just to use the data mapping tool as "it supports many types of formats including XML". True statement, *but* we still give extra points to any application solutions that were 'designed' to support standard XML business transactions, as it will save you an investment of an analyst (*analyst time* spent creating each XML data map, testing it, and supporting it).

FILL IN THE GAP: COST LEVEL 4 (Medium)   DIFFICULTY LEVEL 5 (Medium)

Standard Interface to Material Handling Equipment

Finding standard interfaces that are "plug and play" are very unusual. Rather, the majority of WMS vendors will bill time & materials to develop a "custom" interface to Material Handling Equipment just for your company. The problem with a customized interface is that it must be continually upgraded as software versions are updated. This means additional time & material for the changes and appropriate testing are done.

Built-in, standard interfaces to sorters, diverters, carousels, AS/RS, and other material handling equipment are commonly lacking from all WMS packages. It would be very wise for the top Material Handling Equipment vendors (such as White for carousels) to partner with the WMS providers on standard interfaces on the top selling equipment. In this manner, one would eliminate customizing & the ongoing costs of custom interfaces. Further, the WMS vendor can continue to develop a WMS product, rather than WMS projects (each installation being a project).

FILL IN THE GAP: COST LEVEL **6 (High)**   DIFFICULTY LEVEL **6 (Difficult)**

Standard Interface to Shipping Manifesting System

A Shipment Manifest System (SMS) rates freight for parcels and LTL. In addition, a shipment manifest system produces shipping labels & manifests, and performs 'rate shopping" on shipments when a carrier has not been specified. In prior times, shipment manifest systems were called "parcel manifest" systems. The newer SMS definition is better, as rating can be for parcels, LTL, TL, LCL, and CL.

Many WMS vendors are willing to build custom interfaces on a time and material basis. This is a major letdown since there is established shipment manifesting systems in the marketplace. See Appendix C for a list of vendors willing to sell & support standalone system capable of rating, manifesting, and producing carrier-shipping labels. These vendors (as well as the WMS vendors) commonly interface to one another's systems. It is time to see more and more WMS vendors build a standard interface to the more popular shipment manifesting systems and support it.

The standard bridge between the WMS and Shipment Manifesting System should also include the ability to "rate shop" (also known as "carrier selection"). Outbound orders then may be downloaded into the WMS as "Best Way", the WMS queries the Shipment Manifesting System on who is the best carrier & service, and the Shipment Manifesting System returns the best carrier & service. Note: the WMS should do this as soon as the outbound order is received. Rate shopping is normally done in one of two basic variations. The first method is to consider the fastest way then lowest cost as a tiebreaker. The second method is to consider lowest cost then fastest way as a tiebreaker.

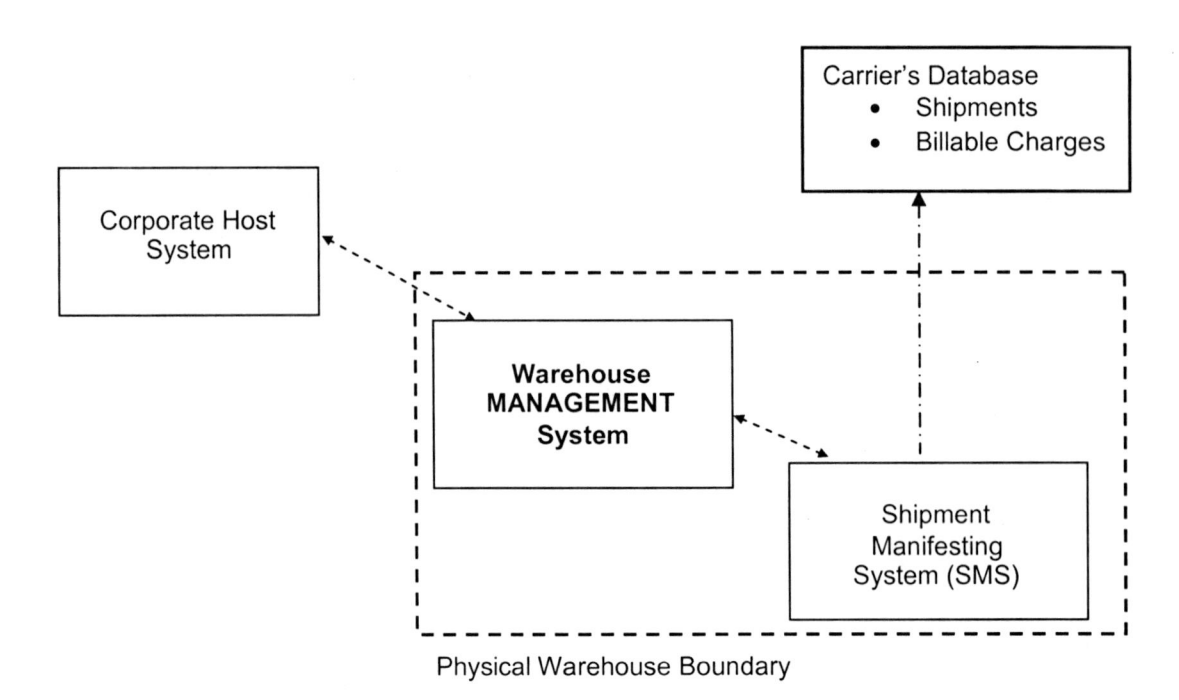

```
                                    ┌─────────────────────┐
                                    │  Carrier's Database │
                                    │  • Shipments        │
                                    │  • Billable Charges │
                                    └─────────────────────┘
┌──────────────┐                              ▲
│Corporate Host│ ◄ ─ ─ ─ ┐                    │
│   System     │         │                    │
└──────────────┘         ▼                    │
                   ┌───────────┐              │
                   │ Warehouse │              │
                   │MANAGEMENT │ ◄ ─ ─ ─ ─ ┐  │
                   │  System   │           ▼  │
                   └───────────┘      ┌──────────┐
                                      │ Shipment │
                                      │Manifesting│
                                      │System(SMS)│
                                      └──────────┘
                         Physical Warehouse Boundary
```

Diagram 8 - Shipment Manifesting & Rating Is a Warehouse Function

As the SMS rates each outbound carton and produces any shipping labels, a tracking number is assigned. The carton information, freight charges & costs, and the tracking number need to be married in the WMS, which can pass this information to the corporate host system.

The SMS will push its manifest of shipments to each carrier. This transmission of data to the carriers occurs during the day. The older SMS solutions will have an end of day transmission. The SMS database is the originating data source of the shipment and the carrier needs this information – for shipping of the shipments, proof of delivery, shipment tracking, and billing.

⚑ Differentiator Alert!

As a differentiator, the WMS should (1) include an outbound carton table that will contain carrier, service, tracking number, ship date & time, freight charges & costs, and what products (with quantities, lot numbers, serial numbers) are in that carton. (2) Have a standard interface as part of the product for major SMS products to assist in shipping product out, and (3) rate shop which carrier via calling the SMS. A WMS product may do none of these three and another may do all three. Some WMS vendors will want the corporate host to do #3 BEFORE the host is downloaded to the WMS.

FILL IN THE GAP: COST LEVEL **5** (Medium)   DIFFICULTY LEVEL **4** (Medium)

Voice Enablement

Voice technology vendors such have partnered with WMS vendors to enable warehouse workers to be directed via hearing from a headset and respond via voice to a microphone. Vocollect, Voxware, and others provide wireless voice equipment that the WMS directs. For each type of warehouse task, the WMS vendor must build "directed voice" software to manage the interaction back & forth to the worker. Another alternative is for the WMS vendor to utilize voice middleware software.

Voice Picking Has Benefits
- Productivity Gains are 10% and Higher in Case Picking and Piece Picking
- Frees Worker's Hands & Eyes
    - Told where to go
    - Voice confirmation of location by **speaking the check-digit of the bin**
    - Voice confirmation of quantity that was picked
    - No Bar Code Scans

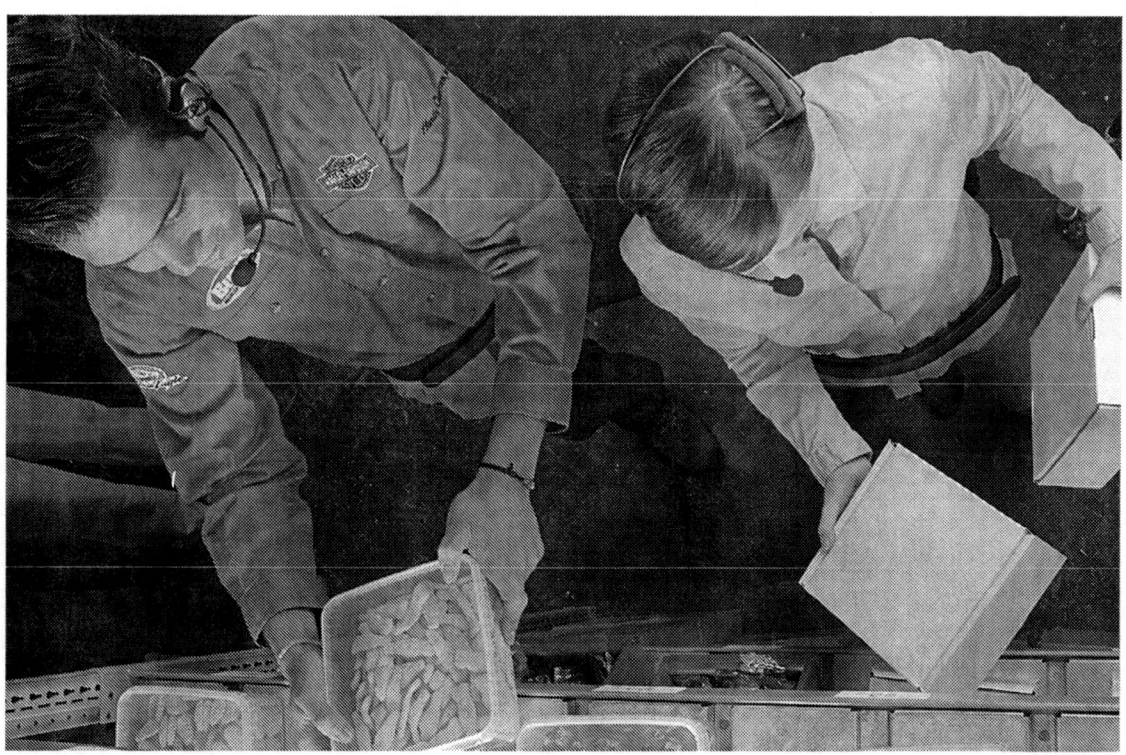

Notice that both hands & eyes are free to focus on picking. Used by Permission of **Voxware**.

Voice picking is the current "first task" that most WMS solutions are doing. This is the largest payback area in productivity. Please note that **just a few WMS providers are providing voice based counting and voice based putaway.**

FILL IN THE GAP: COST LEVEL 7 **(High)**   DIFFICULTY LEVEL 8 **(Very Difficult)**

Chapter 3

Common Deficiencies

Items Not Found in Most Warehousing Software

Summary of Common Deficiencies

Functionality That May Or May Not Be Present	Cost Level 1 to 9	Difficulty Level 1 to 9	Brief Description
Document Imaging / Paper clipping	5	3	WMS must partner with Document Imaging vendor or have built in paper clipping function.
Material Safety Data Sheet (MSDS) Processing	5	3	MSDS must be sent out according to regulations. This includes a history of when the MSDS were sent out. Workarounds exists, but evaluate the costs of each possible solution including labor costs.
Certificate of Compliance Statement (CERT)	5	3	CERTs must be sent with each shipment. This paper document should be automatically printed and attached to the shipment.
Hazardous Material Handling	4	4	This is a coordination of external data sources from carriers and the government, to have the WMS be more intelligent.
Error Analysis Table	3	2	Traps all types of errors. In this manner one may do a vendor, customer, carrier, employee, warehouse, zone, and task type error analysis.
Yard Management on Trailer Tracking	7	6	Tracking trailers in a trailer yard is important.
Order Entry – Enter an Outbound Order	8	5	WMS solutions need the ability to enter an outbound order directly into the WMS.
Automatic Re-Warehousing Optimization	4	3	A re-slotting strategy must be well thought out and implemented. Once a strategy is determined, automate with the WMS package.
Inventory Valuation Report	4	4	Unless the WMS is part of an ERP solution, the WMS will not contain the cost layers needed for an accurate inventory valuation. The corporate host is expected to have the costing layers.
Standard Interface to Load Optimization Software	3	3	WMS has interface to Load Optimization product in order to optimize the building of pallet and/or containers. Interface is standard part of WMS product.
Standard Interface to Route Optimization Software	3	3	WMS interfaces to Route Optimization product in order to load truck in optimal reverse drop sequence.
Standard Interface to a Cubiscan	1	1	WMS has interface to Cubiscan or equivalent product. The Cubiscan easily does weight & cube for the product and the WMS interface updates the WMS with this information.
Standard Interface to Enterprise System	7	6	WMS has certified interface to enterprise wide systems, such as SAP.

Table 5 - Summary of Common Deficiencies

Cost Level	Cost Description	Difficulty Level	Difficulty Description
8 - 9	Very High Cost (Expensive)	8 - 9	Very Difficult Modification
6 - 7	High Cost	6 - 7	Difficult Modification
4 - 5	Medium Cost	4 - 5	Medium Modification
2 - 3	Low Cost	2 - 3	Simple Modification
1	Very Low Cost	1	Very Simple Modification

Table 6 - Cost Level Rating & Difficulty Rating Level

Document Imaging = Paper Clipping Images

Outbound shipments need printed documents in addition to the normal shipping documents and labeling. The most commonly needed are engineering diagrams and material safety data sheets. A better WMS vendor will have an interface to a document imaging system, which is "image enabled". This permits the WMS to dictate a specific command to the document imaging system. For example, prior to the time to close the container, the WMS issues the command "Print document ENGR000077 on printer laser23". The appropriate documents print on the printer at the packing station; the packer drops the documents into the container, and closes the container.

The WMS should have a partnership with an established document-imaging vendor. The document imaging system must be "image enabled". The WMS must have either a cross-reference table of documents to access or receive the document ID's that will be printed as part of the host's outbound order download. Discuss the details on how it works with each WMS vendor.

Deficiency Alert!

Command driving the document-imaging system from the WMS is frequently missing. The document-imaging systems that are "image enabled" have a distinct advantage, as the WMS can command drive the Document-imaging product. This means that the WMS programmers can directly invoke functions of the Document-imaging product. For example, when it is the appropriate time to print a MSDS or engineering diagram for inclusion in an outbound shipment, the WMS issues the command "Print document MSDS00123 on printer laser12". Right away the imaging system prints that document (MSDS images) on that selected laser printer.

Deficiency Alert!

A popular trend with a *few* WMS vendors has been the "paperclip" function, where images are attached to an entity (customer, order, inventory item). This is a very good trend that will lead into more WMS solutions having a mini-document-imaging system.

A weak point with "paper clipped" solutions is that the product master has a limitation of only one or two images attached. Why did these vendors limit themselves and their solution to a small number of product images? Just a short sightedness of the software vendor's design team! Better solutions allow unlimited number of images to the product master.

FILL IN THE GAP: COST LEVEL 5 (Medium)   DIFFICULTY LEVEL 3 (Simple)

Material Safety Data Sheet (MSDS) Processing

Items that are hazardous are numerous – batteries, paint, cleaning solutions, glue, chemicals, and many other items. Review the prior section "Document Imaging Processing" as this will build upon the WMS tapping into a document imaging system.

Most governments require a Material Safety Data Sheet (MSDS) is to be provided to the customer purchasing any hazardous product. A MSDS must be sent out to the customer when either this is the first shipment of the product or the MSDS has had a revision. Practically all WMS have a deficiency regarding MSDS processing and MSDS history tracking.

This critical information needs to get passed from manufacturer to distributor to end user. Fire department personnel, carriers, and hazmat personnel need to have this information available for any accidents onsite at the distribution center facility.

A sample MSDS sheet is on the next two pages. Note the important information on these sheets.

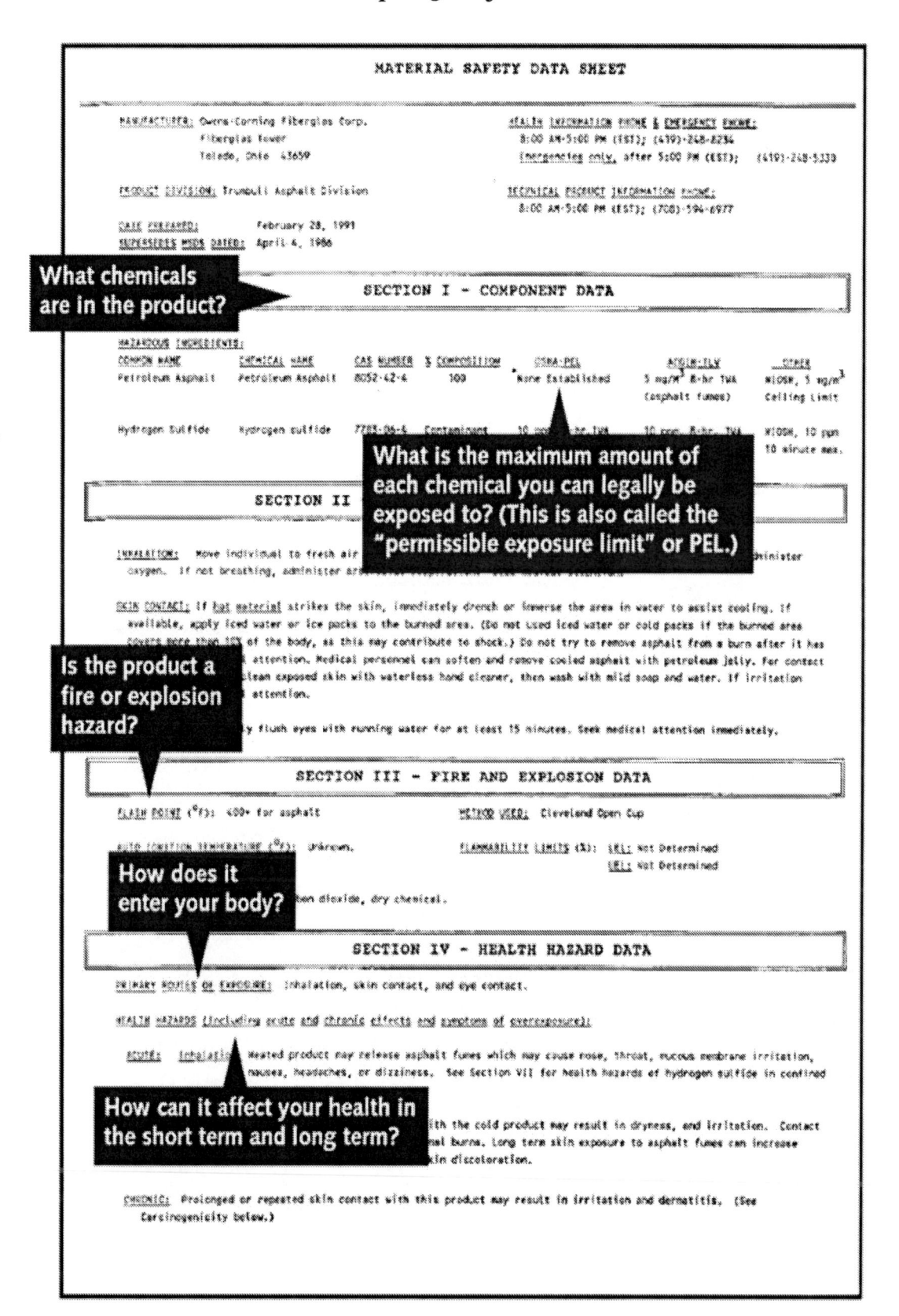

Sample MSDS Page 1 – From eLCOSH and the CDC.

SECTION V - EMPLOYEE PROTECTION

What protection must the employer provide when workers use the product?

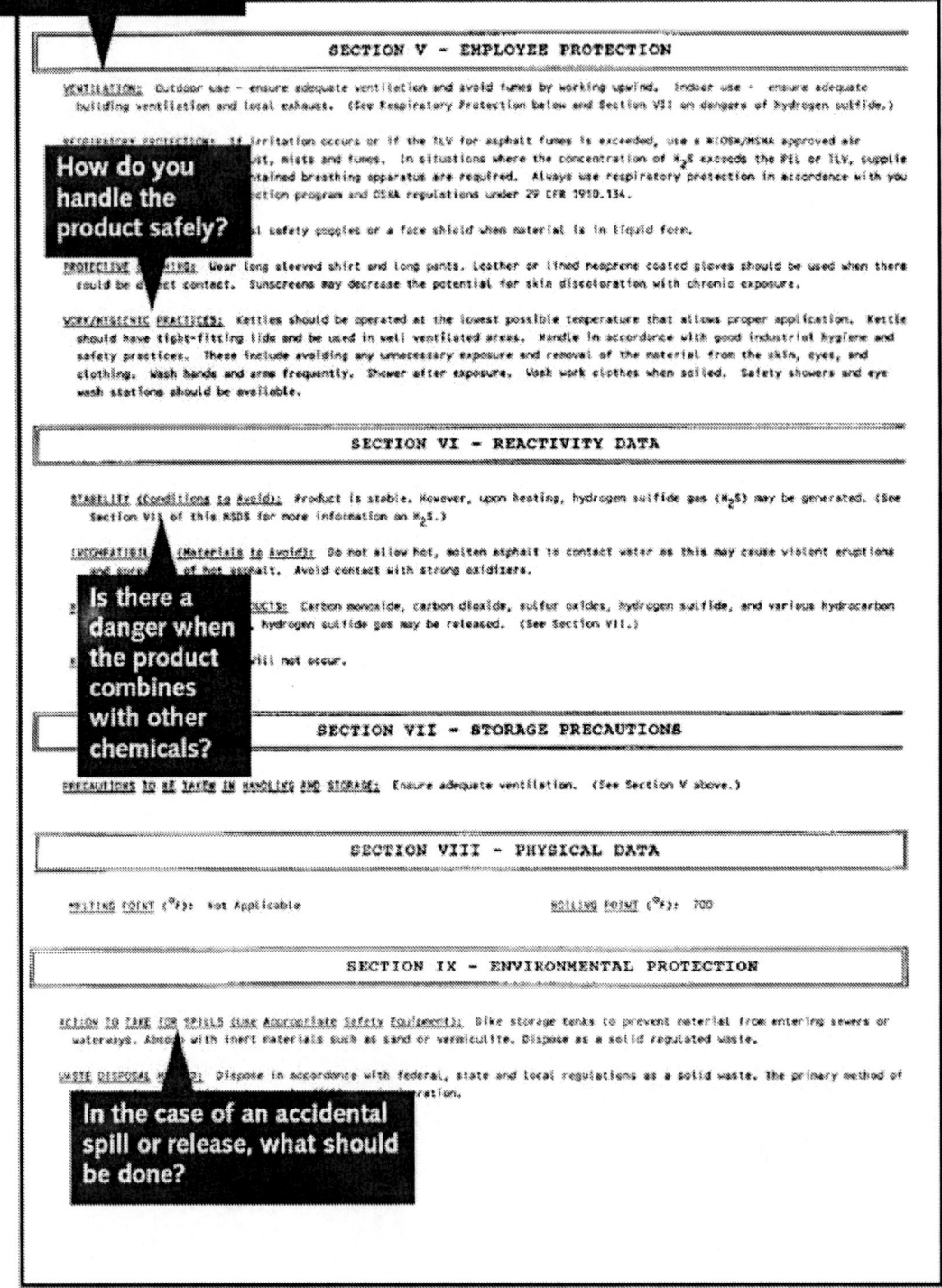

VENTILATION: Outdoor use - ensure adequate ventilation and avoid fumes by working upwind. Indoor use - ensure adequate building ventilation and local exhaust. (See Respiratory Protection below and Section VII on dangers of hydrogen sulfide.)

RESPIRATORY PROTECTION: If irritation occurs or if the TLV for asphalt fumes is exceeded, use a NIOSH/MSHA approved air purifying respirator for dust, mists and fumes. In situations where the concentration of H_2S exceeds the PEL or TLV, supplied air or self-contained breathing apparatus are required. Always use respiratory protection in accordance with your respiratory protection program and OSHA regulations under 29 CFR 1910.134.

How do you handle the product safely?

Wear chemical safety goggles or a face shield when material is in liquid form.

PROTECTIVE CLOTHING: Wear long sleeved shirt and long pants. Leather or lined neoprene coated gloves should be used when there could be direct contact. Sunscreens may decrease the potential for skin discoloration with chronic exposure.

WORK/HYGIENIC PRACTICES: Kettles should be operated at the lowest possible temperature that allows proper application. Kettle should have tight-fitting lids and be used in well ventilated areas. Handle in accordance with good industrial hygiene and safety practices. These include avoiding any unnecessary exposure and removal of the material from the skin, eyes, and clothing. Wash hands and arms frequently. Shower after exposure. Wash work clothes when soiled. Safety showers and eye wash stations should be available.

SECTION VI - REACTIVITY DATA

STABILITY (Conditions to Avoid): Product is stable. However, upon heating, hydrogen sulfide gas (H_2S) may be generated. (See Section VII of this MSDS for more information on H_2S.)

INCOMPATIBILITY (Materials to Avoid): Do not allow hot, molten asphalt to contact water as this may cause violent eruptions and splashing of hot asphalt. Avoid contact with strong oxidizers.

Is there a danger when the product combines with other chemicals?

Carbon monoxide, carbon dioxide, sulfur oxides, hydrogen sulfide, and various hydrocarbons. Hydrogen sulfide gas may be released. (See Section VII.)

Will not occur.

SECTION VII - STORAGE PRECAUTIONS

PRECAUTIONS TO BE TAKEN IN HANDLING AND STORAGE: Ensure adequate ventilation. (See Section V above.)

SECTION VIII - PHYSICAL DATA

MELTING POINT (°F): Not Applicable   **BOILING POINT (°F):** 700

SECTION IX - ENVIRONMENTAL PROTECTION

ACTION TO TAKE FOR SPILLS (Use Appropriate Safety Equipment): Dike storage tanks to prevent material from entering sewers or waterways. Absorb with inert materials such as sand or vermiculite. Dispose as a solid regulated waste.

WASTE DISPOSAL METHOD: Dispose in accordance with federal, state and local regulations as a solid waste. The primary method of disposal is incineration.

In the case of an accidental spill or release, what should be done?

Sample MSDS Page 2 – From eLCOSH and the CDC.

For warehouses with products having MSDS legal requirements, consider that some products have the MSDS imbedded with the product packaging. For example, a hazardous chemical comes in 1-gallon cans, a case with 6 gallons, or a 55-gallon drum. The case has a printed MSDS sheet dropped in it from the manufacturer. The drum has the MSDS sheet printed on it. If the distributor sells an individual gallon can, the need to provide the customer with a MSDS sheet is still there. Therefore, per UOM, there needs to be an indicator whether the UOM has the MSDS imbedded.

By use of a MSDS History table, a WMS can query whether this is the first shipment of the product to the customer or the MSDS has had a revision. If the answer to either one of these is yes, the WMS should direct the document-imaging system to print the MSDS as part of the outbound shipment. The WMS should now record into the MSDS History table that this shipto has been sent the MSDS. Inquiries and reports on the MSDS History table prove that the warehouse is in compliance with OSHA.

The project team must realize that there are workarounds on the MSDS overall problem. Here are some low cost suggestions:

1. Verify all MSDS sheets for all products are regularly updated by a third party website that specializes in MSDS sheets. Customers may access MSDS sheets from the specified website.
2. Regularly provide customers with a CD-ROM that has all products, product information, pricing, and MSDS.
3. Automated process to send MSDS to customer via automated e-mail or fax based on customers requirements. E-mail and fax software products are available for almost all computer systems today.
4. WMS solution with MSDS image processing.

FILL IN THE GAP: COST LEVEL 5 **(Medium)**   DIFFICULTY LEVEL 3 **(Simple)**

Certificate of Compliance and Conformity (CERT) Processing

Review the prior section "Document Imaging Processing" as this will build upon the WMS tapping into a document-imaging system. Manufacturers, labs, and third party calibrators issue CERTs that are a certificate of compliance statements and certificate of conformity statements. These state the product expects or exceeds the expectations stated.

These important documents must be passed unto the end-user of the product. For example, while plastic pellets going into the auto manufacturer, requires a CERT to guarantee the color and chemical makeup of the pellets. Another example is the FAA regulated airports must have a CERT proving that this electronic circuit board has been calibrated (the CERT shows the calibration testing results).

Warehouse operations and 3PL's are expected to process CERT documents, so that they are shipped with the shipment, and transmitted to the appropriate departments of the customer.

FILL IN THE GAP: COST LEVEL 5 **(Medium)**   DIFFICULTY LEVEL 3 **(Simple)**

Hazardous Material Handling

Most WMS vendors have not integrated hazardous material handling (Hazmat) into their systems. There are some software products to handle Hazmat, but this means building a bridge or re-entry of data for the separate software product.

Let's get serious now.

The automation of hazardous material handling is straightforward and can be done.

Here are two ideas on how it can be done effectively and easily maintained:

1. Outbound Shipment Limitation on Carrier's Service. WMS can select the best carrier service based on many factors including the hazard class. All carriers for outbound shipments currently provide service (shipvia) information with limitations on what hazard classes are not allowed. This list of hazard classes not allowed must be stored on every shipvia. In addition, every applicable product SKU must have a UN number (or equivalent government number indicating the hazardous nature of the product). The government publishes the HAZMAT data with the rules on handling, storing, and shipping product based on that UN number. By getting updates to the HAZMAT data, the WMS can eliminate UPS 1 Day Air Service and UPS 2 Day Air Service since UPS does not allow spray paint to be shipped via air. The hazard class is on the HAZMAT data.

2. Storing HazMat Products. The WMS directs the putaway and moving of product, the HAZMAT data can be analyzed to see what bins NOT to locate product in based on two major problem areas. First, the HAZMAT data limits how much product can be stored together in one bin. Second, the data also indicates what products not to locate this product next to. Third, the data sometimes indicates how far away from specific hazard class products it must have as a minimum distance. Out of the three items listed, this third item is the toughest to logically code.

FILL IN THE GAP: COST LEVEL 4 (Medium)   DIFFICULTY LEVEL 4 (Medium)

Error Analysis Table

Most WMS do not have an Error Table that can be analyzed for repetitive problems. An error table would be extremely useful to capture all types of warehouse errors and non-conformance events involving personnel, inventory, customers, vendors, and carriers. The error table could trap the inventory item, employee ID, department, problem code, quantity in error, cost of error, date of error, time of error, vendor ID, customer ID, and so forth.

If an employee picks the wrong product, an entry would be made. If the vendor over ships the product, the WMS could automatically enter an entry into the WMS. *Pareto analysis* can be done on this data via PC based software designed for error analysis ----- if the WMS has an error table.

The goal here is to *assist management and supervisors in eliminating all errors*. An error table in the database is a mark of a better WMS.

⚑ Deficiency Alert!

If the WMS vendor indicates that an error table exists in their WMS, have them print off the error table and all the problem codes for you. See if the problem codes are extensive or not. Please realize that most WMS vendors rely on the report writer to get small snapshots of a few types of problems.

FILL IN THE GAP: COST LEVEL 3 (Low)   DIFFICULTY LEVEL 2 (Simple)

Yard Management on Tracking Trailers

First, tracking trailers and helping the yard is where the WMS products are deficient. Information such as trailer status (date & time checked-in), trailer owner & address, normal due date before rental, rental rate per month, and planned date to return are *not* in most WMS. Yard management system (YMS) alerts and inventory visibility are critical for yard & warehouse operations.

Below is a dashboard that views the current yard information.
Notice:
1. Important alerts for this yard user
2. Elapsed storage time
3. Current equipment
4. Current trailers status

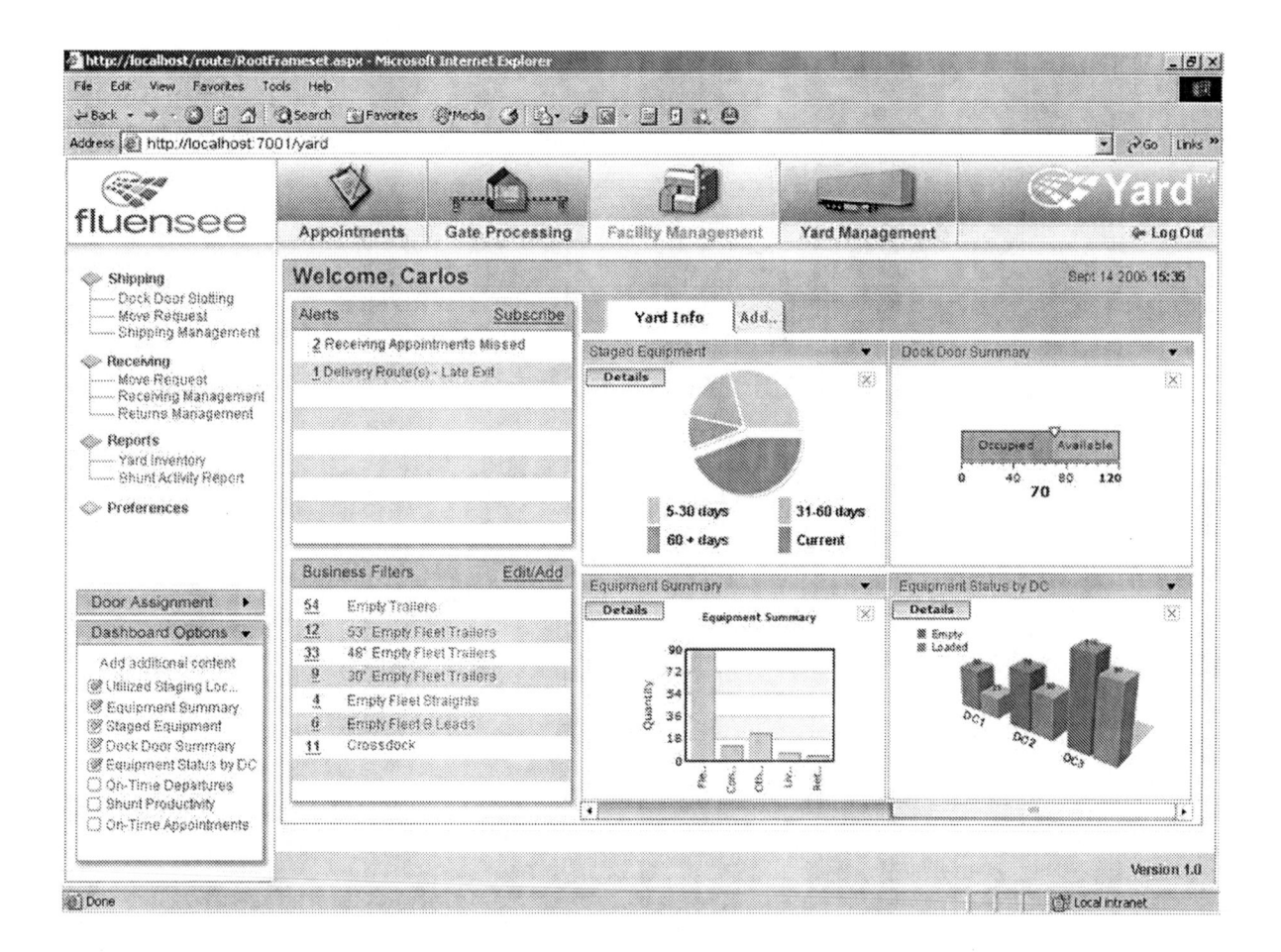

Screen image used by permission of software firm Fluensee. www.fluensee.com

Second, companies use trailers as temporary or permanent bins. For busy and *close to full* warehouses, the trailers can be leveraged to hold inventory for a period of time. Therefore visibility is needed within the trailer – to view quantities, products, and lot numbers with expiration date – so that the "optimal" trailer can be pulled into the dock and needed inventory can be utilized very efficiently.

For example, one of our large manufacturing clients wanted to view the trailers with a specified part and see a list of trailers with the quantities of the part number. The trailer with the smallest quantity meeting the requirements was brought to the dock and fully unloaded of all products. These trailers contained components for the manufacturing process. **Selecting the *right trailer* was very important every time** in this busy and near full warehouse environment. Warehouse space was limited and space was intended for finished goods inventory.

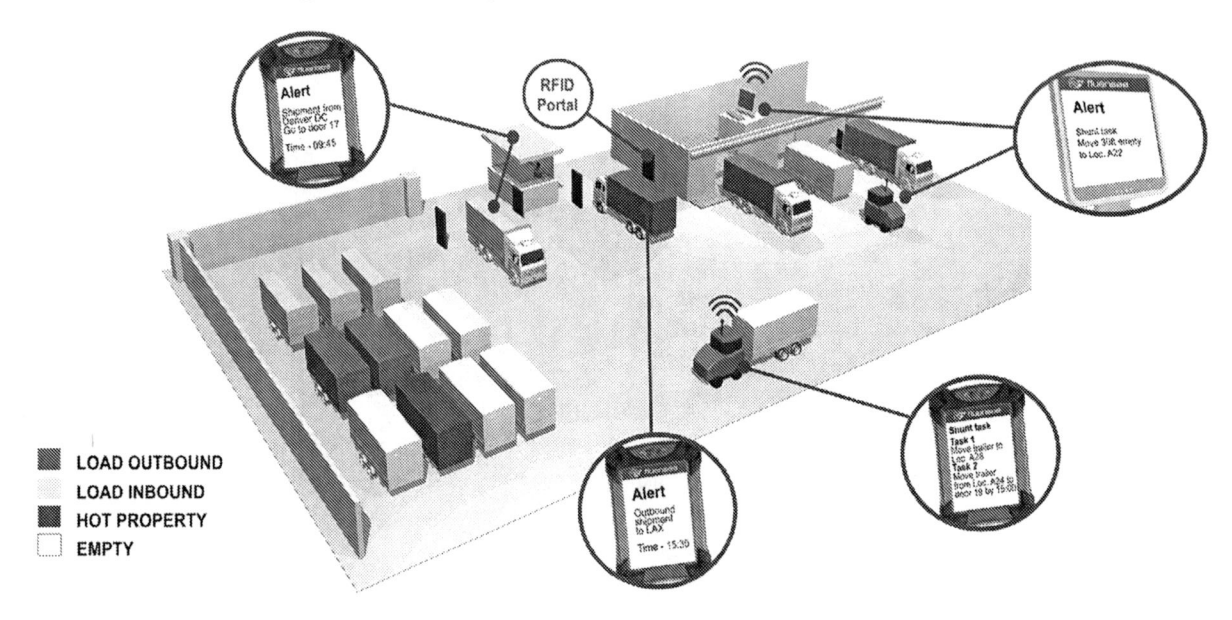

Image by Fluensee and used by permission. **www.fluensee.com**

⚑ Tip! Be Wise on Obtaining the Missing YMS

If any of the final WMS/ERP companies does NOT have an YMS, then push for them to establish a partnership with one of the best-of-breed YMS providers. Encourage the partnership, so data mappings between the software products can be **fully developed and maintained long term by the software firms**.

In addition, YMS providers have their software reasonably priced and have stronger functionality than the WMS vendors with a yard management module.

FILL IN THE GAP: COST LEVEL 7 (High)   DIFFICULTY LEVEL 6 (Difficult)

Order Entry – Enter an Outbound Order

Originally, the WMS was conceived to be a "servant" to the host ERP solution. Therefore it was very focused on the four-wall inventory and orders dropped (downloaded) from the host. Today, with multitudes of collaboration occurring, the ability for the WMS to have the ability to instantly enter an outbound order is critical.

Some of the WMS solutions have a simple order entry system, so a shipment can be executed within in the WMS. This simple order entry design has the shipfrom address, the consignee address, and inventory (quantity needed).

Almost all of these simplistic order entry systems **do *not* have**:
- Inventory costing
- Customer pricing rule matrix
- Commission calculations
- Sales tax computations
- Credit holds logic
- Credit card processing

All WMS vendors supporting 3PLs will have a simple order system. Some of the WMS vendors will surprise with a good & robust order entry system. With the web commerce being popular, the web-based order entry system will process credit cards. The ERP vendors have solid order management systems.

Distributed Order Management

Manhattan Associates and Sterling Commerce (who acquired Yantra) offer a high-powered Distributed Order Management System. This could be a trend for the WMS industry to get serious about order entry.

FILL IN THE GAP: COST LEVEL **8 (High)**   DIFFICULTY LEVEL **5 (Medium)**

Automatic Re-Warehousing Optimization

Re-slotting is an on-going strategy that should be part of the execution of a WMS. Very few WMS vendors have a program to automatically calculate the new slots and automatically release re-slotting tasks. Because of this lack, an optimization after-market has developed to fulfill this need. **WMS vendors should take the time to imbed slotting optimization into their products.**

⚑ Strategy Alert!

Slow movers that turn to fast movers can be reslotted. Fast movers that are out of favor can be reslotted in order to keep those bins for fast movers. One strategy is to have a velocity code on each product and for each bin. The velocity code is re-computed on a regular basis. When velocity code changes on a product, automatically release tasks to re-slot inventory for that product.

Date	Product	Velocity Code	New Action To Take
June 1st	BatteryHD	A	
Oct 10th	BatteryHD	B	Move A inventory to new B slot
Oct 11th	BatteryHD	B	Pick from this new B slot

Another Strategy

Another strategy is to use a pick-to-clean method, and put new receipts in the new bin. In this manner, old product in the non-optimal bin is cleaned out via picking, and the new material is correctly slotted in the optimal bin. Other strategies exist as well. Think out your strategy well for all inventory scenarios. Discuss well with experts and WMS vendor *before* WMS implementation.

The better WMS vendors have a report, which suggests parts that need to be moved for optimal slotting. For the most part, these do not automatically create and release the tasks to move the material. The WMS vendors should take the time to imbed slotting optimization into their products. Why undergo a major re-warehouse operation on once a quarter or once a year basis – when you could be re-warehousing a little bit each day?

FILL IN THE GAP: COST LEVEL 4 (Medium)   DIFFICULTY LEVEL 3 (Simple)

Inventory Valuation Report

A common deficiency found in almost every WMS is the Valuation Report. *WMS are designed to track precisely the inventory movement, but not the inventory cost.* The host corporate system will track the inventory cost. The host has a significant information base, which is updated with inventory quantities from the WMS, such as receipts, outbound shipments, and inventory quantity adjustments.

If the WMS has an Inventory Valuation Report, one should assume the worst, that the report is a ballpark figure from a single cost per item. Please realize there are no costing layers in the WMS. This report should be renamed "<u>Estimated</u> Inventory Valuation Report". Use the host's Inventory Valuation Report to get the actual valuation.

⚑ Deficiency Alert!

Be aware that Enterprise Resource Planning (ERP) solutions that have a WMS module will have an Inventory Valuation Report with actual costs. *Make sure* that the other functional warehousing issues (RF Task Queue, Interleaving, Slotting Optimization…) are strong in the ERP's warehouse solution as well. See ERP vs. WMS chapter for common differences.

⚑ 3PL Alert!

Make sure that the product setup has one or more fields dedicated for a list price and secondary price. Many 3PL clients that are small will commonly ask the 3PL to send them a list of their inventory showing item, quantity, item price, and corresponding totals. FYI - Some client host systems are limited – thereby the client leans on the 3PL to go the extra mile and fill in their reporting gaps.

FILL IN THE GAP: COST LEVEL **4 (Medium)**   DIFFICULTY LEVEL **4 (Medium)**

Standard Interface to Load Optimization Software

Do you frequently build pallet loads or container loads? If so, then having a Load Optimization software solution connected to the WMS is important in your operation. Most load optimization software packages run on PC's and graphically shows how to build the load for best weight & volume distribution. It takes the guesswork out of building a load.

Many WMS vendors overlook this common load building function in the warehouse. This is a common deficiency among most WMS packages.

⚑ Deficiency Alert!

If a WMS vendor plans on adding this to the WMS, plan it out carefully. The interface is a three-step process. The first two steps are relatively easy. Step one; the WMS is to push outbound product information into the load optimization software. Step two, the load optimization product will take the product information and optimization parameters to arrive at the best way to build the load. The challenge for WMS builders is step three, where the outbound product information is returned in optimal load sequence and the WMS must be updated to optimize the picking & delivery of the outbound product to the load building area.

FILL IN THE GAP: COST LEVEL 3 (Low)   DIFFICULTY LEVEL 3 (Simple)

Standard Interface to Route Optimization Software

Do you frequently plan truck or van routes for delivery stops? If so, then having a Route Optimization software product bridged to the WMS is important in your operation. Most route optimization packages run on PC's and is extremely good at getting the optimal route.

Many WMS vendors overlook this common routing function, as they expect a TMS route optimization solution to handle it.

⚑ Deficiency Alert!

If the WMS vendor plans on adding this interface, the same three steps are needed as described above in Load Optimization Software interface to the WMS. In addition, the route must be "frozen" for a snapshot to optimize the route. Are additional outbound shipments allowed after the optimization? If so, then rerun the entire route optimization process. Once the route is perfected, then release the entire route shipments for picking.

FILL IN THE GAP: COST LEVEL 3 (Low)   DIFFICULTY LEVEL 3 (Simple)

Standard Interface to Dimension & Weighing Equipment

The WMS should have a data bridge between a dimensioning unit and itself. This standard interface is primarily a one-way information flow of cubics and weights into the WMS. The WMS vendor should support this interface as part of the WMS product.

Cubiscan Image Provided by Quantronix.   Used by Permission.

Quantronix also offers a broad range of software solutions that will integrate the CubiScan with an existing warehouse or transportation system. For more information please contact Quantronix at 800-488-CUBE (2823) or visit our web site at www.cubiscan.com.

In the picture above, the Cubiscan unit weighs and cubes the carton for the specific SKU. Any type of item can be placed on the unit – whether it is a single unit of the item, carton, or inner pack. The item number, uom, dimensions, and weights are stored in a PC connected to unit. The WMS should have a standard interface to read in this information from the PC and then store it in the WMS product by uom table. Quantronix, Express Cube, and others have these dimensional & weighing units.

Standard Interface to Dimensioning & Weighing Equipment (Continued)

In the image below, the dimensioning unit is electronically capturing the carton's dimensions as cartons are moving on the conveyor. On the outbound, carton dimensions are now required by most parcel carriers. See "Weigh-In-Motion" section in Chapter 2 for more details. On the inbound, dimensions are needed for putaway so that slotting is done correctly via the WMS.

Cubiscan Image Provided by Quantronix. Used by Permission.

CubiScan® dimensioning systems by Quantronix are used to dimension freight in warehousing, and freight transportation applications where dimensional data is used in shipment and logistics planning, storage space planning, carton selection, and computing volume based shipping charges. The CubiScan will electronically capture, store, and send cube and weight information directly to a computerized warehouse systems (WMS) or freight manifesting system.

FILL IN THE GAP: COST LEVEL 1 **(Very Low)**   DIFFICULTY LEVEL 1 **(Very Simple)**

Standard Interface to SAP, Oracle, Baan, PeopleSoft

The WMS should have "certified" interfaces to predominate enterprise solutions. For larger companies, there should be a certified interface to SAP, Oracle financials, Baan, SSA, PeopleSoft, JD Edwards, etc. For smaller companies, a certified interface to Great Plains, MAS, or QuickBooks Professional, is a more practical expectation.

A few WMS solutions have certified interfaces. Look for WMS & ERP vendors that have standard middleware adapters, which are available from the middleware software companies.

⚑ Deficiency Alert!

For many years, a number of WMS providers may have done an interface on a time and material basis. Make sure that one asks specifically if the interface is certified, supported, and available as a purchased product. Our alert here is focusing on standardized & certified interfaces, not those done on a custom per customer basis. Make sure the interface will be used and re-sold to new customers.

⚑ Strategy Alert!

What is the company's long-term plan for its host, enterprise system? If you are planning on moving to a better solution, then put that interface to the probable enterprise systems on your RFP. Plan now for the future by making sure a bridge exists for that future enterprise system. Planning now will save significant bridge building costs later, by avoiding the custom time and material costs in interfacing two separate systems.

FILL IN THE GAP: COST LEVEL 7 **(High)**   DIFFICULTY LEVEL 6 **(Difficult)**

Chapter 4

WMS Strengths vs. ERP

The Strengths of Warehouse Management Systems in Comparison to Enterprise Solutions

Understanding WMS & ERP Differences

Understanding the differences between Warehouse Management (WMS) and Enterprise Resource Planning (ERP) systems is critical, since a few of the ERP solutions have added warehousing functionality to their offerings. Making sound decisions in this "supply chain execution" part of your business is very important.

Warehousing is considered the critical & most important "last mile of a customer order". This is where orders are filled, packaged, touched, documented, notified, and shipped. Many companies are doing value added services in their warehousing, from kitting, private labeling, store ready merchandise, manufacturing, and much more. Accurate inventory receiving must be performed continually in order to insure outbound picks are 100% accurate. Therefore, skimping a full understanding of WMS versus ERP in the execution side of the business is very risky & unwise.

This section contrasts the **average WMS versus the average ERP** solution in the market place today. It will enable a software purchaser to fully grasp what they are and are not buying. This information will assist one in determining whether to obtain a best-of-breed WMS with an ERP or to settle for an ERP solution that has a warehouse module.

Warehouse Management Systems Strengths

A WMS offers greater functionality for inventory, warehousing, logistics, and transportation than an ERP solution does. Our detailed information on the next pages provides an accurate comparison of functionality that a WMS can provide you, which will be either missing or limited in an ERP system. This information is a "high level" view - comparing the realm of WMS solutions to the world of ERP systems. We are not comparing any individual software solution, but rather the two software sectors against one another.

We realize that some ERP solutions are stronger than the average ERP solution in warehouse operations. It is your responsibility to wisely discern individual solutions on their merits - and not assume all packages are alike - they are not.

Use these functional differences as a checklist - to evaluate - to see in a demonstration - and to discuss.

1. Advanced Bin Locator

Explanation	An advanced bin locator system evaluates numerous **rules,** parameters, and setup configurations. The Advanced Bin Locator evaluates product, bin, area, zone, warehouse, owner, and inventory data.
WMS Functionality	**Most** WMS solutions have rule-based bin locator logic for determining the best bin to store newly received product.
ERP Functionality	Limited and/or Not Supported.

2. Slotting Optimization

Explanation	Warehouse managers frequently "re-warehouse" inventory - to minimize travel time and optimize space utilization. This process is called re-slotting or slotting optimization.
WMS Functionality	**Some** WMS solutions have added re-optimization software that is built-in to the WMS or available as a separate module.
ERP Functionality	Not Supported.

3. Dynamic RF Task Queue

Explanation	A task within a warehouse is a pick, pack, ship, receive, putaway, repack, and so forth. A task queue is an active list of tasks that are assignable to warehouse workers. The task is automatically assigned to the worker by the software using rules & parameters.
WMS Functionality	WMS solutions are designed for Radio Frequency (RF) devices that leverage a work task queue. This queue directs workers in an intelligent and optimized manner.
ERP Functionality	Limited and/or Not Supported. RF is not part of the original ERP design.

4. Configurable Warehouse Task "Work Flow"

Explanation	A task within a warehouse is a pick, pack, ship, receive, putaway, repack, and so forth. A task "work flow" permits configuration to indicate the tasks that a specific product needs upon outbound shipment and inbound receipt. E.G., one product needs pick-pack-ship tasks, wherein another product requires pick-qa-repack-ship tasks. The software allows configuration of task workflow at the product level, so proper tasks may be performed and the customer satisfied.
WMS Functionality	**Most** WMS solutions provide workflow, which set the configuration of tasks that a product needs. One product needs to be pick-pack-ship tasks, wherein another product requires pick-QA-repack-ship tasks.
ERP Functionality	Not Supported.

5. Employee Certification Setup

Explanation	Employees are trained and tested for certification. Certification is for equipment and specialized tasks in the warehouse. E.G., forklifts, cycle counts.
WMS Functionality	**Most** WMS solutions require a list of valid tasks that employees are allowed to perform in the warehouse. E.G., Cycle count, Putaway. Most WMS solutions require a list of valid equipment that the employee is certified to utilize.
ERP Functionality	Not Supported.

6. Engineered Labor Standards & Labor Performance

Explanation	Labor Management Systems (LMS) consist of engineered labor standards from warehouse time studies done by Industrial Engineers or existing standards. Also known as Engineered Labor Standards. Based upon these standards, actual time spent versus the standard can be compared for reporting, inquiries, charts, and dashboards.
WMS Functionality	**Some** WMS solutions have engineered labor standards and labor performance measurement tools. Many of the WMS solutions have labor reporting tools.
ERP Functionality	Not Supported.

7. Warehouse Accountability – Transaction History

Explanation	Every work task done by the warehouse worker is recorded in the database. Errors & exceptions are identified and alerts are passed unto the proper supervisors automatically. Supervisors and knowledge workers can fully inquiry and view every movement on an inventory item via the warehouse transaction history log.
WMS Functionality	Fully supported.
ERP Functionality	Limited and/or Not Supported.

8. Recall & Traceability

Explanation	The ability to perform a recall based upon a lot number or production code. Extreme traceability by lot number or production code.
WMS Functionality	Fully supported. Very exact on inventory, where it was sent, and how it was shipped. Can search by lot number, production code, and even the serial numbers.
ERP Functionality	Limited and/or Not Supported.

9. Warehouse Equipment Definition

Explanation	The software has warehouse equipment (E.G., forklifts) defined with limitation concepts and user authorization for this equipment.
WMS Functionality	WMS directs the right equipment through the right aisles at the right levels. E.G., Forklift is limited to authorized users and only directed through aisles wide enough, but not on a mezzanine, nor in a very narrow aisle.
ERP Functionality	Not Supported and/or Limited.

10. Driving Material Handling Equipment via Interfaces.

Explanation	Material handling equipment (MHE) is specialized equipment in the warehouse to handle products being moved and/or stored. The MHE are command driven by external software. The WMS is the "brain in control" and the MHE is the slave. MHE includes Carousels, AS/RS, Pick-to-Light, Put-to-Light, Sorters, Diverters, and other equipment.
WMS Functionality	WMS installations frequently interface to Carousels, AS/RS, Pick-to-Light, Put-to-Light, Sorters, Diverters, and other MHE equipment. WMS solution providers are experienced in these interfaces.
ERP Functionality	Not Supported and/or Limited.

11. Dock Scheduling

Explanation	The dock doors at the warehouse are scheduled for staged outbound shipments and incoming shipments. At a busy warehouse, LTL, TL, and Rail shipments will have appointed dock doors for specified dates & times. Carriers will be notified of their appointment of when to arrive.
WMS Functionality	**Some** WMS solutions offer dock scheduling - approximately 50% have it, especially the Advanced WMS solutions.
ERP Functionality	Not Supported.

12. Trailer Yard Management System

Explanation	A Yard Management System (YMS) assists the warehouse & transportation departments in two areas. First, it extends the warehouse inventory into trailers containing inventory. Second, it keeps track of trailers by location; return dates, rental rate information, and owner of the trailer. A third party manages some trailer yards. Trailer yards may contain truck trailers and/or containers (for import/export).
WMS Functionality	**Some** WMS solutions offer an YMS. Specialized standalone YMS solutions exist for interfacing to a WMS or ERP for a reasonable price.
ERP Functionality	Not Supported.

13. Work Centers

Explanation	Work center logic for value added services including manufacturing, assembly, and repair.
WMS Functionality	**Many** WMS solutions have work center logic as WMS solutions have a strong history of installations in manufacturing. Note: the host system is expected to calculate inventory costing based upon work done & recorded in the WMS.
ERP Functionality	Supported in the MRP module.

14. 3rd Party Logistics Product Ownership

Explanation	3rd Party Logistics (3PL) providers service multiple customers and manage inventory and/or transportation for these customers. Therefore, the software must be able to identify the owner of the inventory, even when the same exact product is stored in the same warehouse for two different customers.
WMS Functionality	**Many** WMS solutions are designed to segment inventory by owner ID. When an order has been received and processed, it will allocate inventory based on owner & part number.
ERP Functionality	Limited and/or Not Supported.

15. 3PL Contract Rates & 3PL Billing

Explanation	3rd Party Logistics (3PL) Providers service multiple customers and bill different rates based upon the contract.
WMS Functionality	**Some** WMS solutions have 3PL billing, which is customer based for storage and tasks. These WMS solutions permit multiple contracts & rates per product line & customer.
ERP Functionality	Not Supported.

16. Advanced 3PL Inventory Allocation Methods

Explanation	3rd Party Logistics (3PL) providers service multiple customers and customers require a large variety of inventory allocation methods.
WMS Functionality	**Some** WMS solutions have more than the basic LIFO, FIFO, and FEFO methods of inventory allocations. Some WMS solutions have more than 20 inventory allocation methods to satisfy customer requirements, which are a simple configuration by customer, product group, or product number. A business analyst or CSR does configuration.
ERP Functionality	Not Supported.

⚐ Private Warehousing Alert!

Private Warehousing Needs 3PL Functionality

3PL WMS functionality can be highly leveraged in private warehousing.

Answer these questions:

- How many times did you need the ability to bill for value added services done in the warehouse?
- How many times did you need storage costs?

Many wholesalers now have customers that dictate how the product is to be allocated, labeled, or packed today. *Consider how many customers have value added requirements, therefore the warehousing software should support billing them for those requirements.*

3PL functionality does invade private distribution & wholesaling to a larger degree than many suspects. The common goal is to please the end user - our customer – by changing how work is performed at the warehouse level. Many wholesalers are doing value added services, which makes them 'similar' to 3PL warehouse operations.

17. Outbound Order Picking Methods

Explanation	Multiple picking strategies for outbound orders. These methods include pick-and-pass, zone picking, batch picking, cluster picking, pick-to-carton, pick-to-clean, and others. In addition, the warehouse might have a planner, who plans waves of orders. In addition, the picking method & strategy selected involves the weight & cube of the item – for pick-to-carton functionality.
WMS Functionality	Fully supported.
ERP Functionality	Limited. The ERP usually picks one order at a time and batch pick. The ERP has no wave planning functionality or a full set of picking methods.

18. Reverse Truck Loading Sequence

Explanation	The ability to pick & stage outbound shipments in reverse truckload sequence. This optimizes warehouse staging space and permits live loading of trailers (if desired).
WMS Functionality	Fully supported.
ERP Functionality	Limited.

19. Transportation Management System

Explanation	Transportation Management Systems (TMS) cover multiple aspects. Our TMS aspect in focus is the **optimization of outbound transportation.** This optimization occurs **before** the pick release of outbound orders. Likewise, inbound shipments can be optimized for transportation. This goes beyond parcel manifesting!
WMS Functionality	**Most** WMS solutions have TMS planning software to optimize and consolidate freight.
ERP Functionality	Limited to Parcel Manifesting.

20. Eliminate Computer Down Time

Explanation	Computer down time is the actual time in hours or minutes that the computer system will be down (unavailable). Warehousing & transportation operations require 24x7 and must run **all** the time, even during backups.
WMS Functionality	Most WMS solutions require no down time, by running dual databases or online backups.
ERP Functionality	ERP systems require scheduled down time, as much as 10 to 15% during a 24-hour period.

21. ERP Interfaces

Explanation	External software must be bridged (interfaced) to the host ERP system. **Why even list this item?** With companies buying other companies, the result is multiple host systems within an organization. The need to connect to more than one ERP exists. 3PL's and 4PL's have this need to connect to hundreds of customers running various ERP solutions.
WMS Functionality	**WMS has multiple interfaces for multiple ERP solutions** (the popular ERP solutions). The interface approach varies from EAI adaptors, middleware, or a WMS vendor's mapping tool. A mapping approach is the norm.
ERP Functionality	**ERP solution is self-contained to its world.** More & more ERP providers are tapping into Enterprise Application Interfaces (EAI) adaptors or middleware.

Conclusion - Focus on Needed Functionality

Our 21 functional areas of contrast between the WMS and ERP solutions have armed you for understanding the common differences. While shopping for software, one needs to build a RFP that clearly represents your short & long term goals.

The warehouse & transportation is expected to work like *precision clockwork*. This is one area NOT to compromise and cut short, as it absolutely mission critical to ship out product at the right time to the right customer. Focus on critical functionality as well as the desired new functionality to leverage in the future.

Don't skimp on the warehouse, transportation, or planning areas!

Chapter 5

Ready... Set... Send RFP

Step By Step Process Explained - Diagram 9

1 - LEARN
Understand the expected, different, and missing functionality. **Use this book!** Tap into consultants as needed. Build the Initial Scope Document.

Do This Step →

2 - BUILD RFP
Based on WMS knowledge and company practices, build a well thought out RFP and send it to all vendors. **Basic RFP is in this book!**

3 - GATHER RESULTS
Enter RFP results into spreadsheet. Challenge vendors on unusual responses to make fair "apples to apples" comparison. One now has a valuable functionality comparison and cost comparison.

4 - DETERMINE FINALISTS
Eliminate all software solutions that do NOT have "must have" functionality. Others may be eliminated on company specific requirements. Call finalists for on-site demonstrations.

Major costs incurred in this step for travel, expenses, and time spent. →

5 - DEMO'S & SITE VISITS
Arrange demonstration of software solution with your inventory items. Indicate important areas that must be demonstrated. After demonstration, go to 2 or 3 sites that are using the software. Insist on sites that are similar in operation, volumes, and size to your operation.

6 - RECALCULATE FINAL COSTS
Have vendors refine cost proposals. Make sure **all costs are included** and updated in the cost comparison. Decide which vendor is #1 and #2. Make written offer to #1. Negotiate. Fall back to #2 vendor, if necessary.

7 - Sign Contacts - Start Installation
With all large computer installations, it takes dedicated staff and a key individual to drive it to successful implementation.

It is a wise idea to do a pilot project, so that the expected and agreed upon procedures can be modeled & changed repetitively before "going live" with the full warehouse.

Reality Check

The Request For Proposal (RFP) should be very clear and be a mirror of the company's needs for a WMS. Once the final RFP is finished, one must step back and ask, "Would this clearly explain our current and future needs?" If it is vague, one will receive vague (and imprecise) answers. But if the RFP is pinpointed and clear, the answers are much more meaningful. *The people receiving the RFP are **not** mind readers* and it is unfair to expect them to "read between the lines" and guess what one means.

In addition to the prior chapters covering base functionality, differentiators, and deficiencies, the RFP needs to include the WMS basics and vendor profiling information. This is a *golden opportunity* to ask and receive *all* the information your company needs to make the very best decision in warehousing software selection. *Take advantage of the opportunity* and get the answers that one needs to make the best decision!

Remember the Basic Functionality

Internationalization

What languages and currencies are important for both warehouse workers and outbound documents? For each warehouse facility, ask the question - If workers are located in Mexico, what language should screens, reports, and documents be displayed in?

What language does the outbound customer documents need to have? These include shipping labels, packing slips, bill of lading, shelf ready tags, and so forth. What currency do outbound customer documents need to show?

Part Number Size

The RFP needs to request the maximum part number size that the WMS supports. Look at the part number size that the company needs for both the future and current business practices.

For example, an industrial wholesaler has utilized a 16-character part number for the last ten years. There has been a recent need for the part number size to be at least 24 characters. The wholesaler should target WMS solutions with a 24 or larger part number size, then later upgrade the distribution/accounting system with a larger part number size.

3rd Party Logistics (3PL) – Public & Contract Warehousing

If your operation is a 3rd party warehousing operation, make sure that this is supported in the WMS. The host interface needs to be able to indicate which company has sent outbound orders to the WMS, as well as push data to the appropriate host. In addition, the WMS inventory must be able to handle duplicate part numbers and segment inventory by company. These are just a few examples that must be addressed in WMS that support public warehousing.

Lot Controlled Items

Many verticals require lot control. Make sure the WMS has lot control for both inbound and outbound processing. Be aware that some WMS packages have manufacturing functionality to assist with work orders, WIP, and some MRP functionality.

Serialized Items

Make sure the WMS has serial number tracking for both inbound and outbound processing. Manufacturing operations will assign the serial # during MRP. As with lot control, some WMS packages handle manufacturing of product and some do not.

Bonded Warehouses

For imported goods, each warehouse must be designated as bonded or regular stocking warehouse. Goods that are received into bonded warehouses are duty free, unless the goods are transferred to the regular stocking warehouse (or sold to a customer within the country). If applicable, verify that the WMS handles bonded warehouses.

Common API for Data Push & Pull

WMS are heavily interfaced as demonstrated in Diagram 3. Therefore expect common application program interface (API). Make sure the WMS has a strong series of programs that are purposely designed for pushing/pulling transactions in and out of the WMS. Many types of transactions exist, such as (1) outbound shipment detail, (2) new product detail, (3) expected receipt detail, and many more. A common API makes interfacing the WMS much easier - for future third party products.

Compliance Labeling & Packing Lists

Major retailers started the trend to require store-ready labeling. They require their vendor to ship goods with their specified tag or label format. This makes their receiving and stocking tasks easier, but puts an additional task on the warehouse - also known as "value added". In addition, packing lists may be customer specific. I.e., packing list showing customer's part numbers and in original PO line item sequence.

Shipping Labels

Requirements for shipping labels vary from carrier to carrier. How many carriers are supported via the WMS or a Shipment Manifesting product? In addition, find out if the WMS supports "blind shipments" when a shipment to a client's customer must show the *client's* address? For some warehouse operations, the *customer* setup table must be examined to see (1) whose address to show on shipping labels & packing lists, (2) preferred carrier, and (3) who's shipper ID will pay the freight charge.

Standard Operating Systems

"Open Systems" has been popular trend in computer software acquisition & development. Does the warehousing software run on Windows, Linux, or UNIX? Windows, Linux, and UNIX are considered "Open Systems". The software vendor should be supporting one or all of these open systems.

Note: For those solution providers that do not support open systems and have no plans to take their package to Windows, Linux, or Unix, one must do a reality check right away (without delay). Ask questions!

Prepare the RFP

Develop Cover Letter

Write up a standard letter to WMS vendors stating your purpose of implementing a WMS and what date is the completed RFP is needed. In this letter, one should state:

- Company Contact Name
- Contact's Address
- Contact's E-mail address
- Contact's Phone # for questions

State clearly the *cut-off date* for the completed RFP. Permit a minimum of 30 to a maximum of 60 days, from the date of mailing the RFP packets to the cut-off date.

State clearly a brief overview of the time line that is currently desired. For example, "ISI is searching for a strong WMS solution to be implemented at the first warehouse **within 6 months of signing a contract**." If you have a specific month and year in mind, say so. For example, "Industrial Supply Inc. plans on going live with the selected WMS **by December 2008** in ALL four distribution centers."

Provide Company Background

With the cover letter, provide a company background sheet. This is a time-saver, as one is providing the common answers to the common questions. Provide the following information:

- Company Name & Address
- Last Year Gross Sales, Current Growth Rate
- Host/ERP Software
- Product Lines
- Current Warehouse Automation - RF/Paper - Shipping Manifest
- Number of Warehouses Currently & Projected for Next Year
- Explain reasons a WMS is currently needed
- Share current problems that are expected to be resolved with new software

Provide Warehouse Details & Statistics

- Facility Status (Current, Planned for MM/DD/YYYY)
- Total number of SKUs stocked
- Outbound shipment type by percentage (%parcel, %LTL, %TL, %LCL, %CL)
- Average # of outbound shipments per day
- Average # of line items in outbound shipment
- Average aggregate quantity in outbound shipment
- Average weight in outbound shipment
- Average volume in outbound shipment
- Average # of inbound shipments per day
- Average # of line items in inbound shipment
- Average aggregate quantity in inbound shipment
- Average weight in inbound shipment
- Average volume in inbound shipment

- Number of shifts that the warehouse is in operation (per day)
- Number of warehouse workers in all shifts

- Total number of bins
- Type of storage by percentage (%bulk, %rack, %mezzanine)
- Number of trailers in the trailer yard

- Special Product Handling Types
  (Hazardous, Cold Storage, Hot Room, Clean Room)

Sample Request for Proposal (RFP)

General Information	Please Provide The Following Information
Company Name	
Address	
City, State, Postal	
Country	
Main Phone #	
Toll Free Phone #	
Fax #	
Year Founded	
Public or Privately Held Company	
Annual Revenue	
Salesperson's Name	
Salesperson's Phone #	
Salesperson's E-mail	
Software Package Name	
Current Version #	
Total # of Installed Customers	
Total # of Installed Sites	
Estimated Initial Costs:	30 active users in WMS, with 17 being RF users.
WMS Software Cost	$
Computer & RF Hardware Cost	$
Professional Services Cost	$
Is WMS Source Code Included?	Yes or No
Source Code Cost	$
Total WMS Cost	$
Estimated Annual Costs	Please estimate annual maintenance costs.
WMS Software Maint. Cost	$
Computer & RF Maint. Cost	$
Source Code Maint. Cost	$
Total Annual Maint. Cost	$

Table 7 - Sample RFP on this page and the following five pages.

ALL responses are to be against the CURRENT version that is released into production. Please note NEW functionality in FUTURE versions in a SEPARATE document, not in the RFP.

Sample RFP (Continued)

A - Functionality	B - Description	C - Vendor Response
GENERAL		
Language - English	Is American ENGLISH written language supported in the WMS screens and reports?	Answer Yes / No
Language - Spanish	Is Spanish supported in the WMS screens and reports?	
Language - French	Is French supported in the WMS screens and reports?	
Other Languages	List other languages that the WMS supports currently:	
Part Number Size	What is the maximum size of the part number?	
Public Warehouse	Does the WMS host interface support more than 1 host computer?	
Public Warehouse	Are downloaded outbound orders required to have a company value?	
Public Warehouse	Can multiple company inventories be in one WMS database?	
Lot Control - Inbound	Does the WMS support inbound lot controlled items being received?	
Lot Control - Manufacturing	Does the WMS assign lot control numbers to items being manufactured in the warehouse?	
Lot Control - Outbound	Does the WMS support outbound lot tracking? (From bin locating to customer shipment information).	
Serialized Item Inbound	Does the WMS tracking inbound serialized items?	
Serialized Item Outbound	Does the WMS track outbound serialized item, from bin slotting through customer shipment detail?	
Bonded Warehousing	Are bonded warehouses supported by the WMS?	
Common API	For all information coming in and out of the WMS, are there established & published application programming interfaces (API's) available for our programming staff?	

ALL responses are to be against the CURRENT version that is released into production. Please note NEW functionality in FUTURE versions in a SEPARATE document, not in the RFP.

Sample RFP (Continued)

A - Functionality	B - Description	C - Vendor Response
GENERAL		
Advance Shipping Notice - Inbound	Can inbound ASN received by EDI transmission be accepted by the WMS?	Answer Yes / No
RF & Paper in Same Warehouse	Can one warehouse have both RF & paper tasks at the same time?	
Cubics Per Uom	Can the WMS store the product's height, width, and depth for every unit of measure (each, case, master pack, and pallet) that the product is defined in?	
Weight Per Uom	Can the WMS store the product's weight for each unit of measure that the product is defined in?	
Unique Paths for Pick, Putaway, Replenishment	Can the user set up separate & unique paths for picking, putaway, and replenishment?	
Equipment Table	Does an equipment table exist in WMS?	
Equipment Table	For a bin in a narrow aisle at 20' in height, does the WMS select the correct equipment every time by evaluating the inventory item, bin characteristics, aisle limitations, and equipment limitations?	
Customer Configurable System	Is the WMS designed to be "configured" so that an end-user can fully re-engineer a process without programming?	
Interleaving of Multiple Tasks	Can all types of warehouse tasks be interleaved? I.E., Can one employee do putaway, cycle count, let down replenishment, and picking?	
Hazardous Material Handling	Is standard government information uploaded into the WMS to limit which products that can slot next to another hazardous product?	
Error Analysis Table	Does an error table exist in the WMS database? Table is a history of all errors (i.e., shortage, overage, etc.)	
Automatic Re-Warehousing Optimization	Can the WMS "automatically" release move tasks based on slotting optimization algorithm?	
Inventory Valuation Report	Can an "accurate" inventory valuation report be generated from the WMS? A NO response indicates that it is the host's responsibility.	
Labor Productivity Information	Is a report writer available to the end-user to create labor productivity reports?	
Labor Productivity Reporting	Does the WMS have standard labor productivity reports?	
Labor Productivity Standards	Can the WMS store and re-compute labor productivity standards?	

Sample RFP (Continued)

A - Functionality	B - Description	C - Vendor Response
PICKING - SHIPPING		
Automatic Release to Picking for Emergency Orders	Can the WMS automatically release an emergency order to picking with no human intervention?	Answer Yes / No
Automatic Grouping & Release to Picking	On a regular schedule, can the WMS automatically group and release a wave of orders to picking, without any human intervention?	
Carton Selection	Does the WMS direct the picker on the size carton that is needed, based on what will be placed in the carton?	
Pick To Carton	Does the WMS support directing the picker to start a new carton, print a carton bar code label, direct the picker to each bin, verify the product picked and placed in the carton, and tell the picker when to close/release the carton?	
Repack Function	Does a repack function exist in the WMS that is based on specific product requirements demanded by specific customers?	
Weigh-In-Motion	Is weigh-in-motion scales supported by the WMS?	
Compliance Labeling	Does the WMS print carton & shelf ready labels based on customer preferences?	
Packing Lists	Does the WMS produce packing slips that include customer part number and can be sorted by customer preference? I.e., sort by customer PO line number sequence?	
Carrier Shipping Labels	Does the WMS produce carrier specific shipping labels?	
Blind Shipments	Are blind shipments (shipping for another party) supported on carton labels, shipping labels, packing lists, etc.? For certain shipments, our company is not displayed on any documentation that the ShipTo will view, but rather the party paying for the material is viewed.	
Advance Shipping Notice - Outbound	Are outbound ASN generated by the WMS for EDI transmission to the customer?	

Sample RFP (Continued)

A - Functionality	B - Description	C - Vendor Response
PUTAWAY - MOVE		
Bin Locator System	For a putaway, does the bin locator system evaluate:	Answer Yes / No
- Frozen Item	Bins that are in a frozen freezer area for a frozen product?	
- Refrigerated Item	Bins that are in a refrigerated area for a refrigerated product?	
- Non-refrigerated Item	Bins that are in a normal, non-refrigerated area for normal product?	
- ABC Classification	Bins with the same ABC classification as the product?	
- Affinity Item	Avoiding bins next to other products that have the same affinity code?	
- Nesting Factor	The product's nesting factor to locate a bin having the needed volume.	
- Maximum Height	Bins at a specific height or lower. To prevent expensive or heavy items being located too high.	
- Maximum Stack	Evaluate the number of existing and proposed product layers in the bin, to not direct the putaway person to add more that N maximum layers (stack).	
Cross Docking	Does the WMS direct the picker to the receiving dock's staging area?	
Cross Docking	Does the WMS direct the putaway person to take product directly to the packing staging area?	

Sample RFP (Continued)

A - Functionality	B - Description	C - Vendor Response
INTERFACE		
Cubiscan	Does standard product have a built-in interface to a Cubiscan?	Answer Yes / No
Route Optimization Software	Does standard product have a built-in interface to Route Optimization Software? List names of these software products:	
Load Optimization Software	Does standard product have a built-in interface to Load Optimization Software? List names of these software products:	
Document Imaging Product	Does standard product have a built-in interface to Document Imaging Product? List names of these software products:	
Material Safety Data Sheets	Does standard WMS product have ability to print MSDS sheets and record MSDS history of who was sent which MSDS?	
Shipment Manifesting System	Does standard WMS product have built-in interface to shipment manifesting and freight calculation software?	
Shipment Manifesting System	Does standard WMS product have built-in interface to "rate shop" by utilizing the freight calculations in a shipment manifesting package?	
Material Handling Equipment	Does standard WMS product have a built-in interface to PLC's?	
Material Handling Equipment	Does standard WMS product have a built-in interface to White Carousels?	
Yard Management	Does standard WMS product have ability to track trailers within a trailer yard?	
ERP Interface	Does a certified interface exist between the WMS and SAP?	
ERP Interface	Does a certified interface exist between the WMS and Oracle Applications?	
ERP Interface	Does a certified interface exist between the WMS and PeopleSoft?	
ERP Interface	Does a certified interface exist between the WMS and Lawson?	

END OF SAMPLE RFP

Advanced WMS RFP with 1,000 Questions and Score Card is available from IDII. See www.IDII.com for more details and pricing.

Reminder - Tailor the RFP

This is a small Request for Proposal (RFP) question set based on this report. The project team should determine additional functionality items, drop items that are not pertinent, and review the RFP with key end-users before sending it to WMS vendors. *If the RFP contains what really are the critical issues to the key end-users, they will agree to use it to score WMS solutions. In this manner the RFP results are utilized to initially screen and quickly get to a short list of vendors. Our common goal is to avoid expense in spending time & trips on solutions that are not a good match in satisfying the company requirements.*

Decide whether to target all WMS solutions OR to limit the scope to either the standalone WMS or the ERP systems that include a WMS. Appendix A contains WMS provider information and appendix B contains ERP provider details. Send the RFP Packet to those providers. The RFP packet will contain the cover letter on company letterhead, the company background sheet, and the RFP. The RFP will only have columns A, B, and C. One may send the RFP on a CD-ROM as a spreadsheet with columns A, B, and C only - as shown on the previous pages.

While Waiting for the Responses

The project team adds two "scoring" columns to the spreadsheet. The first new column is a value from 0 to 10 on how important that RFP item is to the project team. Later, when the RFP responses come back, one may calculate a score for the RFP item by multiplying the Yes/No response times the value it is worth. For example, if an interface to SAP is very important (worth 10 points) and the WMS solution does it (YES=1 NO=0), then the RFP score value is 10 * 1 = 10.

The second new column indicates what RFP items are "knock-outs". The knocks-outs and very important items should be 10 points. Important RFP items should be worth 5 points.

Use a spreadsheet program and add 2 columns per vendor. Place each vendor's response in a new column. Enter 0 for No responses and 1 for Yes responses. Compute the Vendor's RFP score in the second column. Compute total score for each RFP per functional area and for the vendor. Make sure that the RFP responses are for the current version of the WMS software. In this manner, one is doing a fair comparison between solutions on the market place. Compute total functionality score for each RFP returned. The next page has a brief example on this scoring approach.

These two new "scoring" columns are privileged information for internal use only and are not to be disclosed outside of company personnel.

Scoring the RFP

A - Functionality	B - Description	D - Weight 0 to 10	E - Required Item?	G - Vendor A Response Yes = 1 No = 0	H - Vendor A Score
PUTAWAY					
- Nesting Factor	The product's nesting factor to locate a bin having the needed volume.	5	No	1	5
- Maximum Height	Bins at a specific height or lower. To prevent expensive or heavy items being located too high.	10	No	1	10
PUTAWAY	**Sub-Total**				15
INTERFACE					
Document Imaging Product	Does standard product have a built-in interface to Document Imaging Product? List names of these software products:	10	No	0	0
ERP Interface	Does a certified interface exist between the WMS and SAP?	10	Yes	1	10
INTERFACE	**Sub-Total**				10
TOTAL					**25**

Table 8 - Abbreviated RFP to illustrate RFP Scoring

The above table is a sample of how to score a RFP. Vendor ABC scored 25 points. By using yes/no questions, it is possible to score. Yes=1 No=0 Multiple answer times value of the question to determine number of points. Columns I & J would have another vendor's RFP response & scoring.

SUGGESTION: Build another vendor recap table by functional area, i.e., Putaway, Picking, Interface, can be generated to compare all WMS solutions' strengths and weaknesses in a one page management report. Use the subtotals of each functional area and grand total.

Analyze the RFP Responses

Develop a one-page summary showing total RFP functionality score, initial first year, three year, and five year cost analysis. This can be extremely useful. Make sure all costs (i.e., maintenance, hardware, all services) are included. All costs need to be verified - in order to reflect a fair "apples to apples" comparison is accomplished.

While developing this one page cost summary, question the vendor on any large dollar variance amounts between vendor proposals. *The estimated amounts for computer hardware should be similar, with a 10% plus or minus variance.* i.e., the RF costs & maintenance should be the same or very close for all vendors. Costs for computer hardware & maintenance should be the same or very close. If it is not, dig deeper on why it is too high or too low.

Compute the annual maintenance percentage and see if it is exceptionally high or low. A good benchmark on maintenance for software products is normally 18 to 21% of the current list price. Find out whether one is getting 5x8, 5x10, 5x16, 5x24, 7x8, 7x10, 7x16, or 7x24 support. E.G., 7x24 support is 7 days for 24 hours a day. The 21% maintenance fee could go up to 24%, if you need 7x24 support.

This one page summary is an excellent tool as a summary attached to the detailed RFP responses. Table 9 shows an example of this one page cost summary.

Develop a management report with the one page cost summary, vendor summary recap score table, responses from vendors, and a list of finalists. Present this to management and get approval to move ahead to evaluate the finalists.

Decide as a team to eliminate solutions that lack critically needed functionality. A list of finalists is to be developed and let the other WMS vendors know that they have not been selected on the "final cut". The number of finalists should be at least 2 vendors and no more than 5 vendors. If this is not reachable, then have a serious "reality check" --- and get appropriate additional information to make a solid decision. Do your own financial investigation, including a Dun and Bradstreet report.

Each software provider trusts your company with sensitive RFP answers.

Treat each provider's RFP information as privileged information and refrain from sharing it outside of company personnel.

One Page Cost Summary

	Vendor A	Vendor B	Vendor C	Vendor D	Vendor E
Name of Software Company	ABC Inc	BCD Inc	CED Inc	DEF Inc	EFG Inc
Founded	1981	1998	1976	1940	1988
Number of Employees	300	10	40	100	30
# Of Installed Customers	40	4	300	20	50
Cost Analysis					
WMS Software	100,000	85,000	100,000	50,000	75,000
Database	15,000	15,000	15,000	15,000	15,000
Source Code	0	50,000	0	75,000	0
Computer & Computer Hardware	25,000	25,000	25,000	25,000	25,000
RF Equipment & RF Hardware	55,000	49,000	43,000	44,200	49,000
Training, Installation, & Services	90,000	92,000	40,000	85,000	77,000
Total Initial Cost	260,000	301,000	208,000	279,200	236,000
WMS Maintenance Cost	15,000	12,000	15,000	7,500	10,000
Computer & RF Hardware Maintenance.	12,000	12,000	12,000	12,000	12,000
Total Maintenance Cost	27,000	24,000	27,000	19,500	22,000
1 Year Cost	287,000	325,000	235,000	298,700	258,000
3 Year Cost	341,000	373,000	289,000	337,700	302,000
5 Year Cost	395,000	421,000	343,000	376,700	346,000
Vendor Score from RFP	380	400	420	250	375

Table 9 - Cost Summary with Sample Numbers.

Quick Analysis –

1. Vendor CED scored the highest with almost the low costs.
2. Question: Is Vendor CED missing some costs?
   a. Computer & RF Hardware costs are slightly lower.
   b. Training, Installation, and Professional Service costs are very low.
   c. Are these correct? Verify with vendor.
3. Adjust costs and redo analysis.

Note: This one page cost summary is effective for discussions with management. Add a benefit analysis summary on a separate page - as the benefits will have no variance (or an insignificant) per solution selected.

How To Select WMS Software - Diagram 10

1 - LEARN
Understand the expected, different, and missing functionality. **Use this book!** Tap into consultants as needed. Build the Initial Scope Document.

2 - BUILD RFP
Based on WMS knowledge and company practices, build a well thought out RFP and send it to all vendors. **Basic RFP is in this book!**

3 - GATHER RESULTS
Enter RFP results into spreadsheet. Challenge vendors on unusual responses to make fair "apples to apples" comparison. One now has a valuable functionality comparison and cost comparison.

Do This Step →

4 - DETERMINE FINALISTS
Eliminate all software solutions that do NOT have "must have" functionality. Others may be eliminated on company specific requirements. Call finalists for on-site demonstrations.

ARRANGE DEMOS & SITE VISITS →

Major costs incurred in this step for travel, expenses, and time spent.

5 - DEMO'S & SITE VISITS
Arrange demonstration of software solution with your inventory items. Indicate important areas that must be demonstrated. After demonstration, go to 2 or 3 sites that are using the software. Insist on sites that are similar in operation, volumes, and size to your operation.

6 - RECALCULATE FINAL COSTS
Have vendors refine cost proposals. Make sure **all costs are included** and updated in the cost comparison. Decide which software vendor is #1 and #2. Make written offer to #1. Negotiate. Fall back to #2 choice, if necessary.

7 - Sign Contacts - Start Installation
With all large computer installations, it takes dedicated staff and a key individual to drive it to successful implementation.

It is a wise idea to do a pilot project, so that the expected and agreed upon procedures can be modeled & changed repetitively before "going live" with the full warehouse.

Established Vendor Characteristics

Minimum Number of Installed Customers
The warehousing software industry is still maturing and many packages are out there. If yours is an innovative, risk taking company, select a software solution with a minimum of 5 customers. If your company is more conservative, look at software solutions with a minimum of 10 customers. If your company is ultra-conservative, analyze warehousing packages with a minimum of 30 customers.

Customers in Your Industry
Make sure that the RFP has industry specific issues to be addressed by the warehousing solutions. For example, in the food industry, cache weight is a requirement. In the lumber industry, dual quantity tracking is important. Make sure that the industry specific issues are addressed satisfactorily.

Excellent I/O Data Throughput Performance
Very important is the "throughput" of the software to handle large volumes of data. This Input/Output (I/O) of data throughput is very significant. Throughput is how many tasks can be pushed through the WMS is a period of time. For example, make sure the vendor has installed sites with a higher throughput that your largest warehouse. Have the computer "sharpshooter" validate that the suggested computer system, database, and application software will have excellent performance.

Clean Financial History
Do a Dun & Bradstreet Credit Report on each of the finalists. Confront any WMS vendor with slow pays, tax liens, or poor credit rating in order to find out what is going on. *Where there is smoke, there's usually fire.*

This is a sobering reality check on whether the WMS company is healthy or not. Based on a D&B report – we actually eliminated the best vendor due to an IRS tax lien found on this report. Executive management did not *feel comfortable* doing business with this company, even though it had its reasons.

Good Revenue to Employee Ratio
Use this ratio as a reality check to see if the WMS vendor is healthy or spending more than they are taking in. Ratio is annual revenues to total number of employees. Note: a startup software company will be spending more than a mature, established software company.

Excellent References
Once a short list of WMS vendors is determined, request a list of installed customers for reference checking. Reference calling has a two-fold purpose. First, it determines a satisfaction rating for the WMS vendor. Second, we learn from others what to do (and what not to do) on the installation process. If you are hearing *dissatisfied current customers*, call some more *current* customers to determine if there is a problem pattern. If a problem pattern exists, then be realistic about it and drop that WMS vendor off the short list.

Final Selection

With finalists in hand, ask for the following items:

1. Organization chart
2. Financial statement - for stability review
3. Full list of customers with contacts - for reference calling
4. Refinement of any costs due to user counts changing, hardware changes, etc.

Call on current customers and have your questions predetermined. i.e., how long have you been on the package? Did you have problems on going live on it? (All will say yes, unless they are lying to you!) What types of problems did you have? How long did it take between contract signing and going live? What would you do different? How would you rate the support group when there is a problem?

If desired, detail each new proposed procedure for receiving, putaway, picking, shipping, replenishment, and counting. If this can be done now, then this becomes a very effective communication tool during the on-site demo. By encouraging both parties to discuss the details of the new proposed process, one may get a feedback on new ideas, alternative solutions, and missing functionality. Pass these new detailed procedures and demo expectations on to the finalists. Finalists should perform demonstrations at your site and one may wisely indicate what functions will be demonstrated.

Go to the vendor's headquarters in order to get a full demonstration, get answers to outstanding questions, and review the RFP. Expect to actively participate in the following:

1. Demonstration at your company site with your product data demonstrating predetermined specific functions
2. Tour(s) of one or more existing installations that match or exceed your current inventory movement and desired material handling equipment.
3. Vendor headquarters tour & WMS demonstration

In this final selection phase, the team should now be focused on (1) getting a detailed vision on how to install the WMS successfully and (2) final decisions on what to negotiate and what exactly will be purchased.

After the visits to sites and headquarters, review the RFP, cost summary, vendor background, and product functionality. Negotiate.

Selecting the Site to Tour – Site Visit Selection Tips

Option 1 – Select from a Short List of Possible Sites

Have the WMS vendor provide a short list of 2 to 6 applicable warehouse sites and select one site from that list. The WMS vendor can arrange a date and time to visit with this site. An applicable warehouse is one in the same vertical – or - has the same warehousing issues. An applicable warehouse has similar or higher transaction throughput (E.G., number of outbound shipments per day, number of receipts per day).

On this list, it should have the suggested facility location address, description of operations, and their transactional volumes. One wants to see a site that is moving inventory at your current transaction rates or higher.

Ask yourself – Is this site relevant to my industry and situation? Is this site doing the same or a higher number of shipments and line items than our facility?

Option 2 – Here Is "The Site"

Normally, the WMS Vendor will select a site and <u>not</u> ask you for assistance in site selection. <u>Initially</u>, look at the suggested site with suspicion, as you will have an investment of time and travel money into this recommended site.

Ask the WMS vendor: Is this site relevant to our industry and situation? What are the number of inbound & outbound shipments & line items at this site? If it is not a good match in either the industry or the transaction throughput, then switch to a site that is.

Bad Site Visit Will Result in Lost Software Sale

Remember that a realistic and good site visit is worth the extra cost & time. Warehouse and logistics managers want to see sites with higher inbound & outbound volumes than they currently have. We have witnessed clients that were ready to sign a contract with the preferred software vendor, <u>until</u> the wrong site visit happened!

Bad site visits are:
1. Visiting a slow moving warehousing, in comparison to your volumes.
2. The site is using only part of the core functionality. E.G., Full RF functionality was to be expected at this site, but the site was a paper-based warehousing operation.
3. The site did not have the material handling equipment expected.
4. For a 3PL – visiting a site that only has one inventory owner within the DC, rather then a DC containing multiple clients' inventory.

When the vendor selects the wrong site – it *directly* results in the software solution as "looking bad". A complete misfit attitude starts developing within the prospective software buyers. The right site visit(s) are important to verify the software can handle your volumes, material handling requirements, and expectations. **Insist on good sites and avoid bad sites!**

Site Visit Benefits

○ **Viewing software products** in use at a production side. Ask the user to *slow down* on key stroking or scanning so that you can fully understand the steps it took to perform the activity. Many demonstrators, who usually are the expert users, talk fast, and demonstrate fast.

○ **Visit sites that are at the next level.** Plan on moving up to the next step of automation or process re-engineering improvement. Analyze step-by-step how this site is actually performing this level and get informed by asking questions and observing.

○ **Understand current issues with the product** by asking intriguing questions. On a person-to-person level, ask questions to find out what are the current difficulties that they are encountering.

Consider questions like the following, in order to know the current set of problems that they are encountering:

- o Are there times during the day when there are pauses in the software?
- o When does this happen? Is there a pattern? Do you know what is causing these?
- o How responsive is the vendor to resolving critical problems?
- o What are your current problems or new features that need to be added?
- o What customizations did you do to the software? Why?

From an IT perspective on I/O throughput, one should request to visit the site during its busiest times. Compare this to a stress test and view the PC's & RF terminals for any pauses.

o **Build Long Term Relationship.** Be friendly, share business cards, and keep in touch.

o **Learn – Get Ideas.** View advanced modules to better understand the software & how to implement in your operations. E.G., Labor Management System and Advanced TMS.

Vendor Tips

1. Avoid taking prospects to sites with a lower transaction throughput. See above material on what makes a bad site visit.
2. Make sure the site is ready to have the *prospects view and interact with actual users* of the software product.
3. For a 4-hour site visit – keep management overviews and PowerPoint presentations to ½ hour or less. *Skipping PowerPoint presentations is preferred.* The prospect wants to see, touch, feel, and investigate *the product & users* of the software product.

Site Visit Questions

During a site visit, one must ask questions that are precise and dig into the issues. Issues can be slow response time, missing & needed functionality, and current modifications/enhancements that are now being delivered. Consider and evaluate the following questions as a base to build your list of site questions to ask.

Inbound

- Does the software handle **unexpected** receipts well or does it need to be redone?
- How do you do cross-docking and are there better ways to do it? Listen – then ask. Which ways does the software support cross-docking?
- Do you have cubes and weight on each product? Does the software ever tell you to locate product in a bin that is too small or narrow?
- Do you have HAZMAT items and how does the software handle those?

Outbound

- Does the software handle different workflows for outbound shipping, by customer? E.G., one customer wants price stickers applied, while another one does not. How does the software tell the warehouse people to do it and charge for it? To charge for applying the price stickers – is it a manual entry or automatic?
- Have you had an opportunity to try out different allocation methods and adapt the pick route – so that the consignee is happy with the ultimate delivery? E.G., all of one product in one pallet – not mixed across many pallets.
    E.G., Pick to clean strategy.
    E.G., LIFO with N day window for large bin, to avoid dig outs.

Adjustments

- How hard is it to change a part number for current inventory? Lot number?
- What's your process for inventory adjustments?
- What software do you use to handle damaged goods? Take pictures of it?
- Is it a manual process or integrated?

Value Added Services

- What value-added services (VAS) are performed?
- Have you used the *repack* function and does it work well?
- Does your people have to *manually* add VAS as an accessorial charge? Can they do it on a RF device near the work center?
- Are you doing any manufacturing with work centers? Does the software support these work centers well?

Site Visit Questions (Continued)

Customer Service Productivity

- How has level of customer service improved?
- Can customers obtain a data file of available quantities anytime, without any help?
- Can inventory owners obtain a data file of on-hand quantities anytime, without any help?

Management & Client Reporting for a 3PL

- Are you spending considerable time to build a P&L for management?
- Can the system *automatically* generate a customer summary report once a month? Are you doing that?

Data Throughput & Customizations

- Are there times during the day when there are pauses in the software?
- When does this happen? Is there a pattern? Do you know what is causing these?
- How responsive is the vendor to resolving critical problems?
- What are your current problems or new features that need to be added?
- What customizations did you do to the software? Why?

Headquarter Visit Benefits

- **Build Key Manager Relationship.** Meet key executives & management at the software company, which is important if you are planning to become a key part of the user group for the long term. Ask them if it would be OK to call them later on, if you have questions or issues.

- **Expect Canned Presentations.** Multiple departments (E.G., Professional Services, Support, Quality Assurance) will have presentations explaining their department. *Bored of the routine? Here's a way to have fun & benefit:*

  Ask inquisitive questions that go beyond the normal.
    - How do you handle 24x7 support of multiple time zones (one office or multiple support offices)?
    - What is your policy with the user group enhancements?
    - How about committing to the Top 20 Enhancements from the user group each year?
    - Can you agree to take my modifications so that they become part of the standard product, if they are done in a generic form & benefit the majority of the user group?

- **Future Product Presentation & Details.** *Prior to the visit,* request a session that covers what will be in the next few releases with a detailed handout. This is very important, as this will validate expectations of what has already been said in pre-sales demonstrations and meetings. The detailed handout should have new features highly organized & grouped by module. This handout is either the technical details of the new features (a specification) or a derivative of this. Make sure it is not a last minute, thrown together list. If it is, investigate how organized is the product development & testing procedures from current customers.

- **Connect with Development Group.** *Ask in advance* to view coding standards, new product feature process, sample code, database table relationship diagram, and database details. See what testing tools are in use by the vendor.

Visit the software development manager and build a relationship for the long term. If you purchase their product with source code for your IT staff, then this is critical on building a "peer to peer" professional level between organizations. Be energetic, honest, and sincere with these developers. Share business cards, as later you might need to call them with a quick question.

Ask them if it would be agreeable to infrequently call them with a quick question. Once you are up on the product, do the following: only call these developers on development questions and make sure that development questions are short and respecting of their time. Always send the support questions to support. The goal is to build a long-term relationship.

Headquarter Visit Questions (Continued)

- **Last Minute "Product Demonstrations & Detailed Questions".** Normally at the headquarter visit, the product is *not* demonstrated again, unless you request it. Survey the team on what items need to be reviewed again (or for the first time) and build a list. *Prior to the headquarter visit,* send the vendor the list of items the list and request that time be dedicated to seeing and explaining those specific items.

- **Review Company Financials.** Request in advance to see the company's books. Have one of your selection team members that are familiar with financial issues, spend a half hour to an hour reviewing the financial health of the company. Ask questions right away about items that are found, until one is satisfied with the answered depth and details to your questions.

Many software companies are privately held and this is an opportunity to understand how the company earns revenue, expenditures, cash flow, and current debt load. *Many software companies have zero long-term debt.* Most software companies are privately held and this will probably be your *only opportunity* to see "the books".

Understanding the Software Contracts Process

By John Seidl jseidl@kurtsalmon.com and Lori Cox lpcox@kurtsalmon.com

So you've decided to purchase software to improve your supply chain, now what?

In this day and age, a company can't get by without thinking about the information systems that will make its products and services more efficient and thus, more profitable. Once a problem is identified, one of the first decisions to be made is whether to buy, build, or use pre-existing information systems resources (or some combination of all three). For several reasons, including time, money, and advances in the technologies that address today's various business issues, more and more companies are purchasing supply chain software from commercial software vendors rather than developing it themselves.

After an organization has selected a product, however, the process of purchasing the software — from the initial request for proposal (RFP), to contract negotiations, to the final software contract — can be complex, overwhelming, and exhausting. Perhaps the most frustrating aspect of the purchasing process is defining and negotiating the contract.

Understanding the software contracts process and associated risks is what truly makes an informed, knowledgeable buyer, and what results in the best solution for the least investment. This article does not purport to offer legal advice, but rather to simply create awareness of potential issues encountered during the negotiation process.

The Contracts Process

As part of the purchase process, a vendor generally submits a software license agreement as an appendix to the proposal. This agreement is based on criteria from the prospective purchaser's RFP. Many buyers assume they need to accept the vendor's standard terms and conditions as part of this process. While software contracts can be complex and confusing, there is an opportunity for buyers to negotiate to protect their best interests. These contracts are vital to users, as contracted software requires a significant investment of both capital and resources. It is very important to understand even such fundamental items as who owns the source code and whether there are any restrictions, limits, or future payments on use.

> If software users are not knowledgeable about these items, or if they remove themselves from the process too early, they may find themselves in trouble later. In fact, the user's role in the contract negotiation process is critical. Users may not realize, for example, that they may make changes to the vendor agreement or prepare an addendum containing provisions that will take precedence over the standard terms and conditions. The final agreement or contract should be the result of negotiations among the users and vendor, with all attachments — including the original response to the buyer's RFP — signed and included as part of the contract. Bottom line: Treat the contract negotiation process as seriously as the selection decision. Attention, diligence, and patience will save time and money on the back end and ensure the organization receives maximum protection from risk while getting the most for its money.

Contract Provisions from the User's Perspective

During the negotiation process, users will want to consider a number of contract provisions.

1. **Specifications and deliverables** - Articulates software specifications for functions and capabilities and precisely describes deliverables such as software components, documentation, consulting services, etc.

2. **Delivery schedule** - Details the number of days or dates for each deliverable and the vendor's and users' specific responsibilities for installation, conversion, training, and acceptance testing. The schedule may include a provision to extend vendor performance based on user-caused delays or penalties for vendor-caused delays.

3. **Payment terms** - Structures payments so the vendor receives compensation for what is actually delivered, installed, and accepted. For example, an initial payment might be 50% of the licensing fees, with another payment due upon delivery and installation, another upon testing and acceptance, and the final upon acceptance. Definitions of installation, testing, acceptance, and final acceptance are critical. Vendors will typically ask for 100% of the licensing fee and the first year's support payment at contract signing, and then request distributed payments for professional services (consulting). Consider a hold-back percentage on the professional services to maintain leverage throughout the project life cycle. Some clients even seek "pay-for-performance" terms under which the dollar value of the contract is defined based on achieved savings amounts. Obviously, this dictates that the terms and conditions of the contract be clearly articulated to define the baseline, performance metrics, and achieved gains.

    An additional consideration is fixed price vs. hourly (usually labeled "time and materials") payment terms. In general, time and material contracts place the bulk of the risk with the purchaser, as the developer has no direct incentive to complete the project within a set time period unless a specific cap has been put on the number of hours allotted for the project. In contrast, the fixed price contract places the risk with the developer, as time is no longer related to the amount they get paid for the final product. Essentially, the more complex the project is in nature, the less likely a developer will work on a fixed price basis due to the difficulty of defining what needs to be built.

    Finally, when defining payment terms, users should consider basing key dates on milestones vs. on the final project end date, as this will offer added incentive to complete the various project components in a timely manner.

Contract Provisions from the User's Perspective (Continued)

4. **Warranties and remedies** - States who made the warranty and what may be excluded, and outlines the remedies available and procedures for obtaining them. It also includes a minimum warranty of conformance to stated specifications and documentation for an affirmed period of time. This provision specifies time allowed for the vendor to correct breaches of warranty, method of repair, location of warranty services, and any warranty extensions due to ongoing error correction. It outlines the minimum and maximum response times for warranty service, the hours of the vendor's support call center, the location of the support call center, etc.

    If the buyer wants warranty support on site for start-up, this must be stipulated in the contract terms. Vendors commonly charge for software modifications, but users should be aware that most will charge again for support services related to testing and problem resolution of those same modifications. In others words, if the customization doesn't work, the buyer has to pay more for the vendor to fix it. The justification is that the issue resolution process includes a discovery period during which the vendor must determine whether the issue is the result of a software, configuration, data integrity, or user training problem. These areas are not all the vendor's responsibility and thus, their desire to be paid for their time.

5. **Testing and acceptance** - Specifies the method of testing, test data to be used, where that test data will be sourced (test data creation can be a major project), and vendor/user responsibilities. It should include a well-defined process for identifying and communicating errors. It is critical to list explicit acceptance criteria in the agreement.

6. **Support and maintenance** – Denotes the time period for support and maintenance, location of service, hours available, and limits on annual fees. Consider defining scenarios such as how remote access will be gained to the client environment if a copy of the client's production system is maintained at the vendor's support center, and ask the vendor to specify the skill sets of support personnel. Annual maintenance fees are typically a percentage of the original software license price – this percentage is also subject to negotiation.

7. **Documentation** - Explicitly defines electronic and printed documentation with references to versions and future documentation. This should include end user documentation (functional specifications, product training materials, etc.) and technical documentation (technical specifications, system configurations, architecture specification, interface specifications, file layouts, etc.)

8. **Software modifications** - Includes specifications for all customization work. The contract should provide for vendor or user development and user review and approval. Acceptance of the entire system, including all customization, should be a condition of final approval. Refine the rate schedule for software modification and other professional services. Billing rates for services are open to negotiation; consider a blended rate across all resources (rather than separate rates for every title in the vendor organization), and one set of rates for development work performed on shore and another set for work completed off shore.

Contract Provisions from the User's Perspective (Continued)

9. **Source code escrow** - Protects the user against a vendor that is unable or unwilling to maintain the software by providing the terms under which source code and documentation will be released to the user with an independent third party acting as the escrow agent.

10. **Scope of license** - Specifies all rights, including the right to use the software for its intended purpose, keep duplicate copies, modify the source code, use software on a backup or duplicate CPU, make copies for training purposes, and assign the contract to a subsidiary or subcontractor. Special consideration should be given if there are any third-party logistics operations or other outside warehouse service providers. Vendors will typically license by number of users, by each site, or as a corporate license (unlimited users/sites). They may also implement a sliding scale – so much per user up to a certain number, then another fee level beyond that, etc. Understand that there is an important distinction between "named users" and "concurrent users" – where "named users" are individual log-in IDs and "concurrent users" are a certain number of users that would be logged into the application suite at one point in time. "Concurrent users" tends to be a better metric of actual planned activity for the application.

11. **Termination of agreement** - Gives the user and vendor prior notice (specify number of days) of alleged default, and allows the opportunity to correct the default condition. Be aware of vendor clauses to reclaim hardware or software, or to lock software.

12. **Dispute resolution** - Includes a provision to use the software while a dispute is being resolved, and specifies the location (state) of dispute resolution. The user may wish to include a mandatory, non-binding, pre-litigation mediation provision to save parties from unnecessary litigation; this allows parties to retain an arbitrator to assist with resolution.

13. **Confidentiality** - Defines confidential information. Users should attempt to negotiate provisions to protect their own confidential information ("restraint of trade" issues make vendor restrictions difficult) and examine and streamline language that protects the vendor's confidential information where possible.

14. **Patent and copyright indemnity** - Indemnifies the user against third-party suits related to patent, copyright, trade secret, or trademark infringement. This means the vendor will protect or insure against any user liability stemming from those infringements.

15. **Risk of loss** - Passes the risk from vendor to user after software or hardware is delivered to user premises (not to carrier) and specifies damages if the loss of hardware or software affects or interrupts business.

16. **Insurance** - Defines expectations as to what types of insurance the vendor is expected to carry and requests a copy of the insurance certificates.

17. **Solicitation** - Defines restrictions around solicitations for employment of each party's employees.

Customizations and the Contract

It is important for prospective purchasers to remember that a vendor's product may need to be customized. Customized software also requires an agreement with user provisions, including:

- Payment mechanisms.
- Changes to scope.
- Progress reports.
- Project organization.
- Software ownership.

These provisions will protect the user's interests and create a fair and equitable agreement.

The Risks

There are several risks involved with software licensing. These include non-performance, cost of modification or integration, vendor bankruptcy, and infringement. To minimize these risks, a prospective buyer may want to enlist the aid of a third party. The third party should be well versed in supply chain technology and have the business perspective and technical expertise to assist with the contract negotiation process. Once enlisted, the third party can ensure proper legal assistance is retained and help identify client issues related to contracts, such as provisions to be changed, deleted, or included, and risks inherent in the agreement.

Conclusion

Software licensing contracts are complex and confusing. Prospective purchasers who are prepared and know their rights in the negotiation process can reach an agreement with provisions that protect their interests without minimizing the vendor's rights. Suitable legal counsel should review software contracts, as these purchases are very different than other types of business contracts. Ensure counsel has the appropriate experience to support the software purchasing process. Making informed, educated decisions will enable all parties to come away from the table as winners.

"Understanding the Software Contracts Process"
Used By Permission of Kurt Salmon Associates

Written by John Seidl *jseidl@kurtsalmon.com*
and Lori Cox *lpcox@kurtsalmon.com*
November 2007.

Kurt Salmon Associates. Committed to *accelerating your results* through our *industry expertise* in global retailing, consumer products, and health care.
Contact the above authors or visit http://www.kurtsalmon.com.

Software Selection Conclusion

The search for selecting the right software is an exciting journey. We encourage you to find the highest quality product. Make sure that you have the right players on the project team. If the company lacks dedicated resources or lacks the appropriate key personnel, one may add missing project team players by adding consultants, where practical.

Best wishes in the pursuit of obtaining the best software. Let us know how this report has helped.

Phil Obal

PhilObal@IDII.com

Remember that one is investing in a product for the long term.
Remember the saying that is so true on these major purchases:

A second time buyer will focus on quality first

And then the price.

It's a long-term purchase and relationship...
Get the best functionality to grow & expand with!

Chapter 6

Implementation of New Software

Can You Increase the 41% Satisfaction Factor?

Major software projects have only a 41% satisfaction factor **where the customer is happy or very happy with the implementation.** That leaves 59% that were left with a perceived "unsatisfied" installation, according to a WERC and Arthur Anderson study.

Whether one is implementing a WMS, TMS, or ERP – studies result in 40 to 44% satisfaction rate. Therefore – any "major" software package being installed is just a very large project – that manages and oversees people, new processes, and resources for a three to twelve month period normally.

Perceptions, expectations, and attitudes from executives, managers, and workers are important during this implementation phase. These must be managed by excellent project managers from client, consultant, and software vendor groups.

These project "people" are the ones who make the project come alive and judge its success. See the article in this chapter called ""The Human Side of WMS Implementations".

Yes! – You CAN increase the satisfaction factor higher!

Implementation Road Map

Ask the vendor for a step by step project plan for a 3 to 6 month implementation.

Make sure that this is provided in Microsoft Project or another planning tool needed for the project managers. Roles and tasks for the players in the WMS implementation should be identified clearly.

One may ask for this implementation plan during the WMS software selection stage. It gives them a chance to study, adjust, and critique it.

Implementation Costs

Total project costs can be determined from the roadmap for labor costs and the RFP Response will have detailed quotes for the software and hardware. **Software firms will not do fixed pricing for professional services.** Here's why... First, custom programming is difficult to estimate and may grow larger than initially expected. Secondly, the software company wants to bill on a "time and material" basis to maximize revenue and profit. Billing for labor is a high profit item.

Billable versus Non-Billable Services

Be up front with the software vendors during the selection phase and contract negotiations to agree upon billable and non-billable items.

Discuss these items at contract signing time:

Whether:
- Time to make travel arrangements is billable or not.
- Travel time to and from our sites - Negotiable
- Regional management time to occasionally review the project, whether it be over the phone or an onsite visit – is this billable or not.
- Enhancement to the core software product based upon our requirements. Agree to a list of free enhancements to core product at contract signing. Other items will most likely be billed on a time and materials basis.
- For the installation, agree upon a tiered rate based upon vendor's personnel experience & role. Vendor will provide staff with various skill sets and experience levels. *An alternative* is to simply negotiate a lower blended rate for all professional services rendered.

How to Be Extremely Successful in the WMS Software Project

Executive Commitment

The executive group must commit money, momentum, and determination.

This includes a strong mindset "we will make this happen".

It's much more than just a money commitment.

Executives must keep management & staff on course – especially during the challenging implementation.

IT hand-in-hand with Operations

Operations, Traffic, and Information Technology groups **working together** is critical, crucial, **and** vital for success! Look at other departments as "important" to the success of this implantation. The right computer, warehousing, and transportation people are very important.

IDII has seen companies where the IT department manager was at odds with the logistics manager. They both desired a new WMS, but had very little desire to work together. Conclusion: a recipe for disaster and a high opportunity to become a statistic. We warned them about the 41% satisfaction rate!

All groups need to work together for an extended period of time for the installation and on a regular basis after a successful "go live" for upgrading and enhancing operations. Be there and be committed for the success of this team project!

Model New Processes via Conference Room Pilot

After the software selection is finalized with a contract - let the vendor perform an operation analysis on your operations. Your key staff with the vendor's team should model warehouse processes aka Conference Room Pilot (CRP). If the new work flows need to be changed, change them, and rerun them through the warehousing software again. Repeat this model and refine steps until completed. This is an excellent opportunity to implement new best-of-breed processes and try them out on the new software.

Employee Buy-In & Employee Training

Warehouse employees need to be made aware of the new software and how it benefits them. Have warehouse employees involved in the CRP, testing processes, and trained well in the new software. Align software training for all workers to occur just prior to the go-live; in this manner the training is fresh in their minds.

Thorough Testing

The testing needs to be thorough and repetitive, until the software has been proven fully. Let's emphasize that one needs to **TEST-TEST-AND-TEST**. Read the article in this chapter called "WMS Software: The Importance of Testing". The following areas are critical for testing:

- Interface between WMS and WCS / MHE
- Interface between WMS and ERP, TMS, SMS, YMS
- Modifications
- Unit & Process Flows
- System

Best Practice: Test, Test, and Test until it works without any problems. The numbers of issues that arise on the "go live" date have been reduced as they were resolved during this testing stage.

Vendor Onsite during Go-Live

Taking the new WMS live is a major event. Have key personnel from the software provider onsite during the first week. In this manner, problems & issues can be resolved *right away*. It is the very best to resolve issues as soon as possible – rather than incur data errors as new transactions continue!

Setting Real Expectations

Set real and explicit expectations with the Initial Scope Document, discussed in previous chapters. Make sure that this document contains all the major & minor goals, expectations, and ROI numbers expected. Refine this at the start of implementation and then share this document with all new project people – from the vendor, your staff, or another company. Discuss and communicate these frequently.

After a successful go-live on the new software – go back to the Initial Scope Document - to see if you have met your goals and expectations. Great satisfaction from the project people is obtained by meeting these goals! Tell others about your success.

Best Practice: Share Scope Document with all new project people.

Avoid Project Creep by Saying "No"

Avoid project creep – as many people will suggest additional requirements – even after the contract has been signed. Find workarounds, make them re-engineer the process to work with the software to avoid a modification, or postpone their requirement to a later phase.

"What part of NO do you not understand?" This is a phrase for spoiled children and for project people that want their functionality added or customized in this phase. *Just say NO or push it into another phase.* Look for feasible workarounds that neither require any customizations of the software nor incur time delays.

Best Practice: A phased approach that plans more functions and modules is better than growing a large initial install.

The Human Side of WMS Implementations

Too many WMS implementations struggle and fail, not because of the system's weak technical performance, but because of a poorly handled project and people management problems. The many tasks associated with implementing a WMS can make the responsibilities of a project manager seem intimidating. Regardless of which system you select and how much support you expect from the vendor, there is a body of knowledge that you must have as a project manager in order to lead your team through a successful WMS implementation.

Your first mandate is to utilize technical resources for assistance with WMS specific issues, such as the selection of both system and vendor, development of test plans and interfaces, and the hardware setup. You are the manager, and that means that you should not try to be an expert in every area of the project.

Your second mandate is to understand that, despite your best efforts, your WMS project may fail. It is a serious mistake to assume that you will never need to return to the system that you had before (the legacy system). Therefore, be prepared with a clear back-out plan. The days before a new system goes "live" are stressful. Chaos could ensue if the system fails and you are not fully prepared to recover quickly. Before you begin the installation, establish a back-out team, define its responsibilities, and describe step-by-step procedures for returning to the legacy system. The team should review this contingency plan several times before start-up.

There are some project management issues common to most WMS installations, and several basic do's and don't's for leading a cohesive project team, developing a positive communication plan, establishing effective communications channels, and identifying essential training activities. Each of these stages is fraught with pitfalls. Some common traps are described below, along with suggestions for managing or, in the best case, avoiding them.

Project Team

Don't underestimate the importance of project team development. Allowing your corporate organization chart to evolve over time by assigning responsibilities to people, rather than people to functional responsibilities, can result in a dysfunctional team shaped by relationships, personalities, and low morale.

Do take the time to assemble a group with clearly defined roles and responsibilities, and one that is capable of maintaining motivation and commitment throughout the duration of the project. No matter how large or capable your crew is in the beginning, it needs to be properly sized so that momentum and energy can be sustained to the finish line. It is difficult to do this with a large group of loosely knit people, so designate both a core and support team based on functional responsibilities. A sample organization chart is shown in Figure 1.

Project Team Development

```
CORE TEAM
                    ┌─────────────────┐
                    │ Project Manager │
                    └────────┬────────┘
         ┌─────────────┬─────┴─────┬──────────────┐
   ┌──────────┐  ┌──────────┐  ┌──────────┐  ┌──────────┐
   │Functional│  │Technical │  │  System  │  │ Training │
   │Operational│ │          │  │Administr.│  │          │
   └──────────┘  └──────────┘  └──────────┘  └──────────┘

SUPPORT TEAM
   — Receiving    — Interfaces    — Hardware         — Materials
   — Picking      — Testing       — S.W. Maintenance — Training Lab
   — Shipping     — Conversion    — Enhancements     — Trainer
```

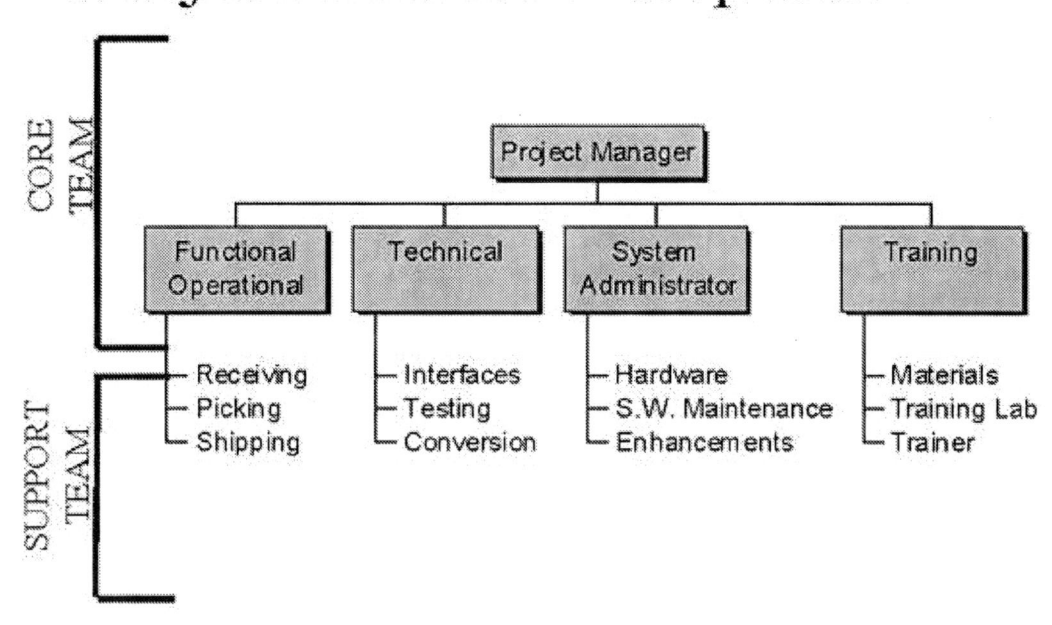

Project Team Development

Don't assume that your team possesses all needed skills and that it will not require additional training.

Do assess the team's capability for achieving a successful implementation. The four main assessment categories are project administration, functional concepts, software modules, and hardware components. To manage a project effectively, the team needs working knowledge in each of these areas. At the very minimum, the team should perform a self-evaluation, but it may be more helpful to have an industry expert conduct the assessment. Based on the assessment results, develop a team education plan outlining the steps required to master the skills needed by the team.

While communication is vital, do not schedule meetings so frequently that you raise the risk of team burnout before the project is completed. Participation and overall project morale wane when people feel that they are not contributing or benefiting from project meetings.

Do schedule full-team meetings monthly or bi-weekly, depending on the project's requirements. These meetings should focus on status updates and discussions of interest to all the participants, including support team members. Core team members, however, should be in constant communication, getting together several times a week in order to handle functional issues that may not always pertain to the entire group. An additional reason for adopting the team structure is that it helps control people's time and the company's resources.

Positive Communication

Don't forget to name your project or it will be done for you. As with all nicknames, once it sticks – it is yours. No one wants to be known for managing Project Hopeless or a name derived from a deliberate mispronunciation of the WMS package name.

Do proactively name your project, preferably with a short, catchy title that imparts a positive message.

It is a mistake to let the project slowly ramp up as activities are initiated. Instead, be sure to kick off the WMS implementation correctly, an essential step in managing a positive project communication campaign. First, hold an executive briefing to introduce the project's name, team, objectives, and benefits. Present the schedule, budget, issues, and risks at the same time. Second, introduce the project to your "customers" – the system's users in the warehouse. A warehouse project kickoff, held during normal shift hours, is very effective. The goal is to announce the reasons for, and the benefits of the project in an upbeat manner. The presentation should include the implementation plans along with the explanation that future updates will be posted on company bulletin boards.

Don't keep project status information secret or attempt to hide problem issues. No news is not necessarily good news when it comes to corporate activities. Perfect projects rarely exist. You will gain respect by facing difficult issues rather than concealing them.

Do provide continued project updates following the kickoff. Informing people of the project status helps mitigate gossip such as "I heard the project has been put on hold ...." People are much more positive and understanding when they are informed. By sharing issues with management, you avoid surprises and may be fortunate enough to receive an unexpected solution. When problems are discovered you need to get pre-approval of contingency plans.

Training

Never underestimate the planning required to develop an effective training program. Weak training programs are a major cause of troubled implementations. Next to having a system that works, a well-trained user group is the most essential component in a successful WMS implementation.

You must develop a training plan that covers the format, approach, course structure and requirements, administration, scheduling, and resources (hardware, software, and trainers). Training can be paper- or computer-based, in a classroom or on the job. It is essential to promptly determine the correct approach for your situation.

Don't Miss the Benefits of Getting Supervisors Involved Early

Do conduct supervisor training. This training provides the opportunity to pilot the training materials and operational concepts. Even though acceptance testing may prove that the system works, it may not identify functional problems that supervisors could uncover during training. Also, users are more receptive when the terminology and examples are correctly tailored for their own facility. When you teach supervisors how to handle exceptions and troubleshoot problems, such as RF communication lapses, you enable them to provide assistance with end user training. This becomes useful if the trainer is a vendor or consultant, because your people are more inclined to ask questions of their supervisor than an outsider. As an added bonus, when your supervisor is in a leadership position, you increase user acceptance.

Don't Limit Training To Only Functions That Users Need To Know

Do explain how the WMS relates to the each person's current job and the impact of his or her actions on the overall operation. It is important to discuss why some activities are no longer required, especially if they are replaced by a new WMS function. A step-by-step correlation between the old and new system and procedures confirms the importance of each part of the user's activities, reduces confusion, and makes any unfortunate return to the old system easier.

Don't Be Too Confident in the System's Reliability During Training

System installation can be tricky, and having a much-touted new system go down during training sends a negative message to users.

Do keep technical support available during hands-on training. Problems will occur, but fixing them immediately keeps the dreaded "it is never going to work" attitude to a minimum.

Don't Rely Completely On Classroom-Based Activities

Do consider building a Mock Warehouse. A "simulation lab" may require time and resources to construct, but the investment is well worth it. Training in a simulated warehouse with actual RF equipment, bar-coded pallet props, and fake storage and staging locations is enormously helpful in relating the classroom instruction to the physical activity on the floor. The mock warehouse should use a training database populated with a sample of the real inventory and locations. Locate the setup in a section of your facility to avoid replicating the RF network, and design receiving, put-away, picking and shipping flows so that they resemble actual operational flows.

Don't Forget To Evaluate And Reward The Participants.

Do certify the participants. Verify that the users have learned how to execute those WMS transactions required performing their job. This will highlight, prior to implementation, areas or workers requiring additional attention. A certification program promotes a sense of achievement. For example, you might try giving each user a card that lists all the classes that he or she attended and then reward completed cards with a token of accomplishment.

Project Documentation

Don't lose track of critical project information or take on the burden of managing a full project library. Project managers begin to lose control when project documentation is spread throughout the company or become overwhelmed by attempting to manage a complete project library. Establishing a balance may seem difficult.

Do develop an electronic project library guide – a fairly easy task if begun early. Create and maintain a spreadsheet that does three things:

- Identifies every document associated with the project.
- Notes whether it is a hard copy or electronic document.
- Describes how or through whom the file can be accessed.

For documents such as status reports, list both current and historical items. Minimal effort is required to keep a spreadsheet like this up to date. With this tool, everyone can find all the project's documents, and the project team is not encumbered with trying to assemble the material in one place and managing a library.

Don't rely solely on what the vendor provides. Documents supplied with the system tend to be encyclopedic, organized by function rather than topic and not handy for a quick reference.

Do Create a Troubleshooting Guide

This time saver can be a struggling user's biggest help on the floor. Customized for your operation, the guide should offer simple diagnostic tests and fast fixes for common problems with barcode scanners, terminals, printers, software, and so forth. At the beginning of the project, designate a spiral notebook as your troubleshooting manual. Encourage team members to record, in simple language, frequently encountered problems and how they were resolved. Before the crunch time of implementation, organize this guidebook by subject, set it in type, and place it in an accessible location on the warehouse floor. It then continues as a living document, with new problems and solutions added on an ongoing basis.

These Do's and Don'ts emphasize the serious attention required for planning implementation activities. Too many WMS implementations struggle and fail, not because of the system's technical performance, but due to poorly handled project management and people issues. Project activities, carefully planned at the start, eliminate wasted time, money, and effort. Your attention to these basics will facilitate a smooth implementation from beginning to end.

This article "**The Human Side of WMS Implementations**" is by Catherine L. Cooper and The Progress Group.   Used by Permission.

The Progress Group LLC is the Atlanta-based international supply chain and logistics consultancy. www.theprogressgroup.com 770-804-9920

Catherine Cooper is President of World Connections. www.worldconnections.com

WMS Software: The Importance of Testing

Tell someone to plan on testing a new WMS installation, and you'll probably get the same response that school children reserve for adults who deliver painfully obvious information: "Well, DUH!" Kids oversimplify things, however, and the person you were talking to might be thinking too quickly and too shallowly when it comes to taking new software for a test spin.

You can smooth your system implementation a lot if you and your consultant devote time and thought to coming up with a rigorous testing plan to make sure the bugs are out of the application and all its interfaces before you trust it with your business. What's more, if you invest time and effort to design and carry out a thorough, planned test of the software application in which you invested your money, you stand a good chance of building teams and finding talent that will continue to pay big benefits long after the implementation project is history.

Testing isn't specific to a brand of software or type of application. It is not limited to making sure software works, either. *Part of the process is trying to make it break.* These guidelines apply whether you're putting in a new WMS, moving transportation decisions to a TMS, or integrating your supply chain partners with an inter-enterprise application integration suite. They apply equally to code on your own servers as well as connections to an application service provider.

Start Testing

Start with an overview of the system and what it is expected to do for the business. Figure out the approach. It sets the scope of system testing, the overall strategy to be adopted, the activities to be completed, the general resources required and the methods and processes to be used. Once the overview is complete, move to a detailed design effort. During this effort, you define exactly what functions the system will use and those you won't. Additionally, you will define the modifications required, including functional specifications, and all interfaces to external systems. This effort will allow you to then define the amount of effort required to complete testing.

Then, move to the test planning stage, which details the activities, dependencies and effort that will be required to conduct the appropriate test, or tests. The next level is called test conditions or cases, which document the tests to be applied, the data to be processed, the automated testing coverage and the expected results. Sound like a lot of work? It is, but it's worth it.

Outline of a Sample System Test Plan

I. Introduction
    A. Overview of this new system
    B. Formal review points
        a. Design documentation
        b. Testing approach
        c. Unit test plans
        d. Unit test conditions and results
        e. System test conditions
        f. Post-system test review
    C. Objectives of system test
    D. Software quality assurance involvement

II. Scope and Objectives
    A. Scope of test approach – system functions
        a. Inclusions
        b. Exclusions
    B. Testing scope
       1. Functional testing
       2. Interface testing
       3. Acceptance testing
       4. Final acceptance testing
    C. Testing process
    D. System test entrance/exit criteria

III. Test Phases and Cycles
    1. Project integration test
    2. Operations acceptance test

IV. System Test Schedule

V. Resources
    1. Human
    2. Hardware
    3. Software
    4. Test environments
    5. Error measurement system

VI. Roles and Responsibilities
    A. Management team
    B. Testing team
    C. Business team
    D. Testing support team
    E. External support team

VII. Error Management
VIII. Reviewing & Status Reporting
IX. Issues/Risk/Assumptions
X. Signoff

Check your assumptions before getting into the work itself. Get your process flow mapping down on paper, numbering each section and detailing procedural as well as system actions. You are starting the documentation package for the entire implementation. Everything you develop – test scripts, standard operating procedures, training materials, job aides and anything else you create or are given – should reference the proper section number on your flow mapping so you can verify all details in the test plan support the desired system configuration. The flow documentation becomes the reference map for changes or upgrades later.

Make sure you and your vendors get on the same page at the outset. Make it clear what you expect from the vendors and what you plan to do. On their side, software will be delivered on time, with modifications if required, and fully tested, with proper version control and all required quality. "Show-stopper" bugs are to get immediate attention from each vendor's development team.

For your part, you'll provide all required resources. No one will make incremental changes that add up to big differences in the project. Management has to approve all changes in scope.

People Are Important

Now, glance back Step VI in the outline. Circle it in red. Blow it up on your copier and put it on your wall. It is about people, people, and people. Get a team together – in practice, not in name only – and do whatever is necessary to make sure everyone on it understands that this is their top priority. Arrange for the team meet weekly and make it clear that no one is to miss any meetings. Ongoing communication leads to clarification about terminology and thinking.

Assign a project leader for testing and give that person full support and the authority to accomplish the mission. Integrate the testing schedule into the master schedule for integrating the system. Identify critical path items and work out solutions early.

The testing project manager should have one eye on deliverables and tasks that are behind schedule. Set up weekly vendor conference calls with the full team. Discuss progress made during the preceding week and review what's coming up over the next two weeks and problem areas you can foresee. Make the people who need to resolve those issues schedule side meetings. The weekly meetings and conference calls breed familiarity, get people used to one another's styles and allow all groups to communicate openly and be part of the team.

Establish the testing team as early as possible. That gives the vendor time to train your people who will do the tests, and thinking about testing will give everyone a better understanding of the integration requirements with legacy systems, other systems you are implementing, and hardware. During heavy testing, meet daily to ensure that all parities are resolving the problems. This process is where you plant seeds to harvest after the implementation is over.

Expect to find people who can be "champions" in your organization, bright people who see the big picture intuitively, who can think cross-functionally. Let them shine in planning and carrying out the testing process. Look, too, for people who show aptitudes that can make them leaders in specific areas of your operation after the new system is in place. These people also should be considered as trainers for other end-users and resources for developing standard operating procedures, job aides and other collateral materials.

Facilities preparation can cause a lot of issues if not managed and can even cause the overall project to be late. IT staff has to be on the testing team. Don't surprise them with setting up and configuring hardware peripherals, arranging system access, or deciding what menu options should be available. IT has to buy in early and help with decisions about establishing the operating environment (testing, training, and production) and with trouble-shooting in general.

Testing takes resources. Establish a conference room as your command post for all testing, with all necessary equipment and supplies. Most software vendors require data lines for remote processing so their programmers and support personnel can access the system for debugging and downloading software patches and upgrades. This is faster and it's cheaper for you because they don't have to be on site. Make it happen very early in the process.

Establishing the Process

Right at the get-go, create definitions for the processes in your testing plan. Make sure everyone's speaking the same language about the new system, about your operation, and about the testing.

Here are some examples of terms to pin down.

Functional Testing – The objective of this test is to ensure that each element of the application meets the functional requirements of the business as outlined in the design documentation.

Integration Testing – This test proves that all areas of the system interface with each other correctly and there are no gaps in the data flow. The final integration test proves that the system works as an integrated whole when all the fixes are complete.

Acceptance Test – This test ensures that the system operates in the manner expected and that any supporting material, such as procedures or forms, is accurate and suitable for the purpose intended. It is high-level testing, ensuring that there are no gaps in the functionality.

Regression Testing – A regression test will be performed after the release of each object code. It means going back and doing exactly what you did before that detected a problem, watching to see that the problem has been fixed. If, for example, you enter five digits of a ZIP code during a test of a customer database and the software populates that field with only four digits, do it after the repair and see if you get five this time.

The level of detail in testing is a judgment call, balancing what you would do in an ideal situation with the expertise of the staff and time available. At any level, tie testing back to the process flow, ensuring that all processes were tested.

The amount of data you need for a thorough test is huge, and it will require a lot of thought to assemble it and resources to enter it. When you're collecting old data or inventing test data, make it as easy as you can to check how the system performs. If, for example, you're entering data about product size and a WMS is supposed to tell you how it cubed out, *use numbers that make it easy for you to tell almost at a glance* if the system got it right. Don't devise tests that require you to spend a day with your calculator checking the system's answers. That's not testing, that's torture.

When the data is ready, do a backup. That will allow for regression testing or volume testing. An error management system is a must and is the yardstick evaluating the software. Set up a spreadsheet to track errors and create categories from serious to minor. You will also want to track the status of each error, such as whether the vendor is correcting, it's ready for regression testing, or it's confirmed as fixed.

Meeting the challenges of software testing is a huge task and shouldn't be underestimated. Remind the team that failing a test is not bad. It shows good work on their part. Remember that most vendors don't warranty the modifications they make to customize your system, and it is your responsibility to find problems and have them corrected before you sign off on project completion.

And the last piece of advice is to keep your sense of humor. It will help get everyone through the process.

"**WMS Software: The Importance of Testing**" is used by permission from the Tompkins Associates. Written by John Seidl, Principal at Kurt Salmon Associates.

Tompkins Associates is the leading operations-focused consulting and integration firm specializing in end-to-end supply chain solutions. Customers look to Tompkins' expertise to develop and implement intelligent solutions in distribution center design, distribution network configuration, transportation planning, systems integration, benchmarking and best practices, logistics outsourcing, and supply chain optimization. For more than 30 years, Tompkins has offered a proven track record and deep industry expertise for solutions that reduce costs and improve supply chain performance. The company is headquartered in Raleigh, NC. For more information on Tompkins, visit www.tompkinsinc.com

Appendix A

A… WMS Software Providers

This appendix contains WMS solutions available currently worldwide. The first section has **stand alone WMS**. A stand alone system is where the provider does not offer an enterprise solution. If you are **replacing software for the entire enterprise**, then go to Chapter 3 (ERP Solutions with a Warehouse Module).

3i Infotech Inc. (International)
450 Raritan Center Parkway
Suite B
Edison, NJ 08837
USA
732-225-4242
Fax: 732-346-1823
www.3i-infotech.com
vbala@3i-infotech.com

3PL Central (USA)
562 E. Technology Avenue
Building C, Suite 1500
Orem, UT 84097
USA
801.494.0512
Fax: 801.494.0512
http://www.3plcentral.com
info@3plcentral.com

7Hills Business Solutions (International)
651 Holiday Drive
Suite 300
Pittsburgh, PS 15220
USA
866.910.3249
Fax: 412-222-9523
http://www.7hillsbiz.com
sales_global@7hillsbiz.com

a-SIS (Europe)
8 rue de la Richelandière
42100 SAINT ETIENNE
France
04.77.49.47.00
Fax: 04.77.49.47.10
http://www.a-sis..com
contact@a-sis.com

Acatech Solutions, Inc. (USA)
2038-B14 Lake Forest Drive
Lake Forest, CA 92630
USA
949.830.6800
Fax: 949.830.6822
http://www.acatech.com
acatech@acatech.com

Accellos, Inc. (North America)
90 South Cascade Avenue
Suite 1200
Colorado Springs, CO 80903
USA
719.433.7000
Fax: 719.433.7039
http://www.accellos.com
matt.petty@accellos.com

Access Data Systems Inc. (USA)
705 Gen. Washington Avenue
Suite 203
Norristown, PA 19403
USA
610.539.6200
Fax: 610.539.5257
http://www.accessdatasys.com
info@accessdatasys.com

Acumen Data Systems, Inc. (USA)
2223 Westfield Street
West Springfield, MA 01089
USA
413.737.4800
888.816.0933
Fax: 413.737.5544
http://www.acumendatasystems.com
acumensales@acumendatasystems.com

ADC Technologies, Inc. (International)
4631 Teller Avenue
Suite 130
Newport Beach, CA 92660
USA
949.752.2328
888.823.2848
Fax: 949.752.2329
http://www.adctech.com
HQ@adctech.com

Advanced Logistics Systems, Inc. (USA)
P.O. Box 4415
Roche Harbor, WA 98250
USA
360.378.5398
Fax: 360.378.6799
http://www.advanced-logistics.com
als@advanced-logistics.com

ASC (International)
4074 E. Patterson Rd.
Dayton, OH 45430
USA
937.429.1428
Fax: 937.429.8575
http://www.ascbarcode.com
sales@ascbarcode.com

Advanta Software (Australia)
82 Waterloo Road
Macquarie Park, NSW 2113
Australia
61.2.9888.4000
Fax: 61.2.9888.4099
http://www.advantasoftware.com.au
contact@advantasoftware.com.au

AHN Corpporation (USA)
P.O. Box 11146
Burbank, CA 91510
USA
818.353.2962
888.807.0958
Fax: 818.353.6053
http://www.ahninc.com
info@ahninc.com

Ames & McBain Inc. (USA)
2601 Grove Bluff Ct SE
Grand Rapids, MI 49546-5618
USA
616.942.1305
800.925.4844
Fax: 616.942.4027
http://www.amesmcbain.com
info@amesmcbain.com

Applied Computer Excellence (USA)
5050 Hillside Drive
West Bend, WI 53095
USA
262.644.4040
888.725.8836
Fax: 262.644-4040
http://www.a-c-e.com
sales@a-c-e.com

AquiTec, Inc. (International)
547 W. Jackson Blvd.
Floor 9
Chicago, IL 60661
USA
312.264.1900
Fax: 312.264.1991
http://www.aquitecintl.com
info@aquitecintl.co.uk

Apollis Inc. (USA)
333 Washington Avenue North
Suite 106
Minneapolis, MN 55401
USA
612-343-0404
http://www.appolis.com
info@appolis.com

Argos Software (USA)
5737 N. Fresno Street
Fresno, CA 93710
USA
888.253.5353
Fax: 559.227.9644
http://www.argosoftware.com
info@argosoftware.com

ASAP Automation (International)
12300 Plantside Drive
Louisville, KY 40299
USA
502.266.9999
800.409.0383
Fax: 502.267.1886
http://www.asapauto.com
info@asapauto.com

Asgard Software Ltd (International)
Oakland Business Centre
2-6 Reeves Way
South Woodham Ferrers
Essex CM3 5XF
England
+44 (0)1245 325 771
Fax +44 (0)1245 325 855
http://www.asgardsoftware.com
sales@asgardsoftware.com

ATL Corporation (USA)
241 East Fourth Street
Suite 200
Frederick, MD 21701
USA
301-695-1703
Fax: 301-695-1506
http://www.atlusa.com
info@atlusa.com

ATMS Ltd. (International)
Number One, Holt Court
Aston Science Park
Birmingham, B7 4EJ
UK
+44 (0)121 628 9000
Fax: +44 (0)121 359 4200
http://www.atms.co.uk
atms@atmsplc.com

Automation Associates, Inc. (International)
7025 Tomken Road
Mississauga, ON L5S 1R6
Canada
905.565.6560
800.223.7080
Fax: 905.565.6570
http://www.rfpathways.com
info@rfpathways.com

Bar Control Systems & Services, Inc. (USA)
P.O. Box 6339
Greenville, SC 29606-6339
USA
864.421-0050
800.947.4362
Fax: 864.421.0051
http://www.barcontrol.com
information@barcontrol.com

BFC Software, Inc. (USA)
245 W. Roosevelt Rd.
Bldg. 8 Suite 51
West Chicago, IL 60185
USA
630.562.0375
Fax: 630.562.0618
http://www.bfcsoftware.com
sales@bfcassociates.com

Boon Software Consulting PTE Ltd (Singapore)
3791 Jalan Bukit Merah
#07-26/27, E-Centre
Redhill, 159471
Singapore
+65 6732-2669
Fax: +65 6276-4149
http://www.boonsoftware.com
marketing@boonsoftware.com

Boxcar Central (USA)
549C College Park Road
Ladson, SC 29456
USA
843.278.8033
info@boxcarcentralims.com
http://www.boxcarcentralims.com

Cadre Technologies, Inc. (USA)
7900 E. Union Ave.
Suite 1007
Denver, CO 80237
USA
303.928.1124
866.25.CADRE
Fax: 303.217.7050
http://www.cadretech.com
info@CadreTech.com

CAIB America Corportation (International)
410 Park Avenue
Suite 1530
New York, NY 10022
USA
917.210.8010
Fax: 917.210.8011
http://www.caibconsulting.com
http://www.kuglerconsulting.com
wilhelm.h.kugler@kuglerconsulting.com

CAL Consult B.V. (Europe)
MarienbergstraBe 78
Nurenborg, 90411
Germany
+49 (0) 911.95219.0
Fax: +49 (0) 9 11.95219.38
http://www.cal-consult.de
info@cal-consult.de

Cambar Software, Inc. (USA)
2387 Clements Ferry Road
Charleston, SC 29492
USA
843.856.2822
800.756.4402
Fax: 843.881.4893
http://www.cambarsoftware.com
sales@cambarsoftware.com

Camelot Consulting. (USA)
10316 Feldfarm Lane
Suite 300
Charlotte, NC 28210
USA
704.554.1670
800.849.2184
Fax: 704.554.1673
http://www.3plsoftware.com
sales@3plsoftware.com

Catalyst International Inc. (International)
8989 North Deerwood Drive
Milwaukee, WI 53223-2439
USA
414.362.6800
800.236.4600
Fax: 414.362.6794
http://www.catalystwms.com
info@catalystinternational.com

CatLogic
Merged. **See GreenCat**

Celution Software Products (USA)
6847 Ellicot Drive
East Syracuse, NY 13057
USA
315.434.8842
800.813.3647
Fax: 315.434.8865
http://www.celution.com
info@Celution.com

Centric Logistic Solutions (Netherlands)
Transistorstraat 2G
1322 CE Almere
Netherlands
+31 (0)36-5498666
Fax: +31 (0)36-5498888
http://www.locuswms.com
logistic.solutions@centric.nl

Ceritar Technologies (Canada)
1205 Rue Ampere
Suite 104
Boucerville, QB J4B 7M6
Canada
450-645-9988
Fax: 450-645-9989
http://www.ceritar.com
info@ceritar.com

CGW, Inc. (USA)
6121A Heritage Park Drive
Suite 200
Chattanooga, TN 37416
USA
423.892.2902
Fax: 423.855.7374
http://www.cgwinc.com
info@cgwinc.com

Chess Logistics Technology Ltd (UK)
Avocado Court, Commerce Way,
Westinghouse Road,
Trafford Park,
Manchester
M17 1HW
UK
44 (0) 161 888 2580
Fax: 44 (0) 161 888 2590
http://www.chess.uk.com
info@chess.uk.com

ClearOrbit (International)
6805 Capital of Texas Hwy
Suite 370
Austin, TX 78731
USA
512.231.8191
800.324.5143
Fax: 512.231.0292
http://www.clearorbit.com
info@clearorbit.com

Click Commerce (International)
233 N Michigan Avenue
22nd Floor
Chicago, IL 60601
USA
312-482-9006
800-899-2641
Fax: 312-482-8557
http://www.clickcommerce.com
click.sales@clickcommerce.com

Codeworks, LLC. (USA)
6388B Fiesta Drive
Columbus, OH 43235
USA
614.389.0692
Fax: 614.389.0697
http://www.ctcodeworks.com
RDeShone@CtCodeworks.com

Consafe Logistics (Europe)
Porfyrvägen 14
224 78 Lund
Sweden
+46 46 280 04 00
Fax: +46 46 15 10 74
http://www.consafelogistics.com/
sales@se.consafelogistics.com

Control Solutions, Inc. (USA)
10 County Line Road
Suite 25
North Branch, NJ 08876
USA
908.526.9083
Fax: 908.526.8929
http://www.consolut.com
sales@consolut.com

Cool Earth Technologies (USA)
2112 Third Avenue
Suite 402
Seattle, WA 98121
USA
206.770.9061
Fax: 206.770.3354
http://www.coolearth.com
info@coolearth.com

Core Partners (USA)
5 South Market Street
Suite 302
Frederick, MD 21701
USA
301.695.2673
301.695.1705
Fax: 301.695.1506
http://www.corewms.com
sales@corewms.com

Crimson Software
811 Wantland Road
Washougal, WA 98671
USA
360.837.8077
http://www.crimsonsoftware.com
info@crimsonsoftware.com

Cristal Solutions Pte Ltd (Singapore)
26 Hillside Drive
#01-01
Singapore 548945
Singapore
65.6289.7838
Fax: 65.6383.8854
http://www.cristalsolutions.com/
sales@cristalsolutions.com

Dalosy Projecten (Europe)
Nikkelstraat 7
Postbus 168
Ridderkerk, 2980 AD
Netherlands
+31 (0) 180 486 486
Fax: +31 (0) 180 415 442
http://www.dalosy.com
info@dalosy.com

Dastronic NV (Belgium)
Molenstraat 2
3202 Rillaar
Belgium
+32.16.300.960
Fax: +32.16.300.961
http://www.dastronic.be
info@dastronic.be

Data Automation Systems Inc. (USA)
1659 Scott Blvd
Suite 26
Santa Clara, CA 95050-4137
USA
408.983.0449
800.448.5606
Fax: 408.983.0416
http://www.dataautomation.com
sales@dataautomation.com

Datex, Inc. (International)
10300 49th Street N.
Clearwater, FL 33762-5000
USA
727.571.4159
800.933.2839
Fax: 727.571.4301
http://www.datexcorp.com
sales@datexcorp.com

Davanti Warehousing BV (Europe)
Landzichtweg 62
4105 DP Culemborg
Netherlands
+31 (0) 88 345450
Fax: +31 (0) 345520857
http://www.davantigroup.com
info@davantigroup.com

DCS Transport and Logistics Solutions
Aquired. **See Four Soft.**

Delfour Corporation
Acquired. **See Accellos**

Delta Software Ltd. (UK)
Whitwood Lane
Wakefield
WF10 5QD
UK
+44 (0)1977 669930
Fax: +44 (0)1977 668378
http://www.deltasoftware.co.uk
info@deltasoftware.co.uk

Distel Group (Netherlands).
Van der Marckstraat 18
Leiderdorp, 2352 RA
Netherlands
+31 (0)71 - 582 08 00
Fax: +31 (0)71 - 582 02 47
http://www.distel.nl
info@distel.nl

Donachie, Fenton & Associates DFA (USA)
115 South Corona Avnue
Suite 2D
Valley Stream, NY 11580
USA
516-593-1136
Fax: 516-593-1785
http://www.dfa-wms.com
info@dfa-wms.com

DSA Software (USA)
208 North Street
Foxboro, MA 02035
USA
508.543.0400
Fax: 508.543.0856
http://www.dsasoft.com
sales@dsasoft.com

DX Corporation (USA)
111 Nesconset Hwy
Hauppauge, NY 11788
USA
631.584.4740
Fax: 631.584.4761
http://www.dx-corp.com
amaurer@dx-corp.com

E.D.G. Enterprises, Inc. (USA)
1010 Calle Cordillera
Suite 101
San Clemente, CA 92673
USA
949-369-6719
Fax: 949-369-0416
http://www.e-warehousing.com
sales@edgent.com

Eclipse Systems Pvt Ltd. (India)
A-21, First Floor
Sector-58
Noida, 201301
India
+91-120-645- 7009
http://www.eclsys.com
info@eclsys.com

eTeklogics. (USA)
7547 Mentor Avenue
Suite 202
Mentor, OH 44060
USA
440-975-0686
800.452.5251
Fax: 440-975-0876
http://www.eteklogics.com/
sales@eteklogics.com

Ehrhardt + Partner GmbH & Co. (International)
Alte Römerstrabe 3
Boppard-Buchholz, D-56154
Germany
+49 67 42 87 27 0
Fax: +49 67 42 87 27 50
http://www.ehrhardt-partner.com
info@ehrhardt-partner.com

Exact Easy Access (Netherlands)
Van 't Hoffstraat 28
3863 AX Nijkerk
Netherlands
+31 (0)33 - 2470010
Fax: +31 (0)33 - 2470047
http://www.exea.nl
info@exea.nl

FASCOR (USA)
11260 Chester Road
Suite 610
Cincinnati, OH 45246
USA
513.421.1777
888.8.FASCOR
Fax: 513.421.1191
http://www.fascor.com
information@fascor.com

Four Soft Ltd (International)
5Q1A3, Cyber Towers
HITEC City, Madhapur
Hyderabad – 500033, AP
India
+91 40 23100600/601
Fax: +91 40 23100602
http://www.four-soft.com
sales@four-soft.com

Foxfire Technologies (USA)
105 North Main Street
Six Mile, SC 29682
USA
864-868-5243
Fax: 864-868-2288
http://www.foxfiretechnologies.com
info@foxfiretechnologies.com

FWL Technologies
Acquired. See Four Soft.

Gateway Software B.V. (Netherlands)
Barbizonlaan 87
2908 ME Capelle a/d IJssel
Netherlands
31 10 2866070
Fax: (31) 10 - 2866075
http://www.Gateway.nl
info@gateway.nl

Geneva Systems, Inc. (USA)
1290 N Hancock Street
Suite 201
Anaheim, CA 92807
USA
714.701.1955
800-GENEVA-8
Fax: 714.701.1954
http://www.genevasystems.com

Global Concepts, Inc. (USA)
900 S. Shackleford Rd.
Suite 412
Little Rock, AR 72211
USA
501.978.3240
800.459.1168
Fax: 501.312.0180
http://www.gclogistics.com
dstuart@gclogistics.com

GreenCat B.V. (Europe)
Stephensonweg 12
4207 HB
Gorinchem
+31 (0)183 - 646 100
Fax: +31 (0)183 - 641 690
http://www.catlogic.com
info@greencat-it.com

Headwater
Acquired. See Accellos.

HighJump Software (International)
6455 City West Pkwy.
Eden Prairie, MN 55344-3240
USA
800.328.3271
http://www.highjump.com
hjinfo@mmm.com

HK Systems (North America)
2855 S. James Drive
New Berlin, WI 53151
USA
(262) 860-7000
800.424.7365
Fax: (262) 860-7010
http://www.hksystems.com

HotStatus Enterprises, Inc. (USA)
23120 Alicia Parkway
Suite 207
Mission Vejo, CA 92692
USA
949.466.3996
http://www.hotstatus.com
info@hotstatus.com

Howard Way & Associates (USA)
5905 Bonnie View Drive
Baltimore, MD 21209
USA
410.542.4446
Fax: 410.542.9218
http://www.howardway.com
art@howardway.com

ICS, Inc. (USA)
1650 Prudential Drive
Suite 300
Jacksonville, Fl 32207
USA
904-399-8500
Fax: 904.398.7855
http://www.e-logimax.com
info@e-logimax.com

Infinite Functions, Inc. (USA)
P.O. Box 240
Creston, CA 93432
USA
805.238.3082
866.967.2932
Fax: 805.238.3047
http://www.infinitefunctions.com
sales@infinitefunctions.com

Infolog Solutions (International)
13 Avenue de la porte d'Italie
75013 Paris
France
+33 0 1 53 61 65 00
Fax: +33 0 1 53 61 65 01
http://www.infolog-solutions.com
info@infolog-solutions.com

Infor (International)
→ **Has Multiple WMS Solutions**
13560 Morris Road
Suite 4100
Alpharetta, GA 30004
USA
678-319-8000
866-244-5479
Fax: 678-319-8682
http://www.infor.com
sales@infor.com

Infosite Technologies Inc. (Canada)
1919, Lionel Bertrand
Suite 204
Boisbriand, QC J7H 1N8
Canada
450-437-0354
1-888-395-0354
Fax: 450-437-1214
http://www.infositetech.com
sales@infositetech.com

Infoscan Software Systems, Inc.
Acquired. **See Scenic Technology.**

Integrated Visual Systems (USA)
1207 East Crews Road
Matthews, NC 28105
USA
704.847.3379
Fax: 704.847.4655
http://www.ivsi.com
sales@ivsi.com

Integrated Warehousing Solutions (USA)
3075 Highland Parkway
Downers Grove, IL 60515
USA
630.493.7899
800.682.2910
Fax: 630.353.6916
http://www.irmswms.com
iwsinfo@irmswms.com

Intellitrack Inc. (International)
224 Schilling Circle
Suite 130
Hunt Valley, MD 21031
USA
410-771-3060
888-583-3008
Fax: 410-771-3061
http://www.intellitrack.net
sales@intellitrack.net

Intek Integration Technologies, Inc. (USA)
1400 112th Ave SE
Suite 202
Bellevue, WA 98004
USA
425.455.9935
Fax: 425.455.9934
http://www.intek.com
sales@intek.com

Interchain B.V.
Acquired. **See Kewill.**

Interlink Technologies (USA)
5925 Chippewa Trail
Frisco, TX 75034
USA
972.334-9220
800.655.5465
Fax: 972.334-9225
http://www.interlinktech.com
info@interlinktech.com

Inther Logistics Engineering (Netherlands)
5809 AE Venray-Leunen
Netherlands
+31 478 502575
Fax: +31 478 636432
http://www.inther.nl
info@inther.nl

JDH Warehousing Systems Ltd (Canada)
1198 Priory Court
Oakville, ON L6M 1B6
Canada
905.827.7532
Fax: 905.827.7247
http://www.jdh.on.ca
jhall@jdh.on.ca

JMO Systems (North America)
11570 Yonge Street
Richmond Hill, ON L4E 3N7
Canada
905.224.6200
888.527.5555
Fax: 905.224.4088
http://www.jmosystems.com
mark@jmo-systems.com

Kare Technologies, Inc. (USA)
5784 Post Road
Suite 1
Warwick, RI 02818
USA
888.388.KARE
Fax:
http://www.karetech.com
info@karetech.com

Kewill (Europe)
Stationsweg 45
3330 AB Zwijndrecht
Netherlands
+31 (0) 78 6 12 37 44
Fax: +31 (0) 78 6 12 12 66
http://www.kewill.com
infonl@kewill.com

KNAPP (International)
277 Southfield Parkway
Suite 135
Forest Park, GA 30297-2527
USA
404-366-1700
Fax: 404-366-1726
http://www.knappsoftware.com
sales@knappsoftware.com

Knighted Computer Systems, Inc. (USA)
145 North Highland Avenue
Ossining, NY 10562
USA
914.762.0505
Fax: 914.303.5208
http://www.knightedcs.com
sales@knightedcs.com

LDS Corporation
Acquired. **See Cadre.**

Leadtec Systems (Australia)
Suite 14
24 Lakeside Drive,
Burwood East, 3151, Victoria
Australia
+61 3 9847 7040
Fax: +61 3 9847 7070
http://www.leadtec.com.au
sales@leadtec.com.au

Lilly Software Associates
Acquired. **See Infor.**

Logarithme
Is now called a-SIS. **See a-SIS.**

LogControl (Europe)
Blucherstr. 32
Pforzheim, 75177
Netherlands
49 0 7231 580 48 0
Fax: 49 0 7231 580 48 20
http://www.logcontrol.de
info@logcontrol.de

Logility Inc. (International)
470 E. Paces Ferry Road
Atlanta, GA 30305
USA
404.261.9777
800.762.5207
Fax: 404.264.5206
http://www.logility.com
sales@logility.com

Logisoft (International)
Bukit Batok Tech Park 21.
71,Bukit Batok Crescent
#07-11, Prestige Centre, 658071
Singapore
+65 98477257
enquiry@elogisoft.com
http://www.elogisoft.com

Logistics Software Corporation (Canada)
8 Hillcrest Avenue
Suite 2910
Toronto, ON M2N 6Y6
Canada
905.843.7433
http://www.logisticssoftware.com
info@logisticssoftware.com

Made4Net (International)
87 South Fairview Avenue
Paramus, NJ 07652
USA
201-645-4345
http://www.made4net.com
sales@made4net.com

Majure Data (USA)
1455 Bluegrass Lakes Parkway
Alpharetta, GA 30004
USA
770.587.3054
800.353.2520
Fax: 770.594.9224
http://www.majuredata.com
rfnavigator@majuredata.com

Manhattan Associates (International)
→ **Has Multiple WMS Solutions**
2300 Windy Ridge Parkway
Tenth Floor
Atlanta, GA 30339
USA
770.955.7070
Fax: 770.955.0302
http://www.manh.com
info@manh.com

MARC Global
Acquired. **See RedPrairie.**

Maves International Software (Canada)
165 Commerce Valley Dr. West
Suite 100
Thornhill, ON L3T 7V8
Canada
905.882.8300
Fax: 905.882.1550
http://www.maves.com
marketing@maves.com

Microlise (Europe)
Farrington Way
Eastwood
Nottingham, NG16 3AG
UK
44 (0) 1773 537 000
Fax: 44 (0) 1773 537 373
http://www.microlise.com
enquiries@microlise.com

Microlistics Pty Ltd (International)
1/21 Bedford Street
North Melbourne, VIC 3051
Australia
613.9326.7422
Fax: 613.9326.7588
http://www.microlistics.com
melbourne@microlistics.com

Micromation Inc. (USA)
16300 Katy Freeway
Suite 140
Houston, TX 77094
USA
281.578.2900
Fax: 281.578.0414
http://www.micromation.com
mmsales@micromation.com

Minerva Associates, Inc. (USA)
12777 High Bluff Drive
Suite 200
San Diego, CA 92130
USA
858.792.8626
866.MINERVA
Fax: 858.792.8615
http://www.minerva-associates.com
info@minerva-associates.com

Motek (USA)
113 North San Vicente Boulevard
3rd Floor
Beverly Hills, CA 90211
USA
323.653.4333
Fax: 323.653.5763
http://www.motek.com
priyainfo@motek.com

Navis LLC (International)
1000 Broadway
Suite 150
Oakland, CA 94607
USA
510 267 5000
Fax: 510 267 5100
http://www.navis.com
sales@navis.com

NeoSystems, Co., Ltd. (International)
5F, 890-44 Seoyoung Bldg
Daechi
KangNam, Seoul 135-839
Korea
02-566-4813
Fax: 02-566-9935
www.neosys.co.kr
sukyoungk@intraLogis.net

NextView Software (USA)
1401 North Batavia
Suite 104
Orange, CA 92867
USA
714.881.5105
Fax: 714.538.3812
http://www.nextviewsoftware.com
info@nextviewsoftware.com

Omega Technologies, Inc. (USA)
1255 Commercial Drive
Conyers, GA 30012
USA
770-922-9488
877-**OMEGARF**
Fax: 770-922-3228
http://www.omega-rf.com
info@omega-rf.com

OMI International, Inc.
Acquired. **See Retailix.**

Optum Software
Acquired. **See Click Commerce.**

Pantheon Automatisering (Europe)
Leeuwenveldseweg 14
Weesp, 1382 LX
Netherlands
+31 (0)294 - 49 03 30
Fax: +31 (0)294 - 43 14 20
http://www.pantheon-automatisering.nl
info@pantheon-automatisering.nl

Paperless Warehousing Pty Ltd. (Australia)
Unit C9, 391 Park Road
Regents Park
Sydney, NSW 2143
Australia
61.2.9644.4000
Fax: 61.2.9645.3030
http://www.paperless-warehousing.com
sales@paperless-warehousing.com

PathGuide Technologies, Inc. (USA)
8221-44th Avenue West
Suite G
Mukilteo, WA 98275
USA
425.438.2899
888.627.9797
Fax: 425.438.2799
http://www.pathguide.com
BusinessDevelopment@pathguide.com

Peak Technologies Group, Inc. (North America)
9200 Berger Road
Columbia, MD 21046
USA
410.309.6219
800.926.9212
Fax: 410.309.6219
http://www.peaktech.com
info@PEAKtech.com

Perfect Circle Solutions (USA)
1009 Wilshire Boulevard
Suite 221
Santa Monica, CA 90401
USA
310.395.5127
Fax: 310.395.9284
http://www.perfectcircle.com
sales@perfectcircle.com

proLogistik (Europe)
Fallgatter 1
Dortmund, 44369
Germany
49.0231.5194.0
Fax: 49.0231.5194.94
http://www.prologistik.com
info@prologistik.com

Provia Software
Acquired. See Infor.

PSI (Europe)
Rayleigh House
2 Richmond Hills
Richmond, Surrey, TW10 6QX
UK
+44/(0)20 8948 6789
Fax: +44/(0)20 8948 6789
http://www.psi.de
info@psiag.co.uk

Pulse Logistics (Australia)
Suite 5, 2-4 Henley Beach Road
Mile End, SA 5031
Australia
618.8416.7600
Fax: 618.8416.7699
http://www.pulse.com.au
pulseinfo@pulse.com.au

Quality Software Systems Inc (International)
200 Centennial Avenue
Piscataway, NJ 08854
USA
732.885.1919
800.338.4420
Fax: 732.885.1872
http://www.qssi-wms.com
sales@qssi-wms.com

Qurius NC BV (Netherlands)
Hogeweg 129
Zaltbommel, 5301 LL
Netherlands
+31 (0)418 - 68 35 00
Fax: +31 (0)418 - 68 35 35
http://www.qurius.nl
info@qurius.nl

Radcliffe, Inc. (Canada)
Acquired by **Avantce Software.**
7300 Warden Avenue
Suite 210
Markham, ON L3R 9Z6
Canada
905.752-8292
Fax: 905.752.0436
http://www.radcliffeinc.com
info@RadcliffeInc.com

Radio Beacon
Acquired. **See Accellos.**

Red Prairie (International)
→ **Has Multiple WMS Solutions**
20700 Swenson Drive
Suite 200
Waukesha, WI 53186
USA
262.317.2000
866.624.8448
Fax: 262.317.2001
http://www.redprairie.com
info@redprairie.com

Retailix (International)
10 Zarhin Street
P.O. Box 2282
Ra'anana 43000
Israel
+972 9 776 6677
Fax: +972 9 740 0471
http://www.retailix.com
info@retailix.com

Robocom Systems (International)
Acquired by **Avantce Software.**
1111 Route 110
Farmingdale, NY 11735
USA
631-753-2180
Fax: 631-249-2831
http://www.robocom.com
sales@robocom.com

Royal 4 Systems (USA)
5000 E. Spring Street
Long Beach, CA 90815
USA
562.420.9594
Fax: 562.420.7818
http://www.r4-wise.com/
info@royal4.com

RT Systems, Inc. (USA)
210 Collingwood Drive
Suite 200
Ann Arbor, MI 48103
USA
734.662.7099
Fax: 734.662.3662
http://www.rt-systems.com
RTsystems@rt-systems.com

Salomon Automation (Europe))
A-8114 Friesach / Graz (Gray)
FriesachstraBe, 15
Austria
43.3127.200.0
Fax: 43.3127.200.22
http://www.salomon.at
office@salomon.at

Savant Software, Inc. (USA)
2301 West Dunlap Ave
Suite 201
Phoenix, AZ 85021
USA
602.906.3047
Fax: 602.906.3792
http://www.savantwms.com
info@savantwms.com

Scenic Technology (USA)
465 Warren Street
Needham, MA 02492
USA
781-444-3433
Fax: 303-379-7615
www.scenictechnology.com
info@scenictechnology.com

Scancode Systems (Canada)
Centennial Business Court
5535 Eglinton Avenue West
Suite 220
Toronto, ON M9C 5K5
Canada
416-620-5000
868.666.4240
Fax: 416-620-5606
http://www.scancode.com
info@scancode.com

ScanData Systems (USA)
4420 Tuller Road
Dublin, OH 43017
USA
614.766.6622
Fax: 614.766.0065
http://www.scandata.com
scandatasales@scandata.com

SCS Automation, Inc. (USA)
A-130 North Drive
PO Box 1095
Oaks, PA 19456
USA
610.666.3540
Fax: 610.666.3544
http://www.scsautomation.com
info@scsautomation.com

SISTEMA LOGISTICS (Canada)
8130 Cote de Liesse
Saint-Laurent, QB H4T 1G7
Canada
514.733.3599
Fax: 514.733.3539
http://www.sistema-logistics.com
sistema@sistema-logistics.com

Softeon, Inc. (International)
8133 Leesburg Pike
Suite 570
Vienna, VA 22182-2706
USA
703-356-8727
Fax: 703-356-8959
http://www.softeon.com
mferreira@softeon.com

Sologlobe Inc. (Canada)
1751 rue Richardson
Bureau 6.519
Montréal QB H3K 1G6
Canada
514.938.4562
Fax: 514.938.4525
http://www.sologlobe.com
info@sologlobe.com

SPEDE Technologies (USA)
24864 Detroit Road
Cleveland, OH 44145
USA
440.808.8888
888.808.4237
Fax: 440.808.8086
http://www.spede.com
info@spede.com

Steppenwolff Corporation (USA)
82 Horatio Street 1B/2B
New York, NY 10014
USA
212.645.9618
Fax: 212.463.0050
http://www.stepwolf.com
bill@stepwolf.com

Sterling Commerce (International)
4600 Lakehurst Court
PO Box 8000
Dublin, Ohio 43016
USA
614-793-4041
800-299-4031
Fax: 614-793-4040
http://www.sterlingcommerce.com
inquiry@stercomm.com

Swisslog Software (International)
Swisslog Holding AG
Webereiweg 3
Buchs, CH-5033
Switzerland
41 62 837 4141
Fax: 41 62 837 4499
http://www.swisslog.com
wds@swisslog.com

Synergy Logistics Ltd (UK)
Synergy House
Lisle Street
Loughborough LE11 1AW
UK
44 (0) 1509 232706
Fax: 44 (0) 1509 6100186
http://www.synergy-logistics.co.uk
info@synergy-logistics.co.uk

Traker Systems (USA)
43460 Ridge Park Drive
Suite 250
Temecula, CA 92590
USA
909-693-1376
800-314-6863
Fax: 909-693-1386
http://www.trakersystems.com
prodinfo@trakersystems.com

Transformations, Inc. (USA)
P.O. Box 1971
Brentwood, TN 37024
USA
615-317-0077
Fax: 615-371-5062
http://www.transfrm.com
sales@transfrm.com

Turning Point Systems, Inc. (USA)
199 Rosewood Drive
Suite 335
Danvers, MA 01923
USA
978-777-9991
800-370-4500
Fax: 978-777-3335
http://www.turningpointsystems.com
info@turningpointsystems.com

Van Boxtel Software BV (Netherlands)
Kerkstraat 14
Boekel, 5427 BC
Netherlands
+31 (0)492 - 32 73 33
Fax: +31 (0)492 - 32 43 26
http://www.van-boxtel-software.nl
info@van-boxtel-software.nl

VCD Automatisering (Netherlands)
Postbus 917
Groningen, AX 9700
Netherlands
(050) 597 55 00
Fax: (050) 597 55 97
http://www.vcd.nl

Warepak Corporation (USA)
423 Southgate CT SW
P.O. Box 2516
Cedar Rapids, IA 52406
USA
319.365.2518
Fax: 319.364.3426
http://www.warepak.com
webmaster@warepak.com

WICS Solutions (Europe)
Havenstraat 32
Werkendam, 4251 BC
Netherlands
+31 183 507020
Fax: +31 183 404050
http://www.wics.nl
info@WICS.nl

Wireless Data Systems, Inc. (USA)
20423 State Road 7
Suite 6182
Boca Raton, FL 33498
USA
561.488.5540
Fax: 561.451.9072
http://www.wdsinc.com
contact@wdsinc.com

Witron (International)
3721 Ventura Drive
Arlington Heights, IL 60004-7468
USA
847.398.6000
Fax: 847.398.6140
http://www.witronamerica.com
info@witron.com

wmsVision, Inc. (USA)
1016 Copeland Oak Drive
Morrisville, NC 27560
USA
919.863.3388
Fax: 919.863.3389
http://www.wmsVision.com
info@wmsVision.com

Wolin Design Group (USA)

171 S. Anita Drive
Suite 105
Orange, CA 92868
USA
714-937-0700
Fax: 714-937-0701
http://www.wdgcorp.com
information@wdgcorp.com

Yantra Corporation

Acquired. See **Sterling Commerce.**

Zetes (Europe)

Zetes Industries
Investor Relations
Rue de Strasbourg 3
1130 Brussels
Belgium
+3 2 2 728 37 11
Fax: +32 2 728 37 51
http://www.zetes.nl
Info@nl.zetes.com

Zethcon Corporation (USA)

200 W 22nd Street
Suite 218
Lombard, IL 60148
USA
847.318.0800
Fax: 847.318.0807
http://www.zethcon.com
connections@zethcon.com

Appendix B

B… ERP Software with a Warehouse Module

Activant Solutions Inc. (International)
7683 Southfront Road
Livermore, CA 94551
USA
888-448-2636
http://www.activant.com
info@activant.com

Adonix (International)
2200 Georgetown Drive
Sewickley, PA 15143
USA
724.933.1377
Fax: 724.933.1379
http://www.adonix.com
info@adonix.com

American Software Inc (USA)
470 E. Paces Ferry Road NE
Atlanta, GA 30305
USA
404.264.5296
800.726.2946
Fax: 404.264.5206
http://www.amsoftware.com
askasi@amsoftware.com

Apprise Software, Inc (International)
3101 Emrick Boulevard
Suite 301
Bethlehem, PA 18020
USA
610-991-3900
Fax: 610-991-3901
http://www.apprise.com
marketing@apprise.com

APRISO Corporation (International)
One World Trade Center
Suite 1000
Long Beach, CA 90831-1000
USA
562.951.8000
877.246.9393
Fax: 562.951.9000
http://www.apriso.com
sales@apriso.com

Apparel 21 (Australia)
Level 2, 21 Cremorne Street
Richmond, Vic, 3121
Australia
+613 8415 9300
Fax: + 613 9427 1752
http://www.apparel21.com
info@apparel21.com

DPS, Inc. (USA)
3685 Priority Way S. Drive
Suite 100
Indianapolis, IN, 46240
USA
317.574.4300
800.654.4689
Fax: 317.574.4322
http://www.dpslink.com
sales@dpslink.com

Escalate (International)
1615 S. Congress Avenue
Suite 200
Delray Beach, Fl 33445-6368
USA
561.265.2700
Fax: 561.454.4803
http://www.ecometry.com
web@ecometry.com

HarrisData (USA)
13555 Bishop's Court
Suite 300
Brookfield, WI 53005-6277
USA
262.784.9099
800.225.0585
Fax: 262.784.5994
http://www.harrisdata.com
mktg@harrisdata.com

Intentia Americas
Merged. **See Lawson.**

International Business Systems (International)
90 Blue Ravine Road
Folsom, CA 95630
USA
916.985.3900
800.886.3900
Fax: 916.985.4922
http://www.ibsus.com
info@ibsus.com

Intuitive (International)
12131 113th Ave. NE
Suite 200
Kirkland, WA 98034
USA
425.821.0740
877.549.2149
Fax: 425.814.0195
http://www.intuitivemfg.com
info@intuitivemfg.com

Lawson Software (International)
380 St Peter Street
Minneapolis, MN 55102
USA
651.767.7000
800.477.1357
Fax: 651-767-7141
http://www.lawson.com
info@lawson.com

Lilly Software Associates
Acquired. **See Infor.**

Mincron Software Systems (USA)
333 N Sam Houston Pkwy East
Suite 1100
Houston, TX 77060
USA
281.999.7010
800.299.7010
Fax: 281.999.6329
http://www.mincron.com
info@mincron.com

NxTrend
Acquired. **See Infor.**
sales@nxtrend.com

Open Business Solutions Ltd (Europe)
140 Buckingham Palace Road
London, SW1W 9SA
UK
44 (0)20 7881 2500
Fax: 44 (0)20 7881 2501
http://www.openbusinesssolutions.com
marketing@openbusinesssolutions.com

Oracle Corporation (International)
500 Oracle Parkway
Redwood City, CA 94065
USA
650.506.7000
Fax: 650.506.7200
http://www.oracle.com

PeopleSoft
Acquired. **See Oracle.**

PSIPENTA Software Systems (Europe)
Dircksenstrasse 42-44
Berlin, D-10178
Germany
49.30.2801.2000
Fax: 49.30.2801.1042
http://www.psipenta.de
info@psipenta.de

QAD (International)
100 Innovation Place
Santa Barbara, California 93108
USA
805.684.6614
888 641 4141
Fax: 805.566.4202
http://www.qad.com
info@qad.com

Sage (International)
Sage House, Wharfdale Road
Winnersh
Workingham, Berkshire RG41 5RD
UK
+44 (0)1189 270 100
Fax: +44 (0)1189 449 278
http://www.sage.com
sesinfo@sage.com

SAP (International)
http://www.sap.com
sales@sap.com

Sentai Software (Canada)
10509 81st Avenue
Suite 300
Edmonton, AB T6E 1X7
Canada
780.423.3113
888.773.6824
Fax: 780.425.8003
http://www.sentai.com
info@sentai.com

SSA Global
Acquired. **See Infor.**

Technology Group International (USA)
6800 West Central Avenue
Suite I
Toledo, OH 43604
USA
419-841-0295
800-837-0028
Fax: 419-327-9017
http://www.techgroupintl.com/
sales@techgroupintl.com

TECSYS Inc. (International)
87 Prince Street
5th Floor
Montreal, QB H3C 2M7
Canada
514.866.0001
800.922.8649
Fax: 514.866.1805
http://www.tecsys.com
info@tecsys.com

XeBusiness Ltd. (England)
3rd Floor
5, Exchange Quay
Manchester, M5 3EF
England
+44 (0)161-869 0430
Fax: +44 (0)161-869 0431
http://www.xebusiness.com
info@xebusiness.com

Appendix C

C... Shipment Manifesting Systems

Shipping Manifest System (SMS) software rates outbound shipments, whether the shipment is a parcel, LTL, or TL. The SMS also produces manifests for the carrier, shipping labels, and bill of lading. The SMS software listed here are multi-carrier.

FASCOR (USA)
11260 Chester Road
Suite 610
Cincinnati, OH 45246
USA
513.421.1777
888.8.FASCOR
Fax: 513.421.1191
http://www.fascor.com
information@fascor.com

Harvey Software (USA)
7050 Winkler Rd., #104
Fort Myers, FL 33919
USA
800.231.0296
Fax: 800.613.1041
http://www.harveysoft.com
sales@harveysoft.com

Kewill (International)
Phoenix House,
2a Amity Grove,
London
SW20 0LJ
Tel: +44 (0)20 8971 6774
Fax: +44 (0)20 8971 6767
http://www.kewill.com
info@kewill.com

Logicor (International)
1236 N Spencer, Suite 3
Mesa, AZ 85203-4350
USA
888-867-7901
Fax: 480-857-6400
http://www.logicor.com
info@logicor.com

Malvern Systems Inc. (USA)
81 Lancaster Avenue
Suite 216
Malvern, PA 19355
USA
610.295.9642
800.296.9642
Fax: 610.889-2254
http://www.malvernsys.com
sales@malvernsys.com

Neopost (International)
30955 Huntwood Avenue
Hayward, CA 94544-7094
USA
800-636-7678
http://www.neopost.com

Pitney Bowes (International)
1 Elmcroft Road
Stamford, CT 06926-0700
USA
203-356-5000
800-322-8000
http://www.pb.com

Precision Software (International)
651 W Washington Blvd
Suite 303
Chicago, IL 60661
USA
312.334.8600
Fax: 312.334.8606
http://www.precisionsoftware.com
usinfo@precisionsoftware.com

Prophesy Trasportation Software (USA)
204-C West Newberry Road
Bloomfield, CT 06002
USA
860.243.0533
800.776.6706
Fax: 860.243.2619
http://www.mile.com
sales@mile.com

Scancode Systems (North America)
Centennial Business Court
5535 Eglinton Avenue West
Suite 220
Toronto, ON M9C 5K5
Canada
416-620-5000
868.666.4240
Fax: 416-620-5606
http://www.scancode.com
info@scancode.com

ScanData Systems (USA)
4420 Tuller Road
Dublin, OH 43017
USA
614.766.6622
Fax: 614.766.0065
http://www.scandata.com
scandatasales@scandata.com

Varsity Logistics, Inc. (North America)
185 Berry Street
Suite 3500
San Francisco, CA 94107
USA
415.651.5600
800.438.7447
Fax: 415.651.5650
http://www.varsitylogistics.com
sales@varsitynet.com

V-Technologies (USA)
675 W Johnson Avenue
Cheshire, CT 06410
USA
203.439.9060
800.462.4016
Fax: 203.574.1979
http://www.vtechnologies.com
starship@vtechnologies.com

Wolin Design Group (USA)
171 S. Anita Drive
Suite 105
Orange, CA 92868
USA
714-937-0700
Fax: 714-937-0701
http://www.wdgcorp.com
information@wdgcorp.com

Appendix D

D... Load Building Software

Load Building software assists in determing the best way to load a pallet, container, or trailer. Based on volume, weight, and product information – the software graphically recommends how to build the load to the warehouse worker.

Advanced Logistics Systems (USA)
P.O. Box 4415
Roche Harbor, WA 98250
USA
360.378.5398
Fax: 360.378.6799
http://www.advanced-logistics.com
als@advanced-logistics.com

HighJump Software (International)
6455 City West Pkwy.
Eden Prairie, MN 55344-3240
USA
800.328.3271
http://www.highjump.com
hjinfo@mmm.com

MagicLogic Optimization, Inc. (International)
604-532-8662
866-535-5133
http://www.magiclogic.com
info@magiclogic.com

Pulse Logistics (Australia)
Suite 5, 2-4 Henley Beach Road
Mile End, SA 5031
Australia
618.8416.7600
Fax: 618.8416.7699
http://www.pulse.com.au
pulseinfo@pulse.com.au

TOPS Engineering Corportion (International)
275 W Campbell Road
Suite 600
Richardson, TX 75080
USA
972.739.8677
800.889.2441
Fax: 972.739.9478
http://www.topseng.com
sales@topseng.com

Transpack Software Systems (USA)
1040 N. Bethleham Pike
P.O. Box 816
Spring House, PA 19477
USA
215.540.8800
Fax: 215.540.8899
http://www.transpack.com
info@transpack.com

Warehouse Optimization LLC (International)
4650 Everal Lane
Franklin, TN 37064
USA
615.719.8000
Fax: 615.791.4749
http://www.WarehouseOptimization.com
info@WarehouseOptimization.com

Appendix E

E... Warehouse Simulation Software

Simulation software is used to model real-life movement of product.

TIP - Before building a new warehouse, simulate the new warehouse with inventory flows and equipment movement to discover problems. Fix them and do another simulation. Expect to go through four or five iterations. Eliminate the bottlenecks by simulation!

Box Works Technologies (USA)
4190 South Highland Drive
Suite 250
Sandy, UT 84124
USA
801.858.3400
877-495-2250
Fax: 801.858.3399
http://www.box-works.com
info@box-works.com

Catalyst International Inc. (International)
8989 North Deerwood Drive
Milwaukee, WI 53223-2439
USA
414.362.6800
800.236.4600
Fax: 414.362.6794
http://www.catalystwms.com
info@catalystinternational.com

FlexSim Software Products, Inc. (USA)
Canyon Park Technology Center
1577 North Technology Way
Building A, Suite 2300
Orem, Utah 84097
USA
801.224.6914
Fax: 801.224.6984
http://www.flexsim.com
sales@flexsim.com

InControl (International)
Planetenbaan 21
3606 AK Maarssen
Netherlands
+31 346 552500
Fax: +31 346 552451
http://incontrol.nl
http://www.showflow.com
siminfo@enterprisedynamics.com

Inther Logistics Engineering (Netherlands)
5809 AE Venray-Leunen
Netherlands
+31 478 502575
Fax: +31 478 636432
http://www.inther.nl
info@inther.nl

NextView Software (USA)
1401 North Batavia
Suite 104
Orange, CA 92867
USA
714.881.5105
Fax: 714.538.3812
http://www.nextviewsoftware.com
info@nextviewsoftware.com

Simul8 (International)
225 Franklin Street
26th Floor
Boston, MA 02110
USA
800-547-6024
Fax: 800-547-6389
http://www.simul8.com
sales@simul8.com

Wild Mouse Software
Not a simulator… but a
Warehouse Mapping tool - see
http://www.wildmousesoftware.com

Appendix F

F... Slotting Optimization Software

Slotting optimization is re-warehousing product to be placed in the optimal slots (bins) based on product movement, velocity, and product configuration.

Box Works Technologies (USA)
4190 South Highland Drive
Suite 250
Sandy, UT 84124
USA
801.858.3400
877-495-2250
Fax: 801.858.3399
http://www.box-works.com
info@box-works.com

Catalyst International Inc. (International)
8989 North Deerwood Drive
Milwaukee, WI 53223-2439
USA
414.362.6800
800.236.4600
Fax: 414.362.6794
http://www.catalystwms.com
info@catalystinternational.com

HighJump Software (International)
6455 City West Pkwy.
Eden Prairie, MN 55344-3240
USA
800.328.3271
http://www.highjump.com
hjinfo@mmm.com

ids engineering
1717 Alliant Avenue
Suite 12
Louisville, KY 40299
USA
502.657.2600
866.657.2600
Fax: 502.657.2604
http://www.idsengineering.com

Intek Integration Technologies, Inc.
1400 112th Ave SE
Suite 202
Bellevue, WA 98004
USA
425.455.9935
Fax: 425.455.9934
http://www.intek.com
sales@intek.com

Manhattan Associates (International)
2300 Windy Ridge Parkway
Tenth Floor
Atlanta, GA 30339
USA
770.955.7070
Fax: 770.955.0302
http://www.manh.com
info@manh.com

SISTEMA LOGISTICS
8130 Cote de Liesse
Saint-Laurent, QB H4T 1G7
Canada
514.733.3599
Fax: 514.733.3539
http://www.sistema-logistics.com
sistema@sistema-logistics.com

Appendix G

G... Labor Management Systems

Labor productivity & performance can be monitored and reported by labor management software, when it is attached or part of a WMS solution. Many labor management systems require setup of standards and vary in the standards functionality that is offered. These LMS take the engineered labor standard and calculate goal times for each task.

Workload planning is easily done by the LMS as the workload is properly estimated. Most offerings are integrated with a WMS, but **Argent Consulting Group, Kurt Salmon Associates, and Tom Zozel Associates** has a stand-alone LMS solution.

AquiTec, Inc. (International)
547 W. Jackson Blvd.
Floor 9
Chicago, IL 60661
USA
312.264.1900
Fax: 312.264.1991
http://www.aquitecintl.com
info@aquitecintl.co.uk

Argent Consulting Group (International)
→ **Standalone LMS/Incentive**
800 N. Harbor Blvd
Suite 200C
La Habra, CA 90631
USA
562.694.6808
Fax: 562.694.8418
http://www.argentconsulting.com
info@argentconsulting.com

ASC (International)
4074 E. Patterson Rd.
Dayton, OH 45430
USA
937.429.1428
Fax: 937.429.8575
http://www.ascbarcode.com
sales@ascbarcode.com

BFC Software, Inc. (USA)
245 W. Roosevelt Rd.
Bldg. 8 Suite 51
West Chicago, IL 60185
USA
630.562.0375
Fax: 630.562.0618
http://www.bfcsoftware.com
sales@bfcassociates.com

Cadre Technologies, Inc. (USA)
7900 E. Union Ave.
Suite 1007
Denver, CO 80237
USA
303.928.1124
866.25.CADRE
Fax: 303.217.7050
http://www.cadretech.com
info@CadreTech.com

Catalyst International Inc. (International)
8989 North Deerwood Drive
Milwaukee, WI 53223-2439
USA
414.362.6800
800.236.4600
Fax: 414.362.6794
http://www.catalystwms.com
info@catalystinternational.com

HighJump Software (International)
6455 City West Pkwy.
Eden Prairie, MN 55344-3240
USA
800.328.3271
http://www.highjump.com
hjinfo@mmm.com

Infor (International)
13560 Morris Road
Suite 4100
Alpharetta, GA 30004
USA
678-319-8000
866-244-5479
Fax: 678-319-8682
http://www.infor.com
sales@infor.com

Knighted Computer Systems, Inc. (USA)
145 North Highland Avenue
Ossining, NY 10562
USA
914.762.0505
Fax: 914.303.5208
http://www.knightedcs.com
sales@knightedcs.com

Kurt Salmon Associates (North America)
→ **Standalone LMS/Incentive**

1355 Peachtree Street NE
Suite 900
Atlanta, GA 30309
USA
(404) 253-0267
http://www.getgoalpost.com
results@getgoalpost.com

Manhattan Associates (International)

2300 Windy Ridge Parkway
Tenth Floor
Atlanta, GA 30339
USA
770.955.7070
Fax: 770.955.0302
http://www.manh.com
info@manh.com

Motek (USA)

113 North San Vicente Boulevard
3rd Floor
Beverly Hills, CA 90211
USA
323.653.4333
Fax: 323.653.5763
http://www.motek.com
priyainfo@motek.com

NextView Software (USA)

1401 North Batavia
Suite 104
Orange, CA 92867
USA
714.881.5105
Fax: 714.538.3812
http://www.nextviewsoftware.com
info@nextviewsoftware.com

Red Prairie (International)

20700 Swenson Drive
Suite 200
Waukesha, WI 53186
USA
262.317.2000
866.624.8448
Fax: 262.317.2001
http://www.redprairie.com
info@redprairie.com

Retailix (International)

10 Zarhin Street
P.O. Box 2282
Ra'anana 43000
Israel
+972 9 776 6677
Fax: +972 9 740 0471
http://www.retailix.com
info@retailix.com

Tom Zozel Associates (North America)
→ **Standalone LMS Offering**

3880 RFD Salem Lake Drive
Long Grove, IL 60047
USA
847- 540-6543
Fax: 847- 540-9988
http://www.tzaconsulting.com
info@tzaconsulting.com

Appendix H

H… Yard Management Systems (YMS)

Yard Management Systems can save significant time & effort in managing trailers & inventory in the yard. There are a number of YMS offered by independent software companies (C3, Cypress Inland, and Fluensee), while the rest are from the WMS software firms. 7Hills indicates that they have and will sell the YMS separately.

It is nice to have the integration already done between the WMS and YMS, but realize that the standalone YMS solutions will **normally** have a stronger feature set.

Appendix H – Yard Management System

7Hills Business Solutions (International)
651 Holiday Drive
Suite 300
Pittsburgh, PS 15220
USA
866.910.3249
Fax: 412-222-9523
http://www.7hillsbiz.com
sales_global@7hillsbiz.com

ASC (International)
4074 E. Patterson Rd.
Dayton, OH 45430
USA
937.429.1428
Fax: 937.429.8575
http://www.ascbarcode.com
sales@ascbarcode.com

Catalyst International Inc. (International)
8989 North Deerwood Drive
Milwaukee, WI 53223-2439
USA
414.362.6800
800.236.4600
Fax: 414.362.6794
http://www.catalystwms.com
info@catalystinternational.com

C3 Solutions (International)
1751 Richardson
Suite 7103
Montreal, QB H3K 1G6
Canada
514.932.3883
888.932.0171
Fax 514.932.0671
http://www.c3solutions.com
sales@c3solutions.com

Cypress Inland (USA)
12539 Sableaf Drive
Cypress, TX 77429
USA
281-469-9125
Fax 281-582-6004
http://www.yardview.com
info@yardview.com

Fluensee, Inc. (USA)
8310 South Valley Hwy
Suite 300
Englewood, CO 80112
USA
303-799-0700
Fax 303-799-0703
http://www.fluensee.com
sales@fluensee.com

HighJump Software (International)
6455 City West Pkwy.
Eden Prairie, MN 55344-3240
USA
800.328.3271
http://www.highjump.com
hjinfo@mmm.com

Infor (International)
13560 Morris Road
Suite 4100
Alpharetta, GA 30004
USA
678-319-8000
866-244-5479
Fax: 678-319-8682
http://www.infor.com
sales@infor.com

Made4Net (International)
87 South Fairview Avenue
Paramus, NJ 07652
USA
201-645-4345
http://www.made4net.com
sales@made4net.com

Manhattan Associates (International)
2300 Windy Ridge Parkway
Tenth Floor
Atlanta, GA 30339
USA
770.955.7070
Fax: 770.955.0302
http://www.manh.com
info@manh.com

Navis LLC (International)
1000 Broadway
Suite 150
Oakland, CA 94607
USA
510 267 5000
Fax: 510 267 5100
http://www.navis.com
sales@navis.com

NextView Software (USA)
1401 North Batavia
Suite 104
Orange, CA 92867
USA
714.881.5105
Fax: 714.538.3812
http://www.nextviewsoftware.com
info@nextviewsoftware.com

Red Prairie (International)
20700 Swenson Drive
Suite 200
Waukesha, WI 53186
USA
262.317.2000
866.624.8448
Fax: 262.317.2001
http://www.redprairie.com
info@redprairie.com

Retailix (International)
10 Zarhin Street
P.O. Box 2282
Ra'anana 43000
Israel
+972 9 776 6677
Fax: +972 9 740 0471
http://www.retailix.com
info@retalix.com

Softeon, Inc. (International)
8133 Leesburg Pike
Suite 570
Vienna, VA 22182-2706
USA
703-356-8727
Fax: 703-356-8959
http://www.softeon.com
mferreira@softeon.com

INDEX

3pl
   accessorial charges, 18
   allocation methods, 100
   contracts, 18, 99
   inventory ownership, 99
   modules needed, 12
   part number duplication, 106
   profit vs loss analysis, 18
   rates, 18, 99
   Software Needs, 18, 100
856. *See* ASN
ABC Code, 48
advanced ship notice. *See* ASN
affinity code, 48
alerts. *See* SCEM
allocation
   automatic, 38
API, 67, 107
Apparel, 37
Application Programming Interface, 67
appointment scheduling, 98
ASN, 26
BarTender, 28
billable costs, 137
bin locator, 48, 94
   criteria, 48
BizTalk, 67
blind shipments, 107
BOM, 18, 55
bonded warehouses, 107
Boomi, 17, 28
Carrier
   Hazard Class, 81
   shipping labels, 69, 107
carton
   weight tolerance, 44
carton selection, 41
carton table, 41
carton weight, 42
catch weight, 50
Categoric, 27
CERT, 80
Certificate of Compliance Statement. *See* CERT
check digit, 71
code dating. *See* Lot Control
coding standards, 127
computer down time, 102
Conference Room Pilot, 140
configurability
   customer preferences, 54
   GUI screens, 27
   shipment options, 54
   task workflow, 95
contract signing, 137
conveyor
   weigh-in-motion, 44
cost summary, 118

CPFR, 67
cross docking, 54
CRP, 140
cubics, 46
Cubiscan, 17
custom modification
   strategy, 22
cycle count
   opportunity, 53
Data Input/Output, 121
Data Throughput, 121
dead-heading, 53
deficiency
   definition, 22
Diagram
   Basic Host to WMS, 15
   How To Select Software, 14, 120
   Scan Open Orders and Release Wave, 39
   Supply Chain Event Management, 60
   WMS Interfacing Diagram, 16
differentiator
   definition, 22
dock doors, 98
dock scheduling, 98
document imaging, 75
dual quantity, 50
EDI, 26
EDIFACT, 26
emergency orders. *See* rush orders
employee certifications, 95
equipment, 97
   abilities, 36, 97
   limitations, 36, 97
   required on login, 36
   restrictions, 36
   table, 35
ERP vs WMS, 93
Error Table, 82
failure
   59% unsatisfied, 10
   technology ignorance, 11
fill in the gap
   1 = very low cost, 22
   10 = very expensive, 22
   explained, 22
future product, 127
Glossary, 196
Glossary of Supply Chain Terminology, 212
goals
   expectations listed, 13
   modules needed, 13
   new functionality, 9
   new host system, 11
   objectives listed, 13
   preferred database, 11
   preferred operating system(s), 11
GUI, 26

hands free, 71
hazardous, 42, 81
HazMat, 81
   UN Number, 81
headquarter visits, 127
implementation, 136
   human side, 142
   project name, 144
   project team, 142
   testing, 147
   training plan, 144
implementation costs, 137
implementation plan, 136
Initial Scope Document, 13, 141
intelligent alert. *See* SCEM
interleaving. *See* task interleaving
internationlization
   currencies, 106
   languages, 106
inventory
   allocation methods, 25, 100
   ownership, 18
   traceability, 96
   velocity code, 86
inventory control, 25
inventory management, 25
inventory valuation, 87
Item Condition. *See* Part Condition
kitting, 26
   advanced, 18
labels
   barcode printing, 28
   compliance, 28, 107
   UCC 128, 28
labor
   charts, 58
   charts by task, 58
   engineered standards, 59, 96
   report writer, 58
   reporting, 58
labor management system, 185
LMS, 185
Load Building, 179
load optimization, 88
Loftware, 28
lot control, 25
   cross over table. *See*
   expiration date, 49
   inbound, 106
   manufacturer date, 49
   outbound, 106
Lot Control, 49
   masking, 49
lot number
   recall, 96
lot tracking, 25
manufacturing, 18, 55, 98
Material Safety Data Sheet. *See* MSDS
Mercator, 17, 28
MHE. *See* Standard Interface, MHE
middleware software, 17, 28

MRO, 51
MSDS, 76
   History Table, 79
multi-tasking, 53
nesting factor, 48
non-billable costs, 137
OAG, 67
OLTP, 121
OMS, 85
Open Applications Group, 67
optimization
   load, 88
   route, 17, 88
   slotting, 17, 86, 94
order entry, 85
   credit card processing, 85
   credit hold, 85
   customer pricing, 85
outbound open order pool, 38
pallet building, 88
paper, 25
paperclip images, 75
parcel manifesting. *See* SMS
Part Condition, 51
part number size, 106
pick and pass, 101
pick on oldest, 48
pick to carrier shipping label, 43
pick to carton, 41, 101
pick to clean, 48, 86, 101
picking
   batch picking, 101
   cluster picking, 101
   voice picking, 71
   zone picking, 101
picking methods, 101
PM. *See* SMS
private labeling, 93
project creep, 141
Project Road Map, 136
putaway
   directed, 48
QA
   Hold, 51
radio frequency, 25
rate shopping, 69
recall, 96
Red Prairie, 28
reference calling. *See* vendor, references
repack, 45
repair facilities, 51
reverse truckload sequence, 101
re-warehousing, 86
RF Screen Configurability, 56
RF Task Workflow, 56
RFID Tag, 52
route
   optimization, 88
rush orders, 38
SCEM, 27, 56, 60
   build KPIs, 61

non-compliance event, 61
Number of Events, 60
  workflow, 61
security, 27
serial number tracking
  inbound, 106
  outbound, 25, 106
shipping manifest system. *See* SMS
Shipping Manifest System, 176
site visit
  questions, 125
site visit benefits, 124
site visits, 123
  bad, 123
slotting optimization, 86, 94
Slotting optimization, 183
SMS, 28, 176
  rating engine, 28
spare part facilities, 51
standard interface
  ERP, 91
  material handling equipment, 68
  MHE, 97
  multiple ERP Hosts, 102
  Shipping Manifest System, 69
  SMS, 69
standard operating systems, 107
standard reports
  strategy, 29
standards
  collaborative, 67
  xml, 67
store ready merchandise, 93
Sub-Part Number, 37
success factors
  41% satisfied, 10
  best practice - software selection, 21
  employee buy-in, 140
  employee project buyin, 20
  executive commitment, 11, 23, 138
  goals documented, 140
  IT with Operations, 11, 138
  long term focus, 10
  model processes, 140
  product master, 23
  selection process, 11
  testing, 140
  training, 20
  training employees, 11
  vendor onsite, 140
  weight on all products, 23
sucess factors
  list of success factors, 11, 138
supply chain event management. *See* SCEM
Supply Chain Event Management, 56
supply chain events. *See* SCEM, *See* SCEM
task interleaving, 53
tasks
  directed, 25
  employee certified, 95
  manual, 25

RF task queue, 94
transaction log, 96
workflow, 95
testing tools, 127
TMS, 101
transaction history, 96
Transportation Management System. *See* TMS and SMS
travel path, 37
travel time
  wasted, 53
Troubleshooting Guide, 146
UPC, 37
value added services, 93
vendor
  coding standards, 127
  customer list, 122
  customers, 121
  debt load, 128
  established, 121
  financial, 121
  financials, 128
  finanical statement, 122
  headquarter visit, 122
  organization chart, 122
  ratios, 121
  reference calling, 122
  references, 121
  site visits, 122
  testing tools, 127
vendor tips
  site visits, 124
VICS, 67
voice based tasks, 71
voice picking, 71
volumetrics, 46
Warehouse Simulation, 181
wave
  automatic, 38
wave planner, 38
wave release
  manual, 38
  scheduled, 39
web-based, 26
web-enabled, 26
weigh-in-motion, 44
WMS
  base line expectations, 25
  common deficiencies, 72
  common differences, 30
  common expectations, 25
  definition - basic, 15, 18
  definition - identify it, 19
  definition - realistic, 16
  Solutions, 152
  Strengths, 93
WMS RFP
  company background, 108
  cost analysis, 118
  cover letter, 108
  filters out the weak, 13

sample, 110
scoring results, 116
warehouse background, 108
WMS RFP Advanced Question set, 8
WMS RFP Professional Service, 8
WMS vs ERP, 93
work centers, 98

Work Orders, 55
workflow, 95
XML, 67
yard management software, 17, 98
Yard Management System, 188
YMS, 188, *See* yard management software

Glossary

Glossary

Word	Definition of Word
ABC	ABC classification. A user defined strategy for grouping parts within the warehouse (or Org). The grouping strategy is usually by product velocity, where fast movers are A items.
ABM	Activity Based Management
Advanced Ship Notice	Abbreviated ASN. Details on products being shipped with carton id numbers. May be transmitted by EDI, XML, and/or data on a barcode/RFID tag.
Affinity	Affinity code. A user defined code for products that look alike. E.G., 10" and 12" adjustable chrome wrenches.
AGV	Automated Guided Vehicle.
AG/VS	Automated Guided Vehicle System.
Aisle	A corridor or passageway within a warehouse, which allows access to, stored goods. [ka]
Allocated Stock	Inventory that has been reserved, but not yet picked from stock, and thus is not available for other purposes.
Allocation	Allocating inventory to a specific order. Order may be an outbound order (sales order, transfer order, work order, etc.). See Hard Allocation and Soft Allocation.
Alphanumeric	A character set that contains letters, numbers, and other groups of symbols. [ka]
Anniversary Billing	A method of public warehouse billing for storage in which the customer is billed a one-month storage charge for all products as they are received. The same unit, if still in storage, is billed an additional monthly charge on each monthly anniversary date thereafter. This method does not involve any pro-rating of time in storage and so requires that anniversary dates for each item in storage be separately identified. See split-month billing. [ka]
Annual Inventory	See Physical Inventory [ka]
API	Application Programming Interface. A series of programs used to bring data in and out of the database. These programs are developed and maintained by the software application vendor to support interfacing their application to external applications.
ASN	See Advanced Ship Notices.
ASP	Application Service Provider. Provides application software on their computer systems.
ASRS	See Automatic Storage & Retrieval System.
Assembly Area	A warehouse location where materials, components, or finished products are collected and combined. [ka]
ATO	Assemble To Order. A technique to postpone inventory that can be utilized as components and/or finished goods. Purpose is to reduce the inventory required on-hand but still keep service rate high, by assembling a finished goods product at the last moment.
Automated Storage & Retrieval System	Material Handling Equipment - specifically an automated, mechanized system for moving merchandise into storage locations and retrieving it from storage locations.
Available Stock	Inventory that is available to service immediate demand.
Banding	Strapping to hold shipment together. Normally banding is plastic or metal strapping.
Batch Pick, Batch Picking	A method of picking a single SKU to be distributed across multiple orders.

Glossary

Word	Definition of Word
Bay	A designated area within a section of a storage area outlined by markings on columns, posts, or floor. [ka]
Bay Storage	The use of a large designated area for storing merchandise. [ka]
BBS	Business Balanced Scorecard
Beginning Inventory	The inventory count at the beginning of the current period. See Ending Inventory and Physical Inventory. [ka]
Bin	Storage space for inventory at rest or being staged. A bin may be a physical bin or a virtual bin.
BizTalk	A XML standard for business commerce promoted & supported by Microsoft. Other XML standards include OAGIS by OAG and Rosetta Net.
Block Pattern	A method of storing merchandise on a pallet in a pattern to allow a stable pallet load. [ka]
Bonded Warehouse	1. A warehouse approved by the Treasury Department and under bond/guarantee for observance of revenue laws. 2. Used for storing goods until duty is paid or goods are released in some other proper manner. [cnf]
Bottleneck	Congestion or significant slow down at an area due to an inefficient resource or process.
Brick Pattern	A method of storing merchandise on a pallet in a pattern to accommodate items of unequal width or length. See Pinwheel Pattern. [ka]
BTO	Built to Order
Buffer Stock	Safety Stock. The stock held to protect against the differences between forecast and actual consumption, and between expected and actual delivery times of procurement orders, to protect against stock outs during the replenishment cycle. In calculating safety stock, account is taken of such factors as service level, expected fluctuations of demand and likely variations in lead time
Bulk Storage	1) Storage of merchandise and materials in large quantities, usually in original or shipping containers. 2) Storage of unpackaged commodities. [ka]
Carousel	Material Handling Equipment - specifically an automated delivery system to move product from storage to picker, without any travel on picker. Two types of carousels are on the market, horizontal carousels and vertical carousels. Carousels are most productive when pick lists are downloaded from the WMS into the carousel system and optimized for multiple orders being picked at one time.
Carton	A protective outer case that contains products. E.G., carton, tote, pallet.
CFR	Case Flow Rack.
Check Digit	In bar codes or data processing, a character added to ensure accuracy. [ka]
Client Client-Server	Any computer connected on a network that requests services from another computer on the network. Normally the client is a PC and is retrieving data from the server (another computer) that has the primary database(s) on it.
Co-Managed Inventory	A support arrangement similar to Vendor Managed Inventory but where replacement orders for the vendor-owned stock are agreed by the user prior to delivery replenishment cycle. In calculating safety stock, account is taken of such factors as service level, expected fluctuations of demand and likely variations in lead-time.

Word	Definition of Word
Commodity	One of the major outputs of the manufacturing effort, also known as product codes. Within a warehouse, an item uniquely identified to a particular customer.
Consumable Stock	A classification of stock used to describe items that are totally consumed in use - e.g. gift wrap, packing materials, etc.
Container	Anything in which articles are packed. A standardized box used to transport merchandise particularly in international commerce. Marine containers are typically 8'X8' with length of 10', 30', or 40'. These containers may be transloaded from rail cars or ships onto a truck frame and delivered to their final destination. [ka]
Contract Warehouse	See also Third Party Warehouse and Public Warehouse.
Cooler	A refrigerated space that holds material above freezing but usually below 50°. [ka]
Cross-Docking	A method of fulfilling orders that the movement of goods directly from receiving dock to shipping dock, bypassing the putaway of inventory to stock.
Cross-training	Providing training or experience in several different warehousing tasks and functional specialties in order to provide backup workers. [ka]
CSV	Comma Separated Values. A data file where fields are separated ("delimited") by commas.
CTO	Configure To Order. See also ETO and MTS.
CTP	Capable To Promise. See ATP / Available To Promise.
Cube Loading	The process of loading merchandise onto pallets or other unit-loading techniques to allow several unit loads to be stacked for transportation. [ka]
Cube Utilization	The percentage of space occupied compared to the space available. [ka]
Cubiscan	A device that cubes and weighs products that are placed unto it. Cubiscan is a registered Trademark ™ of Quantronix company. Website is http://www.cubiscan.com or see the company's main website at http://www.quantronix.com.
Custom Software	Software specially developed for or by the user. [ka]
Customer Pickup	1) Merchandise picked up by the customer at the warehouse. 2) The act of picking up merchandise at the dock. AKA Will-Call or Walk-In. [ka]
Cycle Counting	Cycle counting is the physical counting of stock on a perpetual basis, rather than counting stock periodically. A cycle is the time required to count all items in the inventory at least once. The frequency of cycle counting can be varied to focus management attention on the more valuable or important items or to match work processes. Some of the systems used are: ABC system with the highest count frequency for items with the highest annual usage value, Reorder system when stocks are counted at the time of order, Receiver system with counting when goods are received, Receiver system with counting when goods are received reached to confirm that no stock is held, Transaction system where stocks are counted after a specified number of transactions.
Date Code	A label showing the date of production. In the food industry, it becomes an integral part of the lot number. [ka]
Database	Abbreviated DB. Data stored in a format that allows for flexible sortation and report generation. Common databases include customer lists, routes, carrier selection maps, rate files, and inventory files. [ka]
DB	Data Base. E.G., Oracle, Sybase, Informix, SQL Server, Progress.
DC	See Distribution Center.
Dead Stock	A product that does not move from its storage location for a long time. [ka]

Word	Definition of Word
Deep-Lane Storage	Storage of merchandise greater than one unit deep on one or both sides of an aisle. See Double-Deep Lane Storage and Single Deep. [ka]
Dekitting, Dekit	When a work order has been canceled, the process to return the components back to inventory is called dekitting.
DIR	See Drive In Rack.
Distribution Center	A modern warehouse that processes inventory based upon the direction of the corporate systems. Abbreviated DC
Dock Receipt	A receipt issued for a shipment at a pier or dock. [ka]
Double-Deep Lane Storage	Rack storage of merchandise two loads deep on one or both sides of an aisle. See Deep-Lane Storage and Single Deep. [ka]
Drive-In Rack	Storage rack which provides side rails to allow high stacking in deep rows. Unlike drive-through rack, it provides access only from the aisle. Abbreviated DIR. [ka]
Drive-Through Rack	Storage rack that provides side rails to allow high stacking of products in deep rows and access to either end of the row. [ka]
DSD	Direct Store Delivery. See also FRM.
DTS	Dock To Stock.
Duty	A taxed assessed by the government for importing and exporting goods. [ka]
Duty Drawback	Refund of customs duties paid on material imported and later exported. Also known as Drawback. [cnf].
Earmarked Material	On-hand material that is reserved an physically identified rather than simply allocated in inventory controls. [ka]
ECR	Efficient Customer Response.
EDI	Electronic Data Interchange that specifies standard data format specifications. Computer-to-computer communication between two or more companies that such companies can use to generate bills of lading, purchasing orders, and invoices. It also enables firms to access the information systems of suppliers, customers, and carriers, and to determine the up-to-the-minute status of inventory, orders, and shipments. See also EDIFACT.
EDIFACT	EDI for Administration, Commerce and Transport. EDIFACT is an EDI standard for international usage and was developed by the United Nations. See also EDI.
EHCR	Efficient Healthcare Consumer Response. To realize supply chain cost savings through the adoption of EDI, bar-coding, and other strategies such as Activity Based Costing. See also ECR.
EI	See Ending Inventory
Emergency Order	As differentiated by an order type, an emergency order is processed in an expedited fashion.
Ending Inventory	Abbreviated EI. A statement of on-hand inventory levels at the end of a period. See Beginning Inventory and Physical Inventory. [ka]
ER	Expected Receipt [em]
ERP	Enterprise Resource Planning. Software to manage accounting – purchasing – customer service – distribution – manufacturing – and more.
ETO	Engineer-To-Order. A product that is designed only when an order requires it. These are usually highly engineered goods and non-commodity items. See also CTO and MTS.
Ex-Dec, X-Dec	Export Declaration Documents.
Expiration Date	Date after which merchandise can no longer be shipped. In Expiration date controlled inventory, inventory must be discarded after this date.

Glossary

Word	Definition of Word
Facility	The physical plant and storage equipment. Permanent storage bins in a warehouse may be considered part of the facility, whereas material handling equipment may not. [ka]
Family Grouping	A method of sorting products, with similar characteristics, into families to be stored in the same area. [ka]
FCS	First Customer Ship
FEFO	Inventory allocation method, first-expired, first-out.
F/G	See Finished Goods Inventory.
FGI	See Finished Goods Inventory
FIFO	Inventory allocation method, first-in, first-out. This method allocates first items stored are the first items utilized.
FILO	Inventory allocation method, first-in, last-out.
Finished Goods Inventory	Products that are completely finished and ready for shipment to customers. Abbreviated F/G or FGI.
Finished Product Inventory	Products available for shipment to customers. AKA Finished Goods. [ka]
First In, First Out	Inventory allocation method, first-in, first-out. This method allocates first items stored are the first items utilized. Abbreviation: FIFO
FISH	First In Still Here. A funny, but real expression of very slow movers that needs to be dealt with.
Flow Rack	In one side and out the other. Product stored in this way is necessarily FIFO within the rack itself.
Flow Through	See Cross Dock.
Flow Through Rack	In one side and out the other. Product stored in this way is necessarily FIFO within the rack itself.
Forklift	A vehicle with horizontal lift that moves product & freight within a warehouse or on the dock. AKA Fork-Lift, Hi-Lo or Lift-Truck.
Forward Location	See Pick Slot.
FPO	Firm Planned Orders
Freezer	Temperature-controlled (below 32°) storage space for perishable items. Also Cooler. [ka]
FRM	Floor Ready Merchandise. Prepared products are received as "floor ready" at the retail store. Before shipping these goods, the warehouse or supplier will add prices, price stickers, tags, security devices, special packaging, etc. so that goods may rapidly be cross docked through RDCs or received directly at the retail stores.
FSL	Forward Stock Location. Primary location for picking of a product. AKA as a "pick face".
Gaylord	Large corrugated carton that is sized to fit a pallet's length and width. Typically used for loose parts or other items stored in bulk. Most commonly found in manufacturing.
Godown	A waterfront storehouse in the Orient. [ka]
GOH	Goods on hanger. Some wearing apparel is shipped on hangers without packaging. [ka]
Gross Weight	Weight of inventory item with packing and container. See also Gross Weight.
GUI	Graphical User Interface.
Handling	The movement of materials or merchandise within a warehouse. [ka]
Handling Charge	A charge for ordinary warehouse handling operations. [ka]
Handling Costs	The costs involved in warehouse handling. [ka]

Word	Definition of Word
Hand Truck	A device used for manually transporting goods. A metal plate is slid under the load, then truck and load are tilted toward the operator and moved. There are two varieties: The western type has its wheels located within the side rails, while the eastern type places the wheels located outside the side rails. [ka]
Hard Allocation	Detailed allocation of inventory that specifies the exact bin, license plate, lot, and/or serial numbers. Hard allocations are done by the warehouse management system at wave release or pick release. Soft allocation has been done previously, which committed a specified quantity only.
Hardware	A computer term that denotes the machinery that makes up a computer system. It includes video screens, memory units, printers, etc. [ka]
HazMat	Hazardous Material. Product is classified hazardous by a government agency or a carrier. Special handling is required on some hazardous items, which may include segregation, separation wall, temperature control, and/or limitations on how the product may be shipped. See also MSDS and Hazard Class.
High	Number of Layers per Pallet
Hi-Lo	Another name for a forklift, or a vehicle with horizontal lift. A vehicle to move freight within a warehouse or on the dock. AKA Fork-Lift, Towmotor, or Lift-Truck. See Fork-Lift.
HMI	Human-Machine Interface
Honeycomb Factor	A term that describes the amount of storage space lost to partially filled rows or to pallet positions not fully filled. [ka]
Honeycombing	A waste of space that results from partial depletion of a lot and the inability to use the remaining space in this area. [ka]
Horizontal Carousel	See Carousel.
Housekeeping	Maintaining an orderly environment for preventing errors and contamination in the warehousing process. Good housekeeping includes keeping aisles clear, trash disposal, sweeping, orderly stacking, and removal of damaged goods. [ka]
HU	Handling Unit.
Inner Packaging	Materials such as paper, foam, or wood shavings used to cushion impacts and prevent the movement of goods within a container. [ka]
Interleave	Multi-tasking. The warehouse worker will be directed to do multiple types of tasks in one trip.
Internal Costs	Those costs generated within the facility and directly under the control of warehouse management these include storage, handling, clerical services, and administration. [ka]
Internationalization	Internationalization is the process of building software so it is not based on the assumptions of one language or country. The internationalized software product can display and process locale-dependent information such as date, time, address, and number formats properly to he user.
KDF Cartons	Knocked down (flat) carton – unassembled packages. [ka]
Kit	A number of separate Stock Keeping Units that are supplied or used as one item under its own Item Number.
Kitting	Light assembly of component parts, often performed in a warehouse. [ka]
Knock-Down	Abbreviated KD. When articles are taken apart for the purpose of reducing the cubic space of the shipment, the disassembly process is referred to as a knock-down shipment. [ka]
Last In, First Out	Inventory allocation method called Last In, First Out. Abbreviation: LIFO

Glossary

Word	Definition of Word
Layer	A group of Commodities residing in one horizontal dimension on a Pallet. Each Pallet consists of one or more Layers. During picking, Commodities are generally depleted from one Layer completely, before the next layer is taken.
Layout	The design of the storage areas and aisles of a warehouse. [ka]
LES	Logistics Execution Systems. Involves transportation management (TMS) and warehouse management (WMS) software. AKA Supply Chain Execution (SCE) or Logistics Resource Management (LRM).
Let Down	Replenishment. Moving inventory from reserve storage to the active picking slots below. Normally the reserve storage is above the forward picking slot, therefore this replenishment is called a "let down".
LF	Logistics Fulfillment [em]
License Plate Number	A unique number that is applied to a container to rapidly identify the contents (products) within. The LPN is normally printed as a barcode on a label or the unique id of the RFID tag.
LIFO	Inventory allocation method called Last In, First Out.
Lift Truck	Another name for a forklift, or a vehicle with horizontal lift. A vehicle to move freight within a warehouse or on the dock. AKA Fork-Lift, Towmotor, or Hi-Lo. See Fork-Lift.
Lineside Warehouse	A supplier warehouse positioned as close as possible to the production location to facilitate Just In Time manufacture.
Live Rack	A storage rack constructed to allow items to move unaided toward the picking point. The rack is slanted so that the picking point is lower than the rear loading point, allowing gravity to draw items to the front. A roller conveyor or other low-friction surface supports the merchandise. [ka]
Location	The place in a warehouse where a particular product can be found. [ka]
Location Audit	A systematic verification of the location records of an item or group of items by checking the actual locations in a warehouse or storage area. [ka]
Logistics	Logistics plans, implements, and controls the efficient, effective forward and reverse flow and storage of goods, services, and related information between the point of origin and the point of consumption in order to meet customers' requirements. [cnf]
Loose	The number of remaining Commodities left on a particular Layer. Ex. Tie, High Loose: 7, 3, 1 means 7 boxes per layer, 3 layers high, and 1 loose box on top of the 3rd layer.
Lot	Product that has a life span with an expiration date, Manufacturing date, and/or code date. A lot is a group of an item that has been made using the same ingredients (like a batch), a production run, or some other grouping to be used for identification purposes, unique from other same items produced in a different batch or run. For instance fabric color in the same SKU may not match, lot to lot.
Lot Number	Identifying numbers used to keep a separate accounting for a specific lot of merchandise. [ka]
Lot Number Traceability	The ability to track an item or group of items by a unique set of numbers based by a vendor or production run. [ka]
Lottable	Specific attributes of a Commodity that, taken together, differentiates like Commodities, and allow like Commodity to be tracked as separate Lots throughout the facility. Owners of the Commodity drive what is considered a Lottable. Examples of Characteristics: color, pack size, original production facility, etc.
LPN	License Plate Number. A unique number assigned to a container. A container is any type of container that can hold inventory – such as a pallet, carton, and tote. WMS use & assign LPNs to track inventory.

Word	Definition of Word
LRM	Logistics Resource Management. Software that includes modules with transportation management, warehouse/inventory management, and contracting/rate negotiations. AKA as Logistics Execution System (LES) and Supply Chain Execution (SCE).
Marking Machine	A machine that imprints or embosses a mark on a label, ticket, tape, package, or tag. [ka]
Master Carton	A single large carton that is used as a uniform shipping carton for smaller packages. It is used primarily for protective purposes, but also simplifies materials handling by reducing the number of pieces handles. See Master Pack. [ka]
Master Pack	
Material Handling	The movement of materials going to, through, and from warehousing, storage, service facility, and shipping areas. Materials can be finished goods, semi-finished goods, components, scrap, WIP, or raw stock for Manufacturing.
MHE	Material Handling Equipment.
MHE	Mechanical Handling Equipment.
Master Pack	An established quantity for a manufacturer's product. The master pack is a carton containing a set number of multiple case quantities.
Mat	A panel of wood, rubber, or other material that is placed on top of unit loads to allow tight strapping of the load without product damage. [ka]
Materials Management	The functions that define the complete cycle of material flow, from the purchase to the distribution of the finished product. This includes functions of planning production materials, control of work in process, warehousing, shipping, value added services at the warehouse, and distribution.
Material Safety Data Sheet	A Material Safety Data Sheet (MSDS) is prepared by a chemical manufacturer, and summarizes available information on the health, safety, fire, and environmental hazards of a chemical product. It also gives advice on the safe use, storage, transportation, and disposal of that product. Other useful information such as physical properties, government regulations affecting the product, and emergency telephone numbers are provided in the MSDS as well. There is a detailed description of how to read an MSDS and a useful glossary of MSDS terms in Hach's Website at http://www.hach.com. [hc]
Materials Warehouse	A warehouse used exclusively for the storage of raw materials. [ka]
MCS	Material Control Software. AKA Material Handling Control Software, Warehouse Control Systems, or Conveyor Control Software. This is the software that interfaces the machinery to the WMS or MES.
Middleware	Middleware software helps separate application software to talk to each other. I.E., Mercator, Boomi, IBM's MQ series.
Min-Max System	An order-point replenishment system. The minimum point is the order point and the maximum is the "order-up-to" level. The order quantity is variable to take advantage of usage patterns and lot-sized ordering economies. [ka]
MLP	Master License Plate
Modifications Mods	Computer people frequently use the term "mods" to indicate a minor or major modification is needed. It can used to discuss a specific modification being designed to do specific business functionality, or it can be used to just indicate that the program would need to be changed in order to perform this.

Glossary

Word	Definition of Word
Moveable Units	The container (the "moveable unit") is identified with a unique id and has a barcode or RFID label on it. The moveable unit / container can be a tote, carton, pallet, Gaylord container, or an outbound container – that holds inventory for shipment or for transit just within facilities. Abbreviated MU. See also License Plate Number (LPN).
MRO	Maintenance, Repair, and Operations.
MSDS	See Material Safety Data Sheet.
MTO	Make To Order. A product that is manufactured only when an order is confirmed for it. These are usually low volume or highly engineered goods. See also CTO, ETO, and MTS.
MTS	Make To Stock. Products are manufactured and placed into warehouse as finished goods. The quantity built is based upon safety stock and re-order point calculations. See also CTO, ETO, and MTO.
MU	See Moveable Units.
Mullen Test	A device to test, or the process of testing packaging material to establish its strength. [ka]
Multi-Tine Fork	Attachment to a forklift truck that allows the movement of two pallets side-by-side, rather than one pallet at a time. [ka]
Negotiable Warehouse Receipt	A legal certification that listed goods are held in public warehouse. The certificate can be purchased or sold, thus transferring title to the goods. See Non-negotiable Warehouse Receipt. [ka]
Nested	The process of packing articles so that one rests partially or entirely within another, thereby reducing the total cubic displacement. [ka]
Nested Solid	Articles nested so that the bottom of one rests on the bottom of the lower one. [ka]
Nesting Factor	Nesting on products that "fit" within each other, therefore the first item is full cube, the 2nd, 3rd just use the "factor" cube. E.G., Buckets would have a .20 (20%) nesting factor.
Net Storage Area	The amount of warehouse space actually used for storage of merchandise. It usually expressed in square feet or meters and excludes aisles, dock areas, staging areas, and offices. [ka]
Net Weight	Weight of inventory item without packing and container. See also Gross Weight.
NIS	Not In Stock.
Non-Negotiable Warehouse Receipt	A legal certification that the goods listed on it are now in the custody of the public warehouse. The certificate cannot be bought or sold. [ka]
Non-Read	Failure of scanner to read a barcode or RFID tag.
NSN	National Stock Number. See also SKU.
OAG	Open Applications Group. Building standard OAGIS via XML for business applications. Focus is on standard data formats and interfacing for inter-operability between external vendor applications. Website is http://www.openapplications.org
Obsolete Stock	Stock held within an organization where there is no longer any reason for holding the stock.
On-Hand Balance	The recorded level of inventory in a distribution center. [ka]
Operating System	Software that interfaces between the user and the hardware, and between applications and the hardware. The operating system allocates the resources of the computer, such as memory and processing time, to applications. Abbreviated OS. [ka]
Order Lead Time, Order Cycle Time	The total internal processing time necessary to transform a replenishment quantity into an order and for the transmission of that order to the recipient.

Glossary

Word	Definition of Word
Order Picker	1) Lift truck which allows the warehouse worker to ride with the pallet and to pick from various levels. 2) A warehouse worker whose prime job is selection of orders. [ka]
Order Picking	Collecting items from a storage location or picking location to satisfy an order.
OSD	See Over, Short, and Damaged.
Over, Short, and Damaged	A report issued at the warehouse when goods are damaged. Used to file a claim with the carrier. [cnf]
Overage	Freight in excess over quantity believed to have been shipped, or more than quantity shown on shipping document. [cnf]
Overhead Cost	Those costs that are not directly related to warehousing and storage, which are still part of the total costs of a facility. These include janitorial services, heat, light, power, maintenance, depreciation, taxes, and insurance. [ka]
Overshipment	A shipment containing more than originally ordered. [ka]
Pack Size	A collection of Units per Measure that describe how a Commodity is packaged. For example, Commodity ABC comes packaged in 24 each per Case, and 50 Cases per Pallet.
Packing and Marking	The process of packaging goods for safe shipment and handling, and appropriately labeling the contents. [ka]
Packing List	List showing inventory that was packed in shipment. Prepared by warehouse personnel. Copy is sent to customer / consignee to help verify shipment received. Packing list detail can be also transmitted to customer / consignee via EDI Advance Ship Notice, if containers are uniquely coded.
Palletization	System for shipping goods on pallets. Permits shipment of multiple units as one large unit. [cnf]
Palletize	To place material on a pallet in a prescribed area. [ka]
Palletizer	A type of materials-handling device suing conveyor or robotics to position cubes or bags on a pallet. [ka]
PBR	See Push Back Rack.
PDM	Product Data Management. Software module that is focused on proper setup, maintenance, and changes to the life of the product.
PDT	Portable data terminals. A rugged hand-held computer with the computing power of a stationary computer. Normally equipped with RF (radio frequency) and an antenna.
Perpetual Inventory System	An inventory control system where a running record is kept of the amount of stock held for each item. Whenever an order is filled, the withdrawal is logged and the result compared with the re-order point for any necessary re-order action.
PF&D	Personal fatigue, and delay times. This is expressed as a percentage of time allowed for completing a task. [ka]
PFR	Pallet Flow Rack.
Physical Inventory	A physical count of every item located within the warehouse. AKA Annual Inventory. Cycle counts can replace physical counts. [ka]
PI	Physical Inventory
Pick-and-Pass	Picking technique used with pick zones, flow racks & conveyors. One picker will pull products into tote (or other container). Tote will be passed to next zone for picker to pull and put products into same tote. This pick-and-pass continues until all zones are completed and then tote is taken away on a take-away conveyor.
Picker	Term used for the person assigned the job of locating and removing stock from storage locations. See Order Picker. [ka]

Word	Definition of Word
Pick List	An output from a warehouse management system designating those items, by item number, description and quantity, to be picked from stock to satisfy customer demand.
Pick Time	The amount of time it takes a worker to select and document an item. [ka]
Pick-to-Carton	Picking technique where picker is directed to put pulled product directly into a licensed plated container (a "carton" normally). Picker may be picking for multiple orders during one trip, by using multiple cartons. When finished the picker puts the cartons on a take away conveyor for the shipping station.
Pick-to-Light	Picking technique used where pickers are directed by lights and/or digital displays at each bin. Very effective technique for high volume piece picking. Requires the WMS to be interfaced to Pick-To-Light MHE interface.
Pick Slot	The location where inventory is stored that is dedicated or picking. The pick slot is commonly replenished via a minimum trigger point to initiate replenishment. The terms forward location, primary location, and picking face are synonyms for this term.
Picking Face	See Pick Slot.
Pinwheel Pattern	A method of storing merchandise on a pallet in a pattern to arrange items of unequal width or length. See Brick Pattern and Row Pattern. [ka]
Post Audit	A study conducted of a new warehouse, fleet, or equipment to ascertain how well it is performing in relation to the proposal and financial analyses used to originally justify it. [ka]
Postponement of Final Assembly	The delay of final assembly until a firm customer order is received. Often, common parts and components can be produced, shipped, and inventoried at lower cost and risk than that associated with completed products. [ka]
Pressure Label	A price ticket or other information ticket that can be affixed to merchandise by pressing it on. [ka]
Primary Location	See Pick Slot.
Private Warehouse	A warehouse operated by the owner of the goods stored there. A private warehouse can be an owned or leased facility. [ka]
Pro Number	A unique number assigned to a freight shipment by the carrier. This Pro Number is utilized on the freight bill and bill of ladings.
PTL	Pick To Light technology uses displays at each location that light up to show where to pick. Picker goes to this location, selects quantity displayed and pushes a button to confirm the pick. Used in high volume items. Cost is estimated to be $200 per light position in 2001.
Public Warehouse	See also Contract Warehouse and Third Party Warehouse.
Push-Back Rack	Rack system that allows palletized product to be stored by being pushed up an inclined ramp. This allows for deep pallet storage.
Putaway	The movement of material from the point of receipt to a storage area. [ka]
QA	See Quality Assurance/Quality Control.
QC	See Quality Assurance/Quality Control.
QR	Quality Review. Check procedure on randomly selected components and/or finished goods product. See also QA, QC.
QS	Quality Standard. See Automotive Industry Action Group requirements. [em]
Quality Assurance, Quality Control	Process of inspecting merchandises being received or shipped to ensure that the merchandise is of adequate quality and that the case content specification is accurate.

Glossary

Word	Definition of Word
Quarantine	An inventory status indicating that this product is not available for inventory allocation but is in process of inspection for QA or another reason. See also QA and QC.
Quarantine	The isolation of goods or materials until they can be checked for quality or conformance with all required standards. [ka]
Rack	A structured storage system (single-level or multi-level) that is used to support high stacking of single items or palletized loads. [ka]
Rack-Supported Building	A warehouse in which the storage rack functions as the structural support for the roof. [ka]
Radio Frequency	A system of mobile devices used to issue tasks, edit entered information and confirm the completion of tasks using either laser scanners or terminal entry. RF allows operations personnel to function in a "point-of-work" mode.
Random Storage	One or more areas of the warehouse that are designed for random storage. Bins in a random storage area are not pre-assigned, but the WMS is allowed to fully evaluate what inventory to locate in these random storage bins.
RDC	Retail Distribution Center. A DC replenishing products directly to the stores. See Distribution Center.
Reach Truck	A forklift with the extended ability to reach forward significantly. Very useful for getting or retrieving the deeper pallet in a double deep pallet bin.
Real Time	Real time means that the new or updated information is instantaneously saved in the database.
Receiving Report	A record of the condition in which merchandise arrived. [ka]
Receiving Tally	The warehouse receiver's independent listing of goods unloaded from an inbound vehicle, sometimes prepared on a blind basis to ensure accuracy. [ka]
Refrigerated Warehouse	A warehouse that provides refrigeration and temperature control for perishable products. [ka]
Release	The authorization to ship material. [ka]
Renewal Storage	The rebilling fee (usually monthly) for products stored in a public warehouse. [ka]
Repack	Task that takes product in one configuration and is repackaged into another. 8 packs into 12 packs.
Replenishment	The task initiated to fill a picking location. Typically a replenishment task can be specific to an item's replenishment quantity and unit of measure.
Reverse Logistics	The requirement to plan the flow of surplus or unwanted material or equipment back through the supply chain after meeting customer demand.
Rewarehousing	The process of calculating the best slotting positions for inventory and moving inventory to those optimized bins. This is done to optimize space utilization and decrease deadheading travel time.
RF	See Radio Frequency.
RFDC	Radio Frequency Data Collection [em]
RFI	Request For Information. A request for a vendor to provide information. Not as intensive as a RFP, but may provide detailed functional answers to what a solution can provide.
RFID	Radio Frequency Identification. Usually refers to RFID tags and readers.
RFP	Request For Proposal. A request for a vendor to do a full proposal including costs, references, project plans (implementation), and detailed functional answers from a vendor to a prospective client. See RFI.
RMA	Return Merchandise Authorization.

Glossary

Word	Definition of Word
ROI	Return On Investment. Calculations that result in a measurement of what a company will gain from an investment.
RosettaNet	RosettaNet. Building standard interface specifications for commerce based on XML. Similar to OAG & OAGIS for inter-operability between vendor applications. Website is http://www.rosettanet.org
RPC	Reusable Plastic Container.
RTLS	Real Time Locating System. Usually in reference to a WMS or YMS ability to move-track-locate inventory.
SCC, SCC-14	Shipping Container Code consisting of 14 digits. This UCC SCC-14 code is frequently put on a pallet or container label. The first two digits are the UCC application identifier. The next digit is the packaging level indicator. The next seven digits is the manufacturer identification number. The next five digits represent the manufacturer assigned product number. The last digit is a modulus 10 check digit. See also UCC 128.
SCE	Supply Chain Execution. Refers to the "execution" side of fulfilling the customer order and supporting functions to do so. Commonly includes warehouse, transportation, data interchange.
SCEM	Supply Chain Event Management software module. Provides "event" based notifications via e-mail, screen pop-ups, fax, pager, and wireless message. Events are also known as alerts. May also include event response logic.
SCES	Supply Chain Execution Systems. Software and processes to enable then execution side of fulfilling customer orders and supporting functions. Includes warehouse operations, transportation, with heavy emphasis on inventory & order entry.
SCU	Speech Control Unit. The Speech Control Unit is a computer that connects to the WMS for exchange of information. The SCU then gives individual instructions to the SDT via a wireless network. See also SDT.
SDT	Speech Data Terminal. In voice-activated devices, mobile workers use small, unobtrusive wearable computers called Speech Data Terminals with an attached headset. This would be used in a pick-to-voice environment. See SCU.
Seasonal Inventory	Inventory held to meet seasonal demand. [ka]
Semi-Finished Inventory	Materials that are no longer in raw-material form, but which have not completed the production cycle to become finished goods. [ka]
Sequencing	The process of organizing items in a load so they will be in the order needed for production. [ka]
Serial Number	A unique identification number assigned to a single item. [ka]
Serpentine	A picking path that is in a serpentine pattern of bins to inventory from. Some call this a Z picking path.
Shelf Life	The length of time a product can be kept for sale or use before quality considerations make it necessary or desirable to remove it. [ka]
Shelter	A cover that protects the space between the door of a rail car or truck and a warehouse from inclement weather. [ka]
Ship-Age Limit	The final date a perishable product can be shipped to a customer. [ka]
Shipment	1. Lot of freight tendered to carrier by one consignee at one place at one time for delivery to one consignee at one place on one bill of lading. 2. Goods/merchandise in one or more containers, pieces, or parcels for transportation from one shipper to single destination. [cnf]
ShipTo	The name and address of where the shipment will be delivered. Also known as the consignee.

Glossary

Word	Definition of Word
Shop Floor Control	The process of monitoring and controlling production or warehousing activities to ensure that procedures are followed. [ka]
Shrinkage	Reduction in bulk measurement of inventory. [ka]
Shrink Wrap	A plastic wrap used by shippers to secure cartons on a pallet. [cnf]
Shroud	A protective sheet that covers the top and sides of a load, but which permits air to circulate from the bottom. [ka]
Single Deep	A bin. See also Double Deep.
Site Selection Model	A program that helps to determine the best location for a distribution center, or other facility. [ka]
SKU	Stock Keeping Unit. A product or a set of products referenced by the manufacturer by a unique part number.
Slot	A position within a storage area reserved for a particular SKU. See also Bin. [ka]
Soft Allocation	Initial allocation of inventory to a specific line item of an order. A "soft" allocation just commits this inventory to the order, but does NOT specifically identify the bin, lot, serial number, or license plate. Soft allocation is done by the ERP system normally. See Hard Allocation.
Sortation	The process of separating packages according to their destination. [ka]
Split-Month Billing	A method of public warehouse billing for storage in which the customer is billed for all inventory in the warehouse at the beginning of the month, as well as for each unit received during that month. Merchandise received during the first half of the month is billed at a full-month storage rate, while merchandise received after the 15th day of the month is billed at a half-month storage rate. See Anniversary Billing. [ka]
Split Shipment	A partial shipment that occurs when a warehouse is unable to fill an entire order. The remainder of the order is backordered. [ka]
Spoilage	1) One form of product deterioration. 2) The reduction in an inventory's value resulting from inadequate preservation or excess age. [ka]
Spot Check	A method of inspecting a shipment in which only a sampling of the total number of containers or items are received are inspected. [ka]
Stacked Loads	Unit loads on pallets that are placed on top of each other to created a column of unitized loads. [ka]
Stacking	The process of placing merchandise on top of other merchandise. [ka]
Stacking Height	The distance as measured from the floor to a point 24 inches or more below the lowest overhead obstruction. Stacking height is usually controlled to maintain clearances required by fire regulations. [ka]
Stacks	Refers to product stacked in the warehouse. [ka]
Staging Area	Temporary storage in a warehouse or terminal where goods are accumulated adjacent to the dock for final loading. [ka]
Stock	1) Term used to refer to inventory on hand. 2) The activity of replenishing merchandise in storage. [ka]
Stock Keeping Unit	Abbreviated SKU. A product or a set of products referenced by the manufacturer by a unique part number.
Stock Locator System	A system that allows all storage spots within a warehouse to be identified with an alphanumeric code, and tracks the items and quantity in each location. [ka]
Stockout	An event that occurs when one is out of stock on a specific product. Some software solutions record this event for information and/or input to purchasing.
Stock Picker	See Order Picker. [ka]
Stock Rotation	The process of moving or replacing merchandise to insure freshness and to maximize shelf life. [ka]
Storage Charge	A fee for holding goods at rest. [ka]

Glossary

Word	Definition of Word
Storage Costs	The sum total of all costs associated with storage, including inventory costs, warehouse costs, administrative costs, deterioration costs, insurance, and taxes. [ka]
Storage Rate	The price charged for storage of merchandise, expressed as a cost per unit per month, or as a cost-per-square-foot (or meter) per month. [ka]
Stretch Wrap	A process and means of applying a sheet of flexible plastic to packages in such a way that they are secured together in a unitized load. [ka]
System	An overall set of computer software, hardware, business processes, and people. I.E., the "ERP system" means the ERP software, plus supporting computer hardware, processes utilized in the business with the ERP software, and people that regularly support or utilize this software.
Tag	A method of identifying an item or shipment. [ka]
Tally	A sheet made up when goods are received to count and record their condition on arrival. [ka]
Tare	The weight of packaging or containers. Tare weight plus net weight equals gross weight. [ka]
Terminals	The term for warehouses in early transportation systems. These storage facilities were at the terminal points for land and sea sport. [ka]
Third Party Warehouse	A warehouse operated by a 3PL that contains the client's inventory. See also 3PL, Public Warehouse, and Contract Warehouse.
Throughput	1) The total number of units arriving at and departing from warehouse divided by two. Used in public warehouse rate making to calculate average movement of product. 2) A measure of the amount of work done by a computer. Throughput is dependent on hardware and software, and is more useful than simple measure of hardware speed. [ka]
Tie	Number of Units per Layer
Tiedown	A system of securing a unit load to a pallet. [ka]
Tier	1) A single layer of boxes or bags forming one layer of a unitized load. 2) A set of storage locations that are the same height. [ka]
Tine	The horizontal load-lifting portion of a fork on a fork truck. It is the portion of a fork that contacts the load. [ka]
TO	Transfer Order. An internal company order to move inventory from one part of the company to another. This could be stock transfer between warehouses, or warehouse to a van, or division to division.
TP, Trading Partner	Trading Partner. With EDI or XML, the data is coming from or going to a "trading partner". The trading partner is usually a vendor, a carrier, or a bank.
Traceability	The ability to track a shipment or an item. Any item with a lot number or serial number should be traceable back to the manufacturer, date and location of assembly. See also Lot Number Traceability. [ka]
Truck Door	The part of the warehouse, which accommodates loading and unloading of trucks. It includes an overhead door, and may include a dock leveler, a dock shelter, and a concrete pad for the trailer. AKA Dock Door. [ka]
UI	User Interface. How the user will view and interact with the computer application software. Many user interfaces exist - including old-fashioned "green screen" (character based user interface), GUI, web page, RF handheld screen, RF forklift screen, PDA screen, and voice & 3D vision user interfaces.
ULD	Unitized Loading Device. Freight is shipped in a ULD for loading in and out of aircraft.

Glossary

Word	Definition of Word
Unitization	1) The consolidation of a number of individual items onto one shipping unit for easier handling. 2) The securing or loading of one or more large items of cargo into a single structure or carton. [ka]
Unitize	To consolidate packages into a single unit by banding, binding, or wrapping. [ka]
Unit of Measure	The degree of detail to which we refer about a Commodity. These are usually expressed as Eaches, Cases, Inner packs, and Pallets. Also known as UOM.
Unit per Measure	A count expressed as a smaller Unit of Measure per so many larger Units of Measure. For example, There are 24 Cans (Eaches) per 1 Case. Cans are the smaller UOM, since more cans fit into the larger Case.
UOM	See Unit of Measure.
Vacuum Packaging	The process of sealing packages by removing nearly all air. [ka]
VAL	Value Added Logistics. See Value Added Services.
Value Added	The contribution made by a step in the distribution process to the functionality, usefulness, or value of a product. [ka]
Value Added Services	Often the distribution center is required to perform services for customer orders other than picking and packing. These services are termed Value Added Services and they include (but are not limited to): Ticketing, Kit Assembly, Packaging, Final Finishing, Private Labeling, Pallet Labeling, Shrink Wrapping, and White Boxing.
Vertical Carousel	See Carousel.
Very Narrow Aisle	Very Narrow Aisle. A warehouse aisle that is purposed designed to be narrow. Normally this type of aisle has a wire imbedded in the center of floor, so that a forklift can sense the wire and stay precisely centered on the wire as it moves down the aisle.
VNA	Very Narrow Aisle.
Wall-To-Wall Inventory	A full physical inventory count, which includes everything in the warehouse. [ka]
Warehouse	Place for receiving/storing goods and merchandise for hire. Warehouseman is bound to use ordinary diligence in preserving goods. [cnf]
Warehouse Activity Report	A report that details all activities occurring within the warehouse facility, including merchandise arrivals, loading and unloading times and movements. AKA Activity Report. [ka]
Warehouse Management System	A management information system that controls warehouse activity, furnishing instructions to warehouse resources to manage operations. These systems typically interface with the Host, and RF devices that collect and disseminate information. Related software that may be included or tightly integrated with a WMS includes a Yard Management System, Parcel Manifesting System AKA Shipping Manifesting System, Slotting Optimization, Load Building AKA Load Optimization, and Transportation Management System.
Warehouse Receipt	A form that contains information describing the merchandise received into a warehouse. [ka]
Warehouse Receipt	A receipt, usually non-negotiable, given for goods placed in a warehouse for storage. The receipt is a legal acknowledgement of responsibility of the care of goods. [ka]

Word	Definition of Word
Warehouse Within A Warehouse	A concept of taking subsets of the warehouse for a dedicated purpose. Each subset would be a "warehouse within a warehouse". E.G., By dedicating a zone (WWAW) for fast moving A items and another zone (WWAW) for B items, this would improve picking productivity.
Wave	A wave is a group of outbound orders to be released into picking together.
Wave Planning	Planning a wave of outbound orders by selection criteria. A person that plans the wave is called a planner. A planned wave may be one time or put on a regular schedule.
WC	Work Center.
Weigh-In-Motion	A specialized weight scale that is imbedded in the conveyor line and connected to shipping software.
WIM	See Weigh-In-Motion.
WM	Warehouse Management. Inventory management & inventory control of product within facilities. Older term. See Warehouse Management System.
WMS	See Warehouse Management Systems.
WWAW	See Warehouse Within A Warehouse.
X12	ANSI EDI standards committee has produced the EDI X12 standards for business documents.
XML	Data format specification called eXtensible Markup Language. Standard groups have defined business transaction standards in XML. See OAG, BizTalk, RosettaNet.
Zero Defects	A long-range objective that strives for defect-free products. [ka]
Zone	A section of the warehouse that has exact characteristics based on material handling types and/or inventory management requirements. The Zone is the highest order in the location definition of: Zone, Aisle, Bay, Level, and Position.

The above glossary is a small set of warehousing definitions from **"Glossary of Supply Chain Terminology For Logistics, Manufacturing, Warehousing, And Technology"** has an extensive set of definitions of terms and acronyms.   ISBN 0-9669345-3-9

Order a printed copy from http://www.Amazon.com or any book distributor. Or one may subscribe to the **online glossary at http://www.scglossary.com.** Organizations and companies may license the online glossary for an annual fee by contacting IDII.